ASP.NET 3.5
Content Management System
Development

Build, manage, and extend your own Content
Management System

Curt Christianson

Jeff Cochran

PUBLISHING

BIRMINGHAM - MUMBAI

ASP.NET 3.5 Content Management System Development

First published: June 2009

Production Reference: 1190609

Published by Packt Publishing Ltd.
32 Lincoln Road
Olton
Birmingham, B27 6PA, UK.

ISBN 978-1-847193-61-2

www.packtpub.com

Cover Image by Vinayak Chittar (vinayak.chittar@gmail.com)

Credits

Authors
  Curt Christianson

  Jeff Cochran

Reviewers
  Jerry L. Spohn

  Brigida Ivan

Acquisition Editor
  James Lumsden

Development Editor
  Dilip Venkatesh

Technical Editors
  Gaurav Datar

  Shadab Khan

Editorial Team Leader
  Gagandeep Singh

Project Team Leader
  Priya Mukherji

Project Coordinator
  Leena Purkait

Proofreader
  Sandra Hopper

Indexer
  Rekha Nair

Production Coordinator
  Dolly Dasilva

Cover Work
  Dolly Dasilva

About the Authors

Curt Christianson has been involved in the tech community since the mid 1990's and has been a professional developer for more than a decade. He is an active community contributor on the ASP.NET forums, as well as a Forum Moderator. He has won six Microsoft **Most Valuable Professional (MVP)** awards for his work with ASP/ASP.NET. He is writing a number of open source add-ins and starter kits. He is based in Wisconsin, U.S.A. as a professional developer, as well as contributing to books and articles, both printed and on the Internet.

Curt is in the process of entering into the life of a married man—thanks to his better half Jessyca. They plan on settling down with lots of little ones running around.

Jeff Cochran is a Senior Network Specialist for the City of Naples, Florida. A large part of his job includes web design and coding, as well as web server management. Jeff has nearly two decades of experience with the Internet, having started one of the first Internet Service Providers in Southwest Florida, and has worked with Windows and Unix-based web servers. Now primarily concentrating on Windows technologies, Jeff has been a Microsoft MVP for Microsoft's Internet Information Server for nearly a decade, and is active in the ASP Classic and ASP.NET communities as well.

Jeff has been married for twenty years to Zina, a graphic designer and, according to most accounts, the driving force that keeps him focused on... Oh look – A Pony! In the off-hours, Jeff and Zina spend much of their time remodeling a 1950's bungalow in Naples, Florida, trying to keep the rain out and the cats in. Jeff also has a long-term addiction to classic pinball machines, tropical fish, and off-road vehicles, all of which compete with home repairs for a share of his income.

About the Reviewer

Jerry L. Spohn is a Manager of Development for a medium-sized software development firm in Exton, Pennsylvania. His responsibilities include: managing a team of developers, and assisting in architecting a large, multilingual, multi-currency loan account system, written in COBOL and Java. He is also responsible for maintaining and tracking a system-wide program and database documentation web site, for which he uses DotNetNuke as the portal.

Jerry is also the owner of Spohn Software LLC., a small consulting firm that helps small businesses in the area with all aspects of maintaining and improving their business processes. This includes helping with the creation and maintenance of web sites, general office productivity issues, and computer purchasing and networking. Spohn Software, as a firm, prefers to teach their clients how to solve their problems internally, rather than require a long-term contract, thereby making the business more productive and profitable in the future.

Jerry currently works and resides in Pennsylvania. He enjoys spending time with his two sons, Nicholas and Nolan.

Table of Contents

Preface

ASP.NET Content Management Systems are often at the heart of many businesses and customer interfaces. They help you to maintain and update content on a web site, even if you have little or no web design or programming experience. Imagine how great you'll feel when you have all the knowledge to get your site up and running quickly and also extend it into the future.

This book walks you through the creation of a functional Content Management System using the ASP.NET programming language. You will learn how to build your site in a number of ways, allowing customization. You can set up users and groups, create valuable content for your users, and manage the layout of your site efficiently when you have this book in hand.

What this book covers

Chapter 1 covers planning and building your first Content Management System.

Chapter 2 is about how to replace the file-based system with a database version. It also explores SqlDataSource, and using SQL Server 2005 Express as a source for data in our application.

Chapter 3 covers Content Management System architecture. It helps us build the database, a data access layer, a business logic layer, and a presentation layer for our Content Management System.

Chapter 4 discusses how to configure ASP.NET forms authentication, along with how to provide controls for users to log in, as well as ways to secure the content displayed on the pages.

Chapter 5 covers the basics of how to display your articles, how to create them, and how you may want to extend them.

Chapter 6 covers the concepts of why we lay out the site in a particular way, as well as beginning to help us understand all the pieces involved in this process.

Chapter 7 discusses a great deal about dynamically providing content to the users. It explores streaming files and images from the database, as well as generating RSS feeds "on the fly".

Chapter 8 covers maintaining users, adjusting permissions, approving Articles, and viewing site settings and stats—all key aspects of the Control Panel, which could be called the "brain" of any CMS.

Chapter 9 discusses a few additional options such as upsizing SQL server, using base pages and inheritance, and so on that may help extend a CMS.

Who this book is for

This book is for beginning to intermediate ASP.NET users, who have managed to learn Visual Web Developer and want to take on their first real world application. It will help those who have used SQL Server Express, completed a few sample projects, and who now wish to explore a Content Management System.

Conventions

In this book, you will find a number of styles of text that distinguish between different kinds of information. Here are some examples of these styles, and an explanation of their meaning.

Code words in text are shown as follows: To provide further uniqueness, we could name the fields `employee.employee_address` and `customer.customer_address`

A block of code will be set as follows:

```
Protected Sub Page_Load(ByVal sender As Object,
   ByVal e As System.EventArgs) Handles Me.Load
      Dim articlesAdapter As New DataSet1TableAdapters.
ArticlesTableAdapter
      GridView1.DataSource = articlesAdapter.GetData()
      GridView1.DataBind()
   End Sub
```

When we wish to draw your attention to a particular part of a code block, the relevant lines or items will be shown in bold:

```
<%@ Page Language="VB" %>
<%@ Register Src="~/Controls/ImageRotatorControl.ascx"
    TagName="ImageRotator" TagPrefix="cms" %>
```

Any command-line input or output is written as follows:

```
aspnet_regsql.exe -S .\SQLEXPRESS -U sa -P SimpleCMS -d SimpleCMS_
Database -A all
```

New terms and **important words** are shown in bold. Words that you see on the screen, in menus or dialog boxes for example, appear in our text like this: "When you see the registration information, enter your name and company, then uncheck the **Hide advanced configuration options** checkbox".

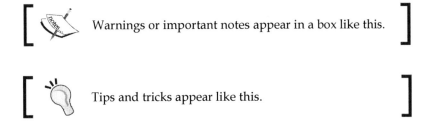

Warnings or important notes appear in a box like this.

Tips and tricks appear like this.

Reader feedback

Feedback from our readers is always welcome. Let us know what you think about this book—what you liked or may have disliked. Reader feedback is important for us to develop titles that you really get the most out of.

To send us general feedback, simply drop an email to feedback@packtpub.com, and mention the book title in the subject of your message.

If there is a book that you need and would like to see us publish, please send us a note in the **SUGGEST A TITLE** form on www.packtpub.com or email suggest@packtpub.com.

If there is a topic that you have expertise in and you are interested in either writing or contributing to a book, see our author guide on www.packtpub.com/authors.

Customer support

Now that you are the proud owner of a Packt book, we have a number of things to help you to get the most from your purchase.

Downloading the example code for the book

Visit `http://www.packtpub.com/files/code/3612_Code.zip` to directly download the example code.

The downloadable files contain instructions on how to use them.

Errata

Although we have taken every care to ensure the accuracy of our contents, mistakes do happen. If you find a mistake in one of our books—maybe a mistake in text or code—we would be grateful if you would report this to us. By doing so, you can save other readers from frustration, and help us to improve subsequent versions of this book. If you find any errata, please report them by visiting `http://www.packtpub.com/support`, selecting your book, clicking on the **let us know** link, and entering the details of your errata. Once your errata are verified, your submission will be accepted and the errata added to any list of existing errata. Any existing errata can be viewed by selecting your title from `http://www.packtpub.com/support`.

Piracy

Piracy of copyright material on the Internet is an ongoing problem across all media. At Packt, we take the protection of our copyright and licenses very seriously. If you come across any illegal copies of our works in any form on the Internet, please provide us with the location address or web site name immediately so that we can pursue a remedy.

Please contact us at `copyright@packtpub.com` with a link to the suspected pirated material.

We appreciate your help in protecting our authors, and our ability to bring you valuable content.

Questions

You can contact us at `questions@packtpub.com` if you are having a problem with any aspect of the book, and we will do our best to address it.

1
Planning and Building your First Content Management System

Welcome, and thank you for picking up this book. The purpose of this book is to walk through the creation of a basic Content Management System using the ASP.NET programming language. During the course of this book you will learn:

- What a Content Management System is and is not
- How to build a very simple Content Management System with very little code
- How to extend that Content Management System to make it more useful
- Why you are building a Content Management System and what it can lead to

This book assumes that you know how to create a basic application in ASP.NET 2.0 using Visual Web Developer and deploy it on an IIS web server. You should also have a basic programming knowledge and you should have worked at least a little with a database. We'll be using both the SQL Server 2005 Express and Visual Web Developer, available free of cost from Microsoft.

In this chapter, we'll cover some basic needs such as setting up your programming environment, and some basic background. You'll need to know about Content Management Systems. We'll also jump right into coding a basic Content Management System, and then step back to analyze what work we've done and why we've done it.

By the end of this chapter, you should be able to:

- Identify the basic functions of a Content Management System
- Understand why ASP.NET is a good technology for building a Content Management System
- Build a simple application that lets a user enter, edit, or delete content on a page
- Explain why this basic application is the main function of any Content Management System

So, let's get going.

What a Content Management System is

A **Content Management System** or **CMS** sounds like an easily defined subject. It's obviously a system to manage content. But what is content, and how do you manage it? And what is managing in the first place? These very basic questions don't have basic answers, and in many cases, the answer depends on who you are and what you need.

For example, a medical facility such as a hospital or clinic has plenty of content, including patient records, billing information, instruction manuals for equipment, employment records, press releases, employee newsletters, photos of the facility, material safety data sheets for chemicals used, shipping and receiving documents, vehicle registrations, medical licenses, email, training videos, contracts, letters to donors, x-rays, and just about everything else you can think of. All are content. Most of it needs to be managed. But is it all worth having a CMS for?

Of course not. Email is best kept with an email archiving system, which is itself a specialized type of content management. Instruction manuals might use a Content Management System, called a file cabinet, which predates computers. And employee newsletters may simply be printed and forgotten. But all of this content could potentially qualify for a Content Management System.

So, how do we narrow and define content? In our situation, we're going to narrow the content by defining the type of Content Management System we're going to build — a **Web Content Management System**. Web content consists of anything you might want to put on a web site, mostly text and images.

Web Content Management Systems

Web Content Management Systems are designed to allow users with little or no web design or programming experience to maintain and update content on a web site. They often provide a **What You See Is What You Get (WYSIWYG)** editor for the content, along with security for granting access to update or delete content, and some kind of workflow management for the content. Workflow management may include entry, approval, and publishing steps so that a user can enter new content. However, another level of security is required to approve and publish that content. Content is often dated, sometimes with an expiration date, and reusable on other pages of the site.

The site itself is usually templated in some manner, separating content from the presentation layer of the CMS, and the coding for the site is hidden from the users. In this setup, a programmer would create the application and provide enhancements to it, a designer would create the look and feel, and content authors and editors would work solely with the content to be displayed.

In many cases, there may be restricted content, viewable by only a specific class of users, and there would be a user management system to handle the creation of users and assignment of permissions. There will normally be some sort of navigation mechanism, and a search mechanism would make retrieving content easier for the end user. For a Content Management System to be useful, content should be dynamic, and should be displayed to specific users, based on specific queries or navigation choices.

A CMS is not necessarily a portal, a community site, a group of forums, or an e-commerce site. While these sites will often have content management as part of their functionality, they are not part of a CMS by default. On the other hand, blogs are purely content management—articles and comments are the content, and it's only the fact that the template creates a blog style which makes them a blog. There's really no difference between an online newspaper and a blog, or a site full of product documentation. All of them have specific content, whether articles, blog posts, or documents, which needs to be managed.

Over the course of this book, we will develop a Web Content Management System, and we'll use the acronym CMS for this. We'll program a basic content system based on articles, along with workflow for the process. This will require a user security system, based on membership of groups that are allowed to perform certain tasks, and we'll add a template system to provide for the layout of the pages separate from the content. We'll use ASP.NET, Visual Web Developer, and SQL Server 2005 Express as our environment, although you should feel free to use tools you are comfortable with, provided they are compatible.

Why use ASP.NET

Why should we choose ASP.NET? There are plenty of suitable programming languages and frameworks, including PHP, Ruby on Rails, Java, and even Classic ASP, which would work fine. Content Management Systems have been developed in pretty much every language and technology ever developed for computer systems, and you might even be more familiar with them than you are with ASP.NET.

ASP.NET, specifically ASP.NET 2.0, has some definite advantages for developing a Content Management System quickly and conveniently. A security system, complete with membership features, is already part of the framework, and so are standard design templates in the form of master pages. Easy configurations for database connections and controls for displaying the data are built in, and by using Visual Web Developer (or Visual Studio) we can take advantage of rapid development techniques to speed up our time to deploying a usable application.

ASP.NET 2.0, as well as the extensions to it (curiously named ASP.NET 3.0 and ASP.NET 3.5), is not a programming language, but a framework to develop applications within. ASP.NET is language independent. You can use any language that supports the ASP.NET framework, but for our application we will use Visual Basic .NET. Visual Basic is a simple, forgiving language that is easy to follow in code and has been used for hundreds of millions of lines of code in web applications around the world. If you feel comfortable translating VB to C#, please feel free to follow along in the language of your choice. Compiled application code resulting in **Dynamic Link Libraries** (DLLs) can be accessed by any language, meaning we could program in both VB and C# for separate parts of the application, but that would make this book harder to follow.

ASP.NET membership and profiles

ASP.NET 2.0 introduced membership and profiles to create users, assign security roles, and provide for authentication and validation of security credentials, all within the ASP.NET framework. This means developers don't have to build an authentication system for applications (unless they want to), and accounts can be protected by one-way hashed passwords, while allowing a simple assignment of access and authority to application pages.

Until the release of ASP.NET 2.0, developers were left to craft their own security system for their applications, including user management functions such as assigning and changing passwords. Add to it the functionality provided by roles in ASP.NET, and an entire security and authentication system for a site can be built with mouse clicks. User profiles are icing on the cake, allowing administrators and users to control their online profile, which can be easily integrated into an application.

ASP.NET Master Pages and Themes

ASP.NET 2.0 introduced the concepts of Master Pages and Themes to help in designing a consistent look and feel to the pages throughout a web application. Master Pages contain common elements, including menus, controls, and graphics, which are displayed on all pages. Content pages contain the individual content that changes on a web page, and are merged with the Master Page when ASP.NET renders the final HTML to the browser.

Master Pages contain ContentPlaceHolders where dynamic content is injected when the page is rendered. A browser requests the content page, which has a declaration for the Master Page, and ASP.NET places the content defined on the content page into appropriate content place holders on the Master Page. The result is that should you want to change the look and feel of your site, you change the Master Page once for your application without touching the content pages. This allows for very simple styling by designers without the need for them to touch the underlying code or having to edit any content to change the look.

ASP.NET 2.0 also introduced Themes, which can be used to alter the look of a site, including controls used on the site. Themes are a combination of control skins (`.skin` files), style sheets (CSS), and graphics that are applied as a group to a page, site, or even an entire server. Even more than with Master Pages, which require at least minimal ASP.NET programming to use, designers can create themes that can be used on a site to alter the look and feel, without touching any other files on the system.

ASP.NET 3.5

Microsoft has done the programming community a disservice in the numbering of ASP.NET versions. ASP.NET 1.0 was the first version released to the public, and was upgraded to a 1.1 version. The next release, ASP.NET 2.0, was an entirely new framework with many enhancements, including Master Pages and membership that are important to our application in this book. ASP.NET 2.0 also included data access and display controls, as well as navigation controls, which we will use.

ASP.NET 3.0 added the **Windows Presentation Foundation (WPF)** and **Windows Communication Foundation (WCF)**, but used the same ASP.NET 2.0 framework to run these extensions. ASP.NET 3.5 added AJAX and LINQ, but still just extended the 2.0 framework. So, ASP.NET 3.5 is really ASP.NET 2.0 with "extra stuff" that makes the framework more usable, but it doesn't really change the framework. Microsoft would have been better off numbering these as ASP.NET 2.1 and 2.2 to avoid confusion in the community, but we're stuck with the confusing numbering for now. Microsoft does have some logic in changing its numbering, but it makes sense mostly to the marketing folks and not programmers.

For this book, we will use ASP.NET 3.5—partly because it's the most current and default version for Visual Web Developer 2008 and also because it adds some functionality that we'll be using later. **LINQ (Language Integrated Query)** provides a uniform query language to access any data source, treating the data as an object and making the application extremely extensible to third-party data sources. We'll use LINQ to SQL for a portion of our application.

ASP.NET 3.5 also provides some new data display options such as `ListView` and `Datapager`, and provides much better support for nested Master Pages than earlier versions. AJAX, included in ASP.NET 3.5, also allows for a richer user experience, though we won't be making use of it in our basic application.

Setting up your environment

To do any programming, it's important you set up your development environment in a way that is conducive to easy, quick, and manageable programming techniques. This doesn't just mean stocking up on Mountain Dew and Hot Pockets, but also configuring your computer to best develop the specific application you're working on. In our case, we're going to configure ASP.NET 3.5, IIS, and Visual Web Developer on a workstation operating system. We'll also use Microsoft's SQL Server 2005 Express in our project. You always want a development environment as close to the environment you will deploy your application in, so we'll use IIS instead of the built-in development server in Visual Web Developer. If you are working on a system that doesn't support IIS, such as Windows XP Home, you can work with the development server and deploy to a web server with IIS, though you may need to reconfigure more settings that way.

Installing IIS

Internet Information Services is Microsoft's web server, and comes with all versions of Microsoft's Windows Server products and many of its workstation operating systems such as Windows XP Pro and Windows Vista Ultimate. The version of IIS is tied to the operating system—Windows XP has version 5.1 and Windows Vista has version 7.0. For our development, it really won't matter which version you use, but there may be some configuration changes based on the version you have. IIS, regardless of version, is not normally installed on a system by default. If your system does not have IIS installed, you will need to install it using your original operating system disk.

Operating systems and IIS versions

Not all Windows operating systems have IIS, and some have only a limited version of IIS included. The following table lists what versions you'll find on which operating systems:

Operating System	Version	Limitations
Windows XP Home	None	No IIS available
Windows XP Pro	5.1	Only one site, 10 connections
Windows Vista Home Basic	None	No IIS available
Windows Vista Home Premium	7.0	Throttled to 10 concurrent connections
Windows Vista Business	7.0	Throttled to 10 concurrent connections
Windows Vista Ultimate	7.0	Throttled to 10 concurrent connections
Windows Server 2003	6.0	None
Windows Server 2008	7.0	None

European editions of Windows Vista, N editions, have the same IIS version as their counterparts.

Installing IIS in Windows XP Pro

In Windows XP Pro, IIS is installed using the **Add or Remove Programs** applet found in the **Control Panel**.

1. Choose **Add/Remove Windows Components** on the left menu.
2. Highlight **Internet Information Services (IIS)** and click the **Details** button.
3. Check **Documentation**.
4. Check the **Internet Information Services Snap-In**.
5. Highlight **World Wide Web Service** and click **Details.**
6. Check the **World Wide Web Service**.
7. Click **OK** twice and then **Next**.

The IIS installation progress dialog will open and installation will complete quickly. You may be asked to insert the CD for the files.

Installing IIS in Windows Vista

To install IIS in Windows Vista, you must be an administrator or run as an administrator. In Windows Vista, IIS is installed using the **Programs** option in the **Control Panel**.

1. Click on **Start** and then **Control Panel**.

2. Choose **Programs**, then **Turn on or off Windows features**.

3. Expand **Internet Information Systems** and make sure the following are checked:

   - **Under Web Management Tools:**
     - IIS Management Console
     - IIS Management Scripts and Tools
     - IIS Management Service
   - **Under World Wide Web Services:**
     - **Application Development Features** — all
     - **Common HTTP Features** — all except Directory Browsing

4. Accept all other defaults and click **OK** to start installation.

You may be asked for the Windows Vista DVD, depending on how your system is configured. Don't worry about ASP.NET installation at this time.

Installation order

It is important that you install IIS before you install ASP.NET so that ASP.NET will recognize that it will be used in IIS. If you have ASP.NET installed first, you will need to register IIS with ASP.NET before using it. You can do this using the `aspnet_regiis.exe` command found in all versions of the ASP.NET framework.

Installing ASP.NET 3.5

For our application, we'll be installing ASP.NET version 3.5, along with the 2.0 and 3.0 versions of the framework. The easiest way to install the ASP.NET frameworks is to use Windows Update, available in Windows XP and higher versions. Simply connect to Windows Update, expand the Optional Software section, and then choose everything related to ASP.NET. Repeat this process until you have installed all the security fixes and updates for all versions of ASP.NET.

Installing Visual Web Developer Express 2008

You can download Visual Web Developer Express 2008, or VWD, from the Microsoft web site at `http://www.microsoft.com/express/`. Install VWD by following these steps:

1. Download Visual Web Developer Express and run the setup file.
2. Choose **Next**, and then accept the **license terms**.
3. Check the **MSDN library** option unless you are short on drive space or have a slow download link.
4. Accept the default installation location and click **Install**.
5. Restart your system when asked.

If ASP.NET is not installed, the VWD 2008 setup will install it for you. You can choose to use VWD 2005, but you will not have the IntelliSense or settings for the 3.5 framework as part of the IDE. You must register Visual Web Developer 2008 Express to continue using it after 30 days, but registration is free.

Configuring and testing your setup

With all the software installed, your development environment still needs to be configured and tested. We do this in stages so that a failure at any stage is easy to diagnose. If we configured everything and then tested, it could be a problem with IIS, ASP.NET, SQL Server Express, Visual Web Developer, or almost anything else. The basis for serving a web site is web server software. In Windows it's IIS, so the first thing we'll configure and test is IIS.

Configuring IIS on Windows XP

As we'll be developing our application in IIS, it's important that we configure IIS appropriately. Start by opening the **IIS Manager** in **Administrative Tools** and selecting the **Default Web Site**. Right-click this and choose **Properties**, displaying the properties dialog shown below:

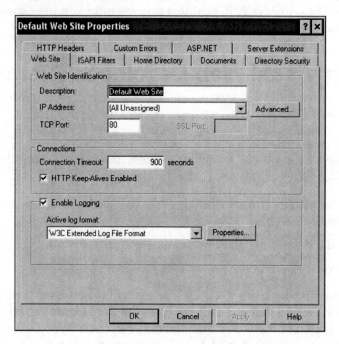

The two tabs we are most interested in are the **ASP.NET** tab and the **Documents** tab. On the **Documents** tab, we set the default document and the file that IIS serves when no file is specified on the URL. Select the **Documents** tab and you will see a predefined list of default documents, in the order IIS will use if it finds them. For our application, we will use only `Default.aspx` as our default document. To help secure our site, we will remove all the other file names listed so that IIS will not serve them, even if they exist. After deleting these, and adding `Default.aspx` if it wasn't in your list to start, your **Documents** tab should look like the given screenshot:

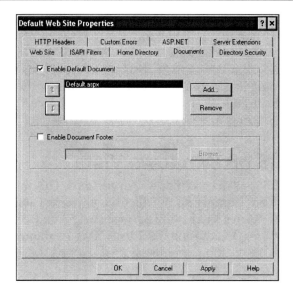

The other tab we need to configure is the **ASP.NET** tab. On this tab we will set the ASP.NET version that our application will use. This can be confusing, as even though we will be using ASP.NET 3.5, the version set in IIS is ASP.NET 2.0. Remember, ASP.NET 3.0 and 3.5 are just extensions to ASP.NET 2.0, not a completely new version of the framework.

In the IIS Manager, select the **ASP.NET** tab. In the **ASP.NET** drop-down list, make sure that you select the **2.0 version** of the framework, as shown in the following screenshot:

For IIS to serve ASP.NET applications, the folder that the application is in has to be defined as an application in IIS. By default, the root folder of a web site is an application, and that's what we will use for our CMS project. This is why you see the file location of `c:\inetpub\wwwroot\web.config` in the IIS ASP.NET configuration tab. If you are developing in a virtual folder or a subfolder of the root of your site, you will need to set that folder as an application in IIS. Chapter 12 has a section on setting folders as applications in IIS.

Configuring IIS on Windows Vista

Windows Vista uses IIS 7, as does Windows Server 2008. This makes Vista an excellent development environment if the deployment server will be Windows Server 2008, as both Windows Vista (with Service Pack 1) and Windows Server 2008 share identical IIS versions. In addition, IIS 7 uses XML configuration files, making it very easy to deploy an application or entire site.

Open the **IIS Manager** in Vista under **Administrative Tools** and navigate to the default web site in the left menu. The **Default Web Site** page is displayed, and under the IIS section you'll find **Default Document**. Double-click it and the **Default Document** pane will open. Highlight any document that is not `Default.aspx` and delete it. If you do not have a `Default.aspx` document listed, click **Add** under the **Actions** menu on the righthand side and add it. When you have finished, the **Default Document** pane should look as shown in the following screenshot:

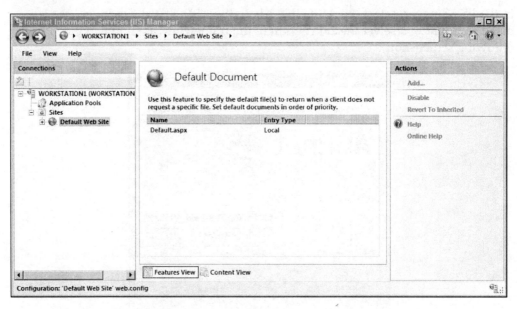

Windows Vista is easier than Windows XP when it comes to configuring the
ASP.NET framework version. To begin with, Windows Vista and IIS 7 install out
of the box, and configure for the ASP.NET 2.0 framework. Also, Windows Vista
ASP.NET versions are configured on an application pool basis, so selecting the
correct application pool is all you need to do for your application to run under
ASP.NET 2.0. The default installation of IIS 7.0 includes two application pools,
one using the new IIS 7 integrated pipeline and the other using the classic ASP.NET
pipeline found in earlier versions.

This means that in the integrated pipeline, all requests to the server are processed by
the ASP.NET DLL, while in the classic pipeline, requests are processed based on the
file extension mapping. You normally need to worry about this only when you are
migrating an application, but you can find a list of breaking changes for ASP.NET
2.0 applications running in the integrated pipeline at `http://learn.iis.net/page.`
`aspx/381/aspnet-20-breaking-changes-on-iis-70/`.

For Windows Vista and IIS 7, all you need to do at this time is verify that the default
application pool is set to version 2.0, as shown in the following screenshot:

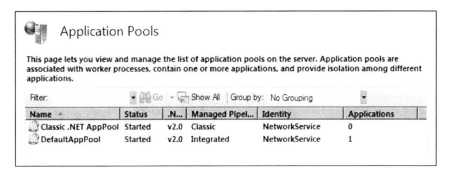

Setting NTFS permissions

There is one additional step we need to take in setting up our web site. Since we
will be altering files on the site using ASP.NET, we need to give permission to the
ASP.NET process account to do so. For this we use NTFS permissions, also known
as Windows file and folder permissions, to allow the proper account access to
the system.

The default ASP.NET process account in Windows XP and IIS 5.1 is the ASP.NET
account, while in Windows Server 2003 and IIS 6, as well as all versions of Windows
with IIS 7, it is the **NETWORK SERVICE** account. These are less privileged accounts
that the ASP.NET process runs under to provide additional security. Unless you
have changed the default account, these are the accounts that need access to our
web site files and folders.

To set NTFS permissions for these accounts, we need to open the file system using **Windows Explorer** or **My Computer**. In Windows Vista, you must be signed in as a local administrator to set permissions. Navigate to the root of your web site, the default is C:\inetpub\wwwroot\, and right-click on the folder, choosing **Properties**. On the **Security** tab, we need to add the proper account for our version of Windows. These accounts are hidden accounts, so simply type in the proper account name rather than searching for it. Also, these are local accounts. Therefore, if your system is part of a Windows domain, you may need to specify the system name such as {SystemName}/ASPNET before the account. Grant this account **Full Control** to the web folder. When you're finished, the Security dialog should look something like this:

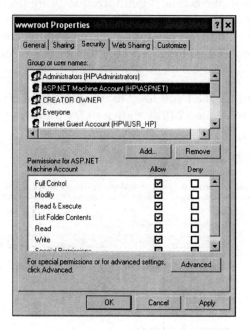

Testing IIS

There is no point in writing any application code if it won't work, so we need to test our installation and make sure that IIS will serve an ASP.NET page. The traditional test method for programming and web sites is with a "Hello World!" application, basically one that simply prints some text to the screen. We want one that uses some ASP.NET functionality, so ours won't simply display "Hello World!" in a browser window, which can also be done in plain HTML. What we need is an application like this:

```
<%@ Page Language="VB" %>

<script runat="server">
    Sub Page_Load(Sender As Object, E As EventArgs)
        HelloWorld.Text = "Hello World!"
    End Sub
</script>

<html>
<head>
<title>ASP.NET Hello World</title>
</head>
<body>
<p><asp:label id="HelloWorld" runat="server" /></p>
</body>
</html>
```

Save this code as `Default.aspx` in the root of your web site, `c:\inetpub\wwwroot\` would be the default, and you have a simpler application that uses an ASP.NET label control to display "Hello World!" in a browser. You can display this within Visual Web Developer, but that uses the development server contained in VWD 2008. What we want is to display this in the same way a browser would display it when browsing our CMS application.

Open a web browser and browse to `http://localhost/`. You should see a display similar to this:

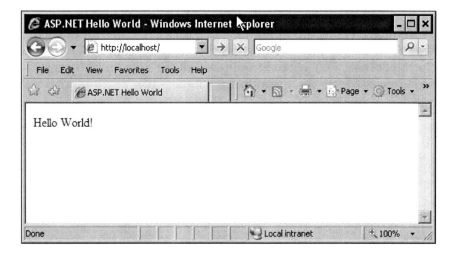

Okay, nothing spectacular, but it does prove that IIS is configured correctly to serve ASP.NET pages.

Localhost

The location "localhost" that we browsed to has special meaning in the networking world. This name resolves to an IP address of 127.0.0.1, which is reserved in networking to mean the system that you are sitting at. In other words, using `http://localhost/` in a browser will always bring up the web server on the system you are physically browsing from. It cannot be used from a second system, as "localhost" resolves to that second system on that second system.

Writing a simple content management application

Alright, we've spent half this chapter just setting up a development system, and now it's time to actually develop something. This application will be the world's simplest Content Management System, and pretty much useless in the real world, but we'll be getting our hands dirty on creating the basics of all web Content Management Systems.

At the heart of any Content Management System is the ability to change content without doing any programming. Most CMS users will be unskilled in development, web design, or even the basics of HTML, but they will be skilled in creating the content they wish to be managed. This application will allow them to add, delete, and change simple content on a very simple web page.

We'll walk through creating this application in Visual Web Developer, though in future chapters I'll assume that you can find your way through VWD well enough to write the application with just code snippets. All the code for every chapter is available for download (see the appendix for instructions).

Default.aspx

Our application is going to consist of two pages:

- `Default.aspx`: The page presented to the viewer
- `Edit.aspx`: The page that handles the editing of the content on `Default.aspx`

We're going to use a few simple ASP.NET controls to accomplish this. First, let's create the `Default.aspx` page.

Open Visual Web Developer, and create a new file by choosing **File | New File** on the menu, and then selecting a Visual Basic **Web Form** as shown in the following screenshot:

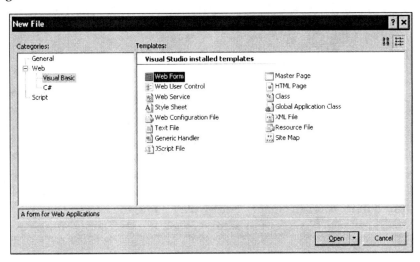

Visual Web Developer creates an ASP.NET form with basic HTML and a script block, and we'll use that as our base for this application. Immediately save this file as `Default.aspx` in the root of your web site, normally `C:\inetpub\wwwroot\` on a fresh installation of IIS. Go ahead and overwrite the "Hello World!" `Default.aspx` we created earlier. We know that our development environment is working.

We'll first need a place for the content. In this example, we'll be using only text as the content, and a Textbox control will do fine. We will also need a link to take us to the `Edit.aspx` page so we can edit the content. We'll use a simple Hyperlink control for this. The following code will create a Textbox control and the Hyperlink when inserted in the `<div>` in the `Default.aspx` created by VWD:

```
<asp:Label ID="Label1" runat="server"
   Height="300px" Width="500px"
   Text="This is where the content will be." >
</asp:Label>
<br />
<asp:HyperLink ID="HyperLink1" runat="server">Edit Text
</asp:HyperLink>
```

You'll notice we have no NavigateURL for the Hyperlink control yet. We still need to create the `Edit.aspx` it will point to. We also need to populate the Label control with the text for our content, and we need to store that content for future use or editing. Right now it is being populated with the `Text` attribute of the Label control. However, to change the text, you would need to open the ASP.NET code and edit it—something that a CMS is designed to avoid.

In our main CMS project, we'll use a database for content. However, as databases aren't fully covered until Chapter 2, for this example, we'll use a simple text file to store our content. The principal is the same as using a database, and many content management systems have been built that store content in the file system instead of a database.

Content.txt

Before we can read a text file into the Label control, or edit it with Edit.aspx, we need to have the text file. Create a simple text file named Content.txt in the root of your web site, using any text editor such as Notepad. For this example we've used "Greeked" text—a publishing layout tool that consists of random Latin words and phrases, which when printed on a page or viewed in a web page, have the general look of text that will eventually appear there. You've probably seen this used in sample web sites, and it's often referred to as Lorem Ipsum text after the first words normally found in it. You can create your own by using the Lorem Ipsum generator at http://www.lipsum.com/ For our sample, we'll use two paragraphs, saved in the Content.txt file.

We need to alter our code to display the Content.txt file in the Label control, and it should look something like this:

```
<%@ Page Language StreamReader ="VB" %>
<%@ Import Namespace="System.IO" %>
<!DOCTYPE html PUBLIC "-//W3C//DTD XHTML 1.0 Transitional//EN"
"http://www.w3.org/TR/xhtml1/DTD/xhtml1-transitional.dtd">
<script runat="server">
    Sub Page_Load(ByVal sender As Object, ByVal e As EventArgs)
        Dim Filetext As String = Server.MapPath("Content.txt")
        Dim objStreamReader As StreamReader
        objStreamReader = File.OpenText(Filetext)
        Dim Content As String = objStreamReader.ReadToEnd()
        Label1.Text = Content.Replace(vbCrLf, "<br>")
        objStreamReader.Close()
    End Sub
</script>
<html xmlns="http://www.w3.org/1999/xhtml">
<head runat="server">
    <title>Basic CMS</title>
</head>
<body>
    <form id="form1" runat="server">
    <div>
        <asp:Label ID="Label1" runat="server"
```

```
            Height="300px"
            Width="500px">
        </asp:Label>
        <br />
        <asp:HyperLink ID="HyperLink1" runat="server">Edit Text
        </asp:HyperLink>
    </div>
    </form>
</body>
</html>
```

We used a `StreamReader` class to read the text file `Content.txt`, and then replaced the CR/LF characters in the text file with `<br>` characters, which are understood by the browser and loaded the result into the Label control. Let's run through the code for this.

We needed to import the `System.IO` namespace because we'll use the `File` class to open the text file and read it, so we added the line:

```
<%@ Import Namespace="System.IO" %>
```

Our script uses the `Page_Load` event to run so that our text file will be loaded into the `Label` control whenever the page is loaded into a browser. We are reading the file through a `StreamReader` object that is returned by the `OpenText` method of the `File` class, so the following lines define the name of the file and create the `StreamReader` object:

```
        Dim Filetext As String = Server.MapPath("Content.txt")
        Dim objStreamReader As StreamReader
```

Then we open the `Content.txt` file and create a string using the `StreamReader` object with these lines:

```
        objStreamReader = File.OpenText(Filetext)
        Dim Content As String = objStreamReader.ReadToEnd()
```

In the next line, we set the `Text` attribute of our `Label` control to be the contents of the string, but we replace the CR/LF characters of the text file with a `<br>` HTML command that the browser will understand:

```
        Label1.Text = Content.Replace(vbCrLf, "<br>")
```

We then close the `StreamReader` object. If you don't do this, you can get unpredictable results from future attempts to access this file. And good programming dictates that if we open something, we close it when we're done.

```
objStreamReader.Close()
```

We've also modified our `Label` control to remove the `Text` attribute we had assigned, as this will now be assigned by our application code:

```
<asp:Label ID="Label1" runat="server"
    Height="300px"
    Width="500px">
</asp:Label>
```

When you test this code, you will see results similar to this:

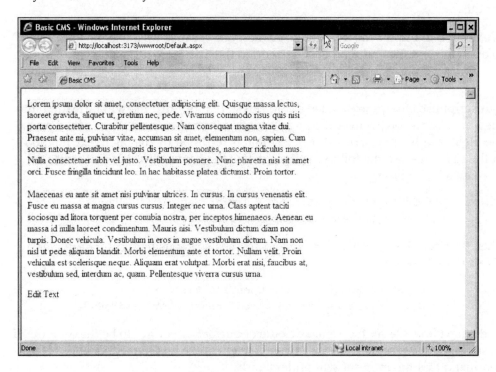

Our content is displayed in the web page and we no longer need to edit the code directly to change it. Of course, we still need to edit the `Content.txt` file to change it, which is only possible by someone with direct access to the file through the Windows file system. That's better than having to edit the code, but it's not very convenient and it certainly can open security risks if you need to provide access to the files in the root of your web site. We need to create a better way to edit the content, without needing physical access to the content storage file.

FCKEditor

We will create a second ASP.NET page to handle editing the Content.txt file. While we could simply write new text to the Content.txt file, that isn't a very clean way of handling editing of content, so we'll use a third-party application called the FCKEditor. This program is distributed under the GPL, LGPL, and MPL open source licenses, and is perfect for open source projects or your own personal projects. FCKEditor got its name from the program's author, Frederico Caldeira Knabben, and can be integrated into an ASP.NET application using the FCKEditor.Net control, licensed in the same manner.

FCKEditor may be downloaded from http://www.fckeditor.net/, and you will need both the editor and the ASP.NET control. Once you have downloaded the compressed files, the ZIP file you download can be unzipped directly to your web site's root and it will expand into the properly named folders. You can test the installation by browsing to http://localhost/FCKeditor/_samples/ default.html. This should bring up a sample of the FCKEditor.

To use FCKEditor in an ASP.NET page, we need to install the second file you downloaded, the FCKEditor.Net control. Expand the downloaded file, open the folders, and find the path /bin/Release/2.0/. The FredCK.FCKeditorV2.dll file in that folder is all we need to install in our application. Create a /bin folder under your web site root, at c:\inetpub\wwwroot\bin\, and copy the FredCK.FCKeditorV2.dll into it.

Edit.aspx

Now that we have the FCKEditor installed in our application, we need to create the Edit.aspx page that uses it to edit our content. Start a new Visual Basic web form in Visual Web Developer, and just below the <%@ Page Language="VB" %> line, add this line of code:

```
<%@ Register Assembly="FredCK.FCKeditorV2" Namespace="FredCK.
FCKeditorV2" TagPrefix="FCKeditorV2" %>
```

This will register the FredCK.FCKeditorV2.dll in our page. To add the editor to the page itself, add this line of code between the <div> statements:

```
<FCKeditorV2:FCKeditor ID="FCKeditor1" runat="server"></FCKeditorV2:
FCKeditor>
```

This creates an instance of the editor in our page. If you browse to your page with the URL `http://localhost/Edit.aspx`, you should see a page something like this:

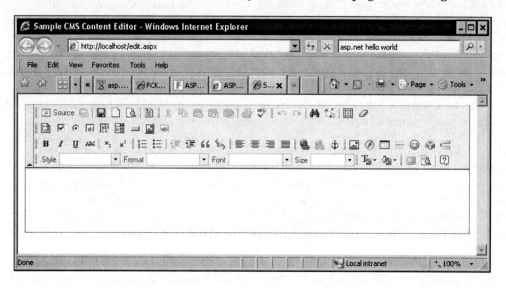

You can use the control to enter text, format it, and... well, not much else. We need a way to save this text as the `Content.txt` file we use for our `Default.aspx` page. You can download the code for our `Edit.aspx` page from Packt's official web site, or you can type the code in from the following walkthrough of the code:

```
Creating and Understanding Edit.aspx
```

Let's walk through the `Edit.aspx` code, so you can understand the process the code follows. See the following block of code:

```
<%@ Page Language="VB" Debug="True"%>
<%@ Import Namespace="System.IO" %>
<%@ Register Assembly="FredCK.FCKeditorV2"
   Namespace="FredCK.FCKeditorV2"
   TagPrefix="FCKeditorV2"
%>
```

This block of code imports the `System.IO` namespace that we use to read and write our `Content.txt` file, just as in our `Default.aspx` page. See the next line:

```
<!DOCTYPE html PUBLIC "-//W3C//DTD XHTML 1.0 Transitional//EN"
   "http://www.w3.org/TR/xhtml1/DTD/xhtml1-transitional.dtd">
```

It simply identifies the Doctype for the browser, so it knows how to interpret the rendered HTML. This was the default inserted in our code by Visual Web Developer when we created a new form. If you want to know more about the Doctype specification, you can refer to the Word Wide Web Consortium's list of recommended doctypes at http://www.w3.org/QA/2002/04/valid-dtd-list.html.

Our script block consists of two subroutines. The following snippet is the first subroutine:

```
<script runat="server">
    Sub Page_Load(ByVal sender As Object, ByVal e As EventArgs)
        If Not Page.IsPostback Then
            Dim Filetext As String = Server.MapPath("Content.txt")
            Dim objStreamReader As StreamReader
            objStreamReader = File.OpenText(Filetext)
            Dim Content As String = objStreamReader.ReadToEnd()
            objStreamReader.Close()
            FCKeditor1.Value = Content
        End If
    End Sub
```

This subroutine is nearly identical to our Default.aspx page code for loading the Content.txt file into the Label control. You will notice the following two changes:

1.   We only do this if the page is not a postback from itself, to prevent reading the text file again after we have edited it but not saved it.

2.   Instead of setting the text in the Label control to match the Content.txt file, we set the Value of the FCKEditor control. This loads the Content.txt file into the FCKEditor, so we have what already exists and can edit it.

The second subroutine is new to the Edit.aspx page.

```
    Protected Sub Button1_Click(ByVal sender As Object, ByVal e As
        System.EventArgs) Handles Button1.Click
        Dim Outfile As String = Server.MapPath("Content.txt")
        Dim objStreamWriter As StreamWriter
        objStreamWriter = File.CreateText(Outfile)
        objStreamWriter.Write(FCKeditor1.Value)
        objStreamWriter.Close()
        Server.Transfer("Default.aspx")
    End Sub
</script>
```

This subroutine is almost the opposite of the first. Instead of a `StreamReader` object, we use a `StreamWriter` object, which will write our text to the `Content.txt` file. The `StreamWriter` writes the value of the FCKEditor control to `Content.txt`. The subroutine closes the `StreamWriter` and uses a `Server.Transfer` to send the browser back to the `Default.aspx` page, where the `Content.txt` file is again read and displayed, this time with the altered content.

Server.Transfer vs HyperLink

ASP.NET provides a number of methods for browsing from one page to another. We've used a `HyperLink`, which merely sends a request for the new page from the browser, and we now use a `Server.Transfer` to move back to the `Default.aspx` page. Using `Server.Transfer` ends control of the current ASP.NET page and transfers control to the destination page, and can be used to maintain session information between pages. In this case, we are using it simply because it has a slight performance boost over other possible methods, though in this application you would never notice. It is also easier to code in a `button_click`.

The page code displays our page with the FCKEditor control, the button that activates the subroutine to save the content, and a hyperlink that simply returns the browser to the `Default.aspx` page without saving anything to the `Content.txt` file.

```html
<html xmlns="http://www.w3.org/1999/xhtml">
<head runat="server">
    <title>Sample CMS Content Editor</title>
</head>
<body>
    <form id="form1" runat="server">
    <div>
    <FCKeditorV2:FCKeditor ID="FCKeditor1"
      runat="server"
      Height="400"
      Width="800">
    </FCKeditorV2:FCKeditor>
    <br />
    <asp:Button ID="Button1" runat="server" Text="Save Content" />
    <br />
    <asp:HyperLink ID="HyperLink1" runat="server"
      NavigateUrl="Default.aspx">
      Cancel and Return to Original Page
    </asp:HyperLink>
    </div>    </form>
</body>
</html>
```

The final `Edit.aspx` page should look something like:

Let's try out our simple CMS. Change some of the text, add your own, make some of it bold or italics, and save it. Your changes will show in the `Default.aspx` page. Of course, it's still ugly. Let's give it at least a little formatting, a title, and some structure. In later chapters, we'll deal with much more advanced formatting and design work, but we'll start with a few simple HTML changes for now. In the `<body>` of your `Default.aspx` page, add or change the highlighted lines:

```
<body>
  <form id="form1" runat="server">
    <table width="500" border="0" cellpadding="4"
      cellspacing="0" align="center">
      <tr>
        <td>
          <h1>The World's Simplest CMS</h1>
          <hr />
          <asp:Label ID="Label1" runat="server"
            Width="500"></asp:Label>
          <hr />
        </td>
      </tr>
      <tr>
```

```
        <td align="center">
          <asp:Button ID="Button1" runat="server"
           Text="Edit Content" />
        </td>
      </tr>
    </table>
  </form>
</body>
```

We have created a table for our page to be displayed in, centered that table, and added a headline. We also added horizontal lines to define our content block, and centered the button used to edit our content. These are some extremely simple changes, using only basic HTML. However, these changes dramatically improve the look of our basic CMS, or at least make it look like we didn't just concentrate on writing code.

Summary

In this chapter, you learned what a Content Management System is and why ASP.NET is a good technology to use in developing a CMS. We walked through getting installed the Internet Information Services, the ASP.NET 3.5 framework, Visual Web Developer 2008 Express, and Microsoft SQL Server 2005 Express. We also configured a development environment to use VWD and IIS on our system.

The very basic CMS sample we programmed in this chapter shows the basics of a CMS system. We have a storage area for content—the file system and a file named Content.txt in this case. We have a mechanism for an average user to edit this content, using the FCKEditor control. And we have the code that reads our Content.txt file and writes changes back to the same file. This is what makes a Content Management System work—the ability to store and recall content, the ability to change the content without programming skills, and the permanent retention of content when it is not being accessed.

The final code for this chapter can be downloaded from Packt's official web site. The full code is slightly different from that presented in this chapter in that it is commented for you to understand. This chapter started from scratch, but future chapters will build on this base. Therefore, you will find that the starter code for many of the chapters can be downloaded as well.

In the next chapter, we'll add a database to our CMS as the storage mechanism, allowing us far more flexibility in storage than the file system does. In future chapters, we'll take this rather plain looking site to new design levels, add a security system so that users will only be able to perform tasks they have permission for, and build some more useful content management functions into our application. So, if you're ready, we'll get started with Microsoft SQL Server 2005 Express.

2
Adding a Database to a Content Management System

The simple Content Management System we developed in the last chapter worked, but there were plenty of drawbacks to the system we created. One of the major drawbacks was the use of the file system for storing content. Files can be insecure, text files can be unwieldy in size, and you can hold only text content in one. We could use other file types, maybe save the text as HTML to overcome some issues, but that means our content and our presentation are part of the same file. In a CMS, this is one of the issues we need to avoid.

Imagine something as simple as your boss deciding that headings in the pages will now be formatted as a `<h2>` heading with a purple font color. If we stored 500 pages as simple files that included the HTML, we would have to edit 500 files to change every heading. And you know that, once we finished that task, the company president would want the headings formatted simply as bold text in green. And we would have to change all 500 files again. Even with a search and replace function that works across files, we would still have to check every page to make sure the changes take place. I don't know about you, but I would either rewrite the application or quit the company. As we both need to pay the rent and buy food, let's change the application to use a database to store our content.

In this chapter, we will cover:

- Why to use a database
- How to install, configure, and use SQL Server Express
- How to install and use SQL Management Studio Express
- Creating your database, creating a user, and setting user permissions
- Connecting our CMS to the database
- Managing data from our CMS application

Why use a database

That's actually a fair question. After all, there are other storage mechanisms such as XML files, which could be used. But none of the other storage possibilities allow us the flexibility, and especially the programmability, of a database. A modern database is capable of holding many millions of records, while being able to search for and retrieve records fitting specific conditions. Exactly what we need to store for our CMS—the content or data.

Databases provide additional advantages over file-based storage such as our simple CMS or even an XML file. While a file on the system can get fragmented through constant changing, causing slower access times, data in a database can be changed at will without changing the access time. Compared to XML files, which get unwieldy after the size of the file exceeds the available memory resources, databases have near unlimited storage capacity. This means our CMS can scale from a simple family web site to a corporate publishing portal.

Why use SQL Server Express

Microsoft has a long history in databases, producing one of the most popular database systems on the planet, Microsoft's SQL Server. Over the years, Microsoft has improved SQL Server, and they have always provided a development or personal version for programmers to use. This means programmers don't need to pay outrageous licensing fees to simply develop against SQL Server, and then pay those fees again when the application is deployed. In Microsoft's latest implementations of SQL Server, this development version is called SQL Server Express. Both Microsoft SQL Server 2005 (which we will use) and its recently released SQL Server 2008 come in Express versions.

Licensing for these versions is also very advantageous to our project, as the use of the Express version is free. That's right, a fully functional **Relational Database Management System (RDBMS)** that can be used for no charge. There are limitations such as the size of the database and the lack of management tools built into the database package, but they are not an issue in our case. Our database will never grow too large while we create this project, and Microsoft has a free management tool for SQL Server 2005 Express, which will meet our needs.

There are two other advantages to Microsoft SQL Sever Express versions. The first is that they easily transfer to a full version of the software. The database files in both the full versions and the Express versions are the same. This means that if we ever did run out of space on the Express version, we could super size the database by migrating to the full SQL Server version.

The second advantage is that Visual Web Developer, which we are using for development, already has an understanding of Microsoft SQL Server, including the Express version. This means we can use the tools in Visual Web Developer to create our database and connections, and the connections will just work. As with everything created in a development environment such as Visual Web Developer, there are ways we can improve the default functions. However, when just starting out, it is critical to have a development environment that understands what you're doing.

Installing and configuring SQL Server 2005 Express

When you download Microsoft Visual Web Developer 2008 Express, you have the option of downloading Microsoft SQL Server 2005 Express from the same page. When given an option, choose to download Microsoft SQL Server 2005 Express with Advanced Services. This includes Management Studio Express and Full Text Search, both of which are especially handy to have. The SQL Server 2005 Examples and SQL Server 2005 Books Online are not critical for our CMS application, but you will most likely want them if you intend to do any SQL Server programming or extend the application you create in this book.

Once you download the SQL Server 2005 Express executable, run it and accept the licensing agreement. The installation wizard will configure the required components, and will then check your system. Once that is finished, and you have installed everything it asks for, the SQL Server 2005 Express installation will start. When you see the registration information, enter your name and company, then uncheck the **Hide advanced configuration options** checkbox. We need to change some configuration settings, so your screen should look something like:

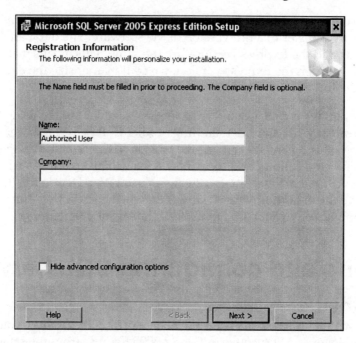

The next installation choice you will have is **feature selection**, which is chosen to run everything from your hard drive. We won't use everything, but it's easier to have it already installed than to install a new feature the first time you choose to use it. The next choice is how you want to install SQL Express, choose **Named Instance** and the default name of **SQLExpress**. Accept the default values for each step, except when you come to the **Authentication Mode** dialog. Here, we want to set SQL Server 2005 Express to allow Windows or SQL logins, called Mixed Mode authentication. Select **Mixed Mode (Windows Authentication and SQL Server Authentication)** and enter SimpleCMS as a password for the **sa logon** account, as shown below:

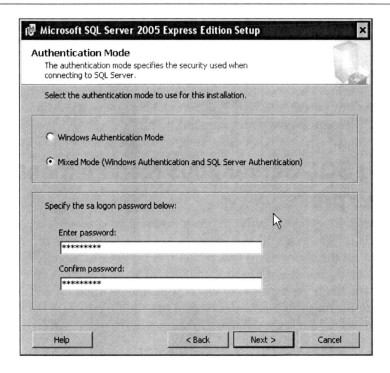

In SQL Server, the **sa** account is the system administration account, similar to the Windows Administrator account. Continue the setup process, accepting the default choices until the setup is complete.

Installing SQL Server 2005 Management Studio Express

If you didn't install SQL Server 2005 Management Studio Express with SQL Server 2005 Express, it can be downloaded individually or as part of the SQL Server 2005 Express Edition Toolkit, which includes **Business Intelligence Development Studio (BIDS)**. BIDS will let you create and manage **SQL Server Reporting Services (SSRS)**, which provides reports on SQL Server operations, as well as allowing you to generate reports from your database. We won't be using BIDS in our project, so we only need Management Studio Express, but you can install either version to work through this book.

When you download Management Studio Express, you will have a Microsoft installation file, or MSI, called **SQLServer2005_SSMSEE.msi** in your download location. In a Windows system, an MSI file can be run as an executable, so simply double-click the filename to begin the installation. Agree to the licensing and accept all the defaults, unless you need to change the installation location. When the installation finishes, you should find SQL Server Management Studio Express in the SQL Server 2005 program group on your start menu.

Running SQL Server 2005 Management Studio Express

When you start Management Studio Express, you will be presented with a login dialog for the SQL Server. It will have your server name and use Windows Authentication for the connection. This works fine on your local system for development, but if you intend to use Management Studio Express on a hosted web site, you will likely be required to use SQL Authentication for access. If that is the case, your hosting service should be able to provide you with the name of the SQL Server, as well as the login details.

Clicking **Connect** will connect Management Studio Express to your SQL Server. If you expand the **Databases** folder, and then expand **System Databases**, you will see four default databases required for SQL Server — **master**, **model**, **msdb**, and **tempdb**.

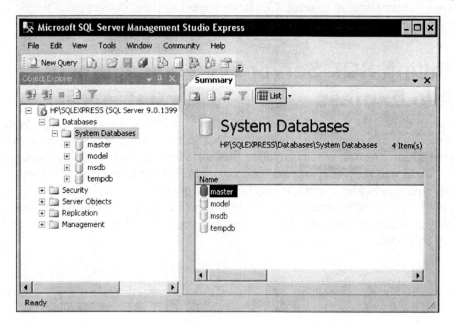

These four databases are used by SQL Server to store information for SQL Server itself, and you should never need to touch them. The database we create for our application will be separate from these and that will be the only database we use. SQL Server 2005 Express allows the creation of multiple databases, but for our application we will only create one, both because it makes our application simpler to manage and because many web hosting services charge extra for hosting additional databases.

Management Studio Express allows us to perform some important tasks on our database. If you right-click on the **master** database and choose **Tasks**, you will see the important **Backup** and **Restore** tasks, as well as a **Shrink** task that allows us to compress the space used by our database. On a web host, this is important because extra space often costs extra. However, in any SQL Server installation, a smaller database will be a better performer. Shrinking the database is a double-edged sword though, since it can lead to fragmentation of the database. It can also be useless, since a database needs some extra space to function and will need to grow larger as it needs the space. Shrinking is most useful in development or updating a database, especially after a table is altered or dropped and large amounts of space may end up empty.

Creating a database for our simple Content Management System

The simple Content Management System we developed in Chapter 1 suffers from many problems, one of which is the limited storage capabilities provided by the file system. The way to overcome the limitations and problems with file system storage is through the use of a database, so we'll create and use an SQL Server 2005 Express database for this project. There are quite a few ways to create this database, some easy and some less so, but we'll work through a process that would be similar to using any other database server, rather than relying on the development shortcuts found in many ASP.NET tutorials.

We are going to create a database and some initial structure using SQL Server Management Studio Express, instead of using wizards to create a database with a mysterious underlying structure, so that you can learn some ASP.NET techniques for working with data connections. At some point you will need a deeper knowledge of the database you use, and databases in general, than an ASP.NET tutorial can give. I apologize in advance that this book won't come anywhere near making you a SQL Server Guru, but I hope that you will at least understand the basics behind the product we'll create.

Creating a new database with Management Studio Express

Open Management Studio Express and right-click **Databases** in the **Object Explorer** pane. Choose **New Database**, and the **New Database** dialog will open. Enter **SimpleCMS** for a name, then scroll the **Database files** window to the right until you can see the **Path** field. The default path for the database is under the Microsoft SQL Server folder hierarchy, but we want to change that. While the database will function fine in the default location, and for many SQL Server applications, you may have a reason to leave it there—we want to simplify our web site management and locate the file within our web site hierarchy. And there is a special place we want to put it.

ASP.NET and Visual Web Developer have some unique folder names that are recognized as special within the VWD development environment. One is the /bin folder we used for the FCKEditor in Chapter 1, and another is the /App_Data folder. This folder has a unique relationship to VWD in that any database in that folder is automatically added to the Database Explorer in VWD for the application this folder appears in.

So, we want our database to be located in the /App_Data folder of our web site. First, in the web site root folder (the default is C:\Inetpub\wwwroot\), create a folder named App_Data. To set the Path for our database, click on the default path and change it to **C:\Inetpub\wwwroot\App_Data** for both the database and log files, as shown below:

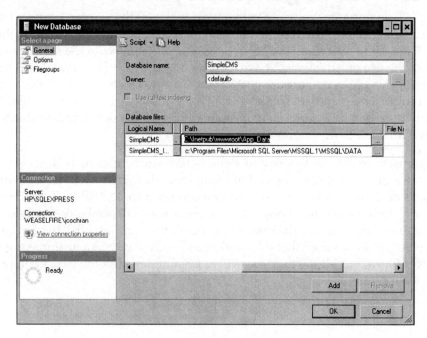

When you click **OK** and finish the new database wizard, you should find that two new files, `SimplCMS.mdf` and `SimpleCMS_log.ldf`, have been created in the `App_Data` folder that you created earlier.

Windows authentication vs SQL server authentication

We are using SQL Server authentication for access to our database to make development and deployment simpler. You will find that many hosts will run SQL Server in such a manner that you can use Windows authentication, though you will need to reconfigure the connection string in your application. If you use SQL Server authentication, the same account will exist on your server and on the development workstation, so developing and deploying your application won't require changes to the connection string when your application is installed on different systems.

Configuring an SQL user account

We are going to use SQL server authentication for our application's connection to the database, so first we need to create a SQL server user account. Open Management Studio Express and expand the **Security** folder in the **Object Explorer** pane. Right-click on **Logins** and choose **New Login**. Enter **SimpleCMSUser** and check the **SQL Server authentication** radio button. Use `SimpleCMS` as a password and uncheck the **Enforce password policy** checkbox. Set the **Default Database** to **SimpleCMS** and leave the **Language** at the default. You should have an account that looks something like this:

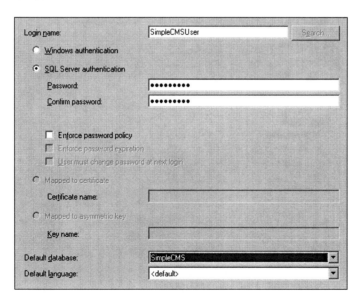

Configuring the database to use the SQL Server account

With the SimpleCMSUser account created, we now need to configure the SimpleCMS database to use this account. In Management Studio Express, expand the **SimpleCMS** database, expand **Security**, and then expand **Users**. You will see a few default users created when we created the database, including **dbo** and **guest**. If you right-click on the **dbo** user and choose **Properties**, you will find this user belongs to the **db_owner** role. As it sounds, the database owner has pretty much full control over the database, much as the Administrator account has full control over Windows. We're going to break with good security guidelines and grant our account the same access to the database. The overall increase in security risk is extremely minimal in our case, and many production systems run with this same security. If you have a database administrator who fully understands SQL server account security, by all means follow their advice. However, for our application and for our specific use, we'll accept the minimal risk increase in return for the greater programming flexibility.

Close the **Properties** window for the dbo user account, and right-click on **Users** then select **New User**. Enter the username of **SimpleCMSUser**, and browse to the **Login name** of **SimpleCMS User**. Now, browse to the **Default Schema** of **dbo** and check the role membership for **db_owner**. The SimpleCMS user should look something like this:

When you click **OK**, you will have the new user created for the SimpleCMS database. This is the user account we will use for accessing the database for our application.

Creating a database table with Management Studio Express

Databases store information in tables, something like a spreadsheet, and we will need at least one table to use in our simple CMS. We'll get into the databases and structures in the next chapter, but for now let's create a very simple table to store our content. All we really need is a column for the content anyway, mirroring our single content.txt file we created in the last chapter. To create the table in Management Studio Express, expand the **SimpleCMS** database we created and right-click on **Tables**, then select **New Table...** as shown below:

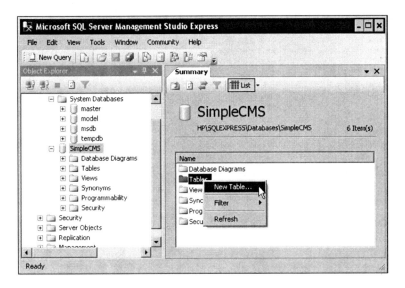

This will create a new table, but we need to define the columns and we'll want to change the default table name to one we can remember. Change the table name in the **Properties** pane to **Content** by clicking on the default name and editing it. The first column in the table has no default name, so name it **Content** as well. When you click in the **Data Type** column, you'll see a drop-down menu, select a data type of **ntext** and make sure **Allow Nulls** is checked. The table should look something like this:

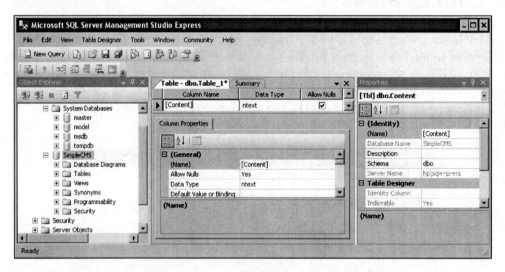

Click on **File | Save All**, and the new database and table are ready for us to use. We've created a very basic table here and made some choices that may not be the best for a production environment. For example, we've allowed a null entry in our content field. In reality, we would never want the content to be null, or non-existent, we would want something in there. Not allowing nulls in the database would be one method of forcing the field to always contain something to display to the end user, even if it was just a line that said, "Sorry, nothing to see here, please move along." But for our immediate purpose, allowing nulls avoids having to write code that deals with attempting to enter nothing into the database and receiving a cryptic error that stops our application from continuing. Besides, at this stage, we don't really want anyone else to look at our web site anyway.

Dealing with null data

There are several ways to deal with null data entries in a web application. One is by not allowing null data into the database, enforcing data integrity through the database structure. This would be the way a database programmer would handle the problem, using stored procedures that supplied data even if the user didn't. A second method would be for the application programmer to write code that created the record with default data, and then accepted user input to change the defaults. This has an advantage that null data fields are always filled with the same data if the user doesn't input any. However, a lazy user may just allow the default to pass through, instead of entering what they really needed to.

Perhaps the most common web application solution is the use of required inputs, and ASP.NET provides developers with the ability to require fields within a data input screen. You've surely seen forms having the name, password, and email fields mandatory, whereas the address or phone fields are optional. This ensures that the name, password, and email fields of a database are never null, but allows null entries in the other fields.

Even though we allow null data, we don't actually want null data in our database because it wouldn't make sense to display nothing. We'll add some simple data so that our application isn't left with nothing to show when a web page is requested. In the **Object Explorer** pane of Management Studio Express, browse to the **Content** table we just created. Right-click it and choose **Open Table** as shown below:

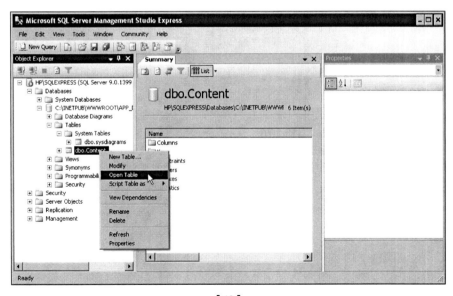

This will open the table in the center pane and allow you to enter data into the **Content** field of the table. Click on the record and a new record will open. Type in "Enter your content here..." without quotes. Exit Management Studio Express, as soon as you move off the field you entered the record is saved. This is the text that will display in our CMS application's Default.aspx page until we edit it.

Using the SimpleCMS database in Visual Web Developer

We've created the database, and now it's time to put it to use. We'll be changing our code in Chapter 1 from accessing a text file to reading and writing to a field in a database table, and really it's not that different from using a text file. The process is the same, with the only change being the data source, a database versus a text file.

The first thing we need to do is make the database usable in Visual Web Developer. Open VWD and open the web site we started in Chapter 1. If you expand the **App_Data** folder in **Solution Explorer,** you should see the SimpleCMS database we created previously, as shown below:

If you right-click the **SimpleCMS.mdf** database file and choose **Open**, you should see the database open in **Database Explorer**. You can expand the **Tables** section and see the **Content** table we created earlier, as shown next:

Chapter 2

Solution Explorer and Database Explorer will be instrumental throughout the process of building our CMS because most of the work we need to do can be accomplished here. If you right-click **Tables** in **Database Explorer**, you will see the option to create a new table, which will bring up a similar table creation dialog to the one we used in Management Studio Express.

System Error 32:'The process cannot open the file...'

You may experience an error similar to **Unable to open the physical file "C:\inetpub\wwwroot\App_Data\SimpleCMS.mdf". Operating System error 32:"The Process cannot access the file because it is being used by another process".** There is an annoying problem with using Microsoft SQL Server Management Studio Express to create the database as we did in that the database is attached to Management Studio Express and we can't also attach it in VWD.

To fix this, open Management Studio Express, expand **Databases** and right-click the **SimpleCMS** database. Choose **Tasks | Detach** and the database will be detached from Management Studio Express. You can then follow the steps above to open the SimpleCMS database in Visual Web Developer without the error.

[45]

Using the SimpleCMS database in the CMS application

Okay, we have a database. Now let's make use of it by replacing our text file in our Simple CMS application with a database as the storage for our content. First, we'll create a data source that uses our database, and then we'll bind our display to the data source. We'll also configure our application to update the data in our database using our FCKEditor control.

Creating a new Default.aspx file

Open Visual Web Developer 2008 and open the web site we created in Chapter 1; it should be in the `c:\Inetpub\wwwroot` folder by default. Delete (or rename if you want them for reference) the files `content.txt`, `Default.aspx`, and `Edit.aspx` from the web root. These files used the file system for storing the web site content, but now we have a database for this purpose. We will change almost all of the code, so it is easier to start from scratch in this case.

In VWD, click on **File | New File** to open the **Add New Item** dialog. Choose **Web Form**, name it **Default.aspx**, and make sure the **Place code in separate file** checkbox is checked, as shown below:

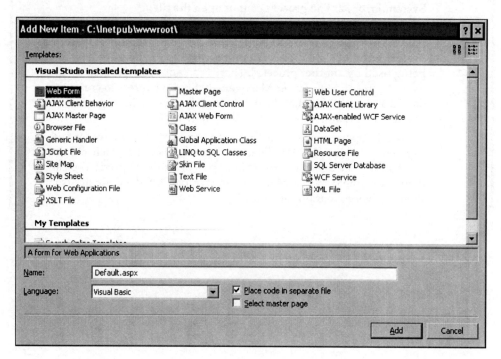

This creates two files, `Default.aspx` and `Default.aspx.vb`, the second one being the code-behind file. In the first chapter, we used inline code because the application was quite simple at that stage. For the rest of the application, we will use the **code behind** technique to separate code from presentation.

Configuring the data source

Using a database in an ASP.NET application requires a data source to be created for the application to access the data. The data source control handles the task of retrieving the specific data with almost no code, making coding quicker and more accurate. Many types of data sources exist, from XML files to OLEDB and ODBC data sources, to databases such as the SQL Server 2005 Express database we are using. Controls for these sources exist in the ASP.NET 2.0 framework such as the XmlDataSource control for accessing an XML file. Using these existing controls makes development faster and reduces potential coding errors.

For our application, we will use the SqlDataSource control. The name of this control makes it seem like it works with SQL Server, but it allows access to any OLEDB or ODBC database, meaning it can be used on Microsoft Access databases as well. For our use the name is perfect, since we'll use SQL Server 2005 Express. We can create an SqlDataSource control for our database quite easily using the drag-and-drop functions in Visual Web Developer 2008.

In **Source View** in VWD, expand the **Data** section in the **Toolbox**, then drag a **SqlDataSource** control to the **<div></div>** section of the code, as shown below:

In the **Properties** window for the **SqlDataSource** control, at the bottom is a link to **Configure Data Source**. Clicking this opens the data source configuration wizard, starting with the **Connection** dialog. Since we have no connections to choose from, we need to create one, so click on **New Connection** and the **Add Connection** dialog appears.

The default data source is **Microsoft SQL Server Database File (SqlClient)**, but we want to connect to SQL Server Express itself, not just our database file. Click on the **Change** button and choose **Microsoft SQL Server** as the data source. The **Add Connection** dialog will change to match the new data source choice. Select the **SQLEXPRESS** named instance from the **SQL Server** drop-down list, there will most likely only be one listed. Select **Use SQL Server Authentication,** and enter SimpleCMSUser as the user account and SimpleCMS as the password, choosing to save the password. Choose the **SimpleCMS_Database** from the database drop-down list. Your **Add Connection** dialog should look something like this:

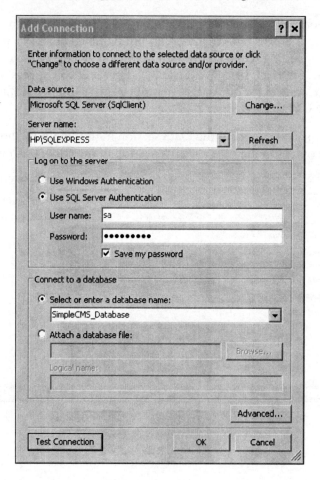

Click on the **Test Connection** button and you should see a message that the connection succeeded. Click **OK** and return to the **Configure Data Source** wizard. Choose **Next**, and then choose to save the connection in the application configuration file. This is the `web.config` file, which is used to hold your application's configuration information.

In the **Configure the Select Statement** dialog, check the checkbox next to **Content** and the **SELECT Statement** should look like this:

```
SELECT [Content] FROM [Content]
```

We'll walk through a few SQL commands later in the chapter, but this statement simply says to "Select the Content field from the Content table", which is the field we created in our database earlier. Click on **Next** and then **Test Query**, and you should see the default content we entered in our database — "**Enter your content here…**".

Finishing the wizard will add the SqlDataSource configuration to both our `Default.aspx` file and a new `web.config` file. The `Default.aspx` code should have changed to something like:

```
<asp:SqlDataSource ID="SqlDataSource1" runat="server"
  ConnectionString="<%$ ConnectionStrings:SimpleCMS_
DatabaseConnectionString %>"
  SelectCommand="SELECT [Content] FROM [Content]">
</asp:SqlDataSource>
```

This sets up our `SqlDataSource`, using the `ConnectionString` stored in the `web.config` file, along with the query we created in the wizard. The new `web.config` file, in addition to a lot of default settings and comments, has a `connectionStrings` section in it that looks something like:

```
<connectionStrings>
  <add name="SimpleCMS_DatabaseConnectionString"
    connectionString="Data Source=HP\SQLEXPRESS;
    Initial Catalog=SimpleCMS_Database;
    Persist Security Info=True;
    User ID=SimpleCMSUsersa;Password=SimpleCMS"
    providerName="System.Data.SqlClient"
  />
</connectionStrings>
```

Now that we have a connection with a data source, we need a way to display that data.

Binding the Data Source to a Repeater control

In ASP.NET, there are a number of controls that can be bound to specific data and data sources. The GridView, FormView, and DetailsView are most common, but even a drop-down control can be data-bound. For our `Default.aspx` page, we'll use a Repeater control. The control in our case is misnamed. As we have only a single piece of data to display, there won't be anything to repeat. However, a Repeater control is a good way to display reoccurring data in a template such as a list of business addresses or books in a library collection. The advantage for us is the ability to use a template for each item—in our case, just the one item in the list of data. A Repeater control is read only, that is, you cannot change the data displayed. We'll handle this when we create our new `Edit.aspx` file.

To create the Repeater control, simply drag a **Repeater** control from the **Data** section of the **Toolbox** to a location just below our **SqlDataSource** control, still inside the **<div></div>** in our web form. We will then add a `<ItemTemplate>` to our Repeater, which will provide the template to display our data retrieved from our SqlDataSource. Add the required code to your `Default.aspx` page, so the Repeater control section looks like:

```
<asp:Repeater ID="Repeater1" runat="server"
 DataSourceID="SqlDataSource1">
  <ItemTemplate>
    <asp:Label ID="Label1" runat="server"
      Text='<%# Eval("Content") %>'
    />
  </ItemTemplate>
</asp:Repeater>
```

In the `<asp:Repeater>` control, we bind the control to our data source by setting the `DataSourceID` to the name of the data source—`SqlDataSource1` in this case. Our `<ItemTemplate>` contains just a simple Label control. However, we set the `Text` attribute to the data we retrieved in the `SelectCommand` from our SqlDataSource—in this case evaluating the `Content` field and displaying it. Once you have saved the code, you should be able to open a web browser and browse to `http://localhost/` and see a page similar to this:

Creating a new Edit.aspx

Okay, displaying the content wasn't so hard. But now we have to edit it in an ASP.NET page, as we can't easily call up a database tool to edit our web content and it's no longer a simple text file. We need to create the Edit.aspx page. Start by adding a new **Web Form** in the Visual Web Developer, naming it Edit.aspx and making sure **Place code in separate file** is checked, just as we did when adding the new Default.aspx file. We will use the same SqlDataSource as we did in Default.aspx to load the content into our FCKEditor control, so add the following code inside the <form> tags in the auto generated code:

```
<asp:SqlDataSource ID="SqlDataSource1" runat="server"
  ConnectionString="<%$ ConnectionStrings:SimpleCMS_
DatabaseConnectionString %>"
  SelectCommand="SELECT [Content] FROM [Content]">
</asp:SqlDataSource>
```

We also need to add the FCKEditor to our page, which requires registering it on the page as we did in Chapter 1. Add the following code to the top of Edit.aspx, immediately below the page definition line:

```
<%@ Register
  Assembly="FredCK.FCKeditorV2"
  Namespace="FredCK.FCKeditorV2"
  TagPrefix="FCKeditorV2"
%>
```

We'll add our FCKEditor in a FormView control, replacing the Repeater control we used in the `Default.aspx` file to display our content, as the Repeater control is a read only control and cannot be used to edit the data bound to it. First, we create the FormView with the following code:

```
<asp:FormView ID="FormView1"
  runat="server"
  DataSourceID="SqlDataSource1"
  DefaultMode="Edit">
</asp:FormView>
```

This creates our FormView control and sets the data source to our SqlDataSource control. A FormView control displays a single record from the data source—our database in this case. However, unlike the Repeater control, we can edit the data returned, and eventually save it back to our data source. The FormView also allows us to specify an `EditItemTemplate`, as we did with our `ItemTemplate` in the Repeater control, which allows us to use the FCKEditor control to edit our content instead of just seeing our record in a table.

Other ASP.NET databound controls that allow editing

In addition to the FormView and Repeater controls, ASP.NET has a number of other databound controls that display data from a DataSource control. These controls are composite controls, and will often have other controls such as a Label or TextBox within their layout. The Gridview control does as its name suggests, display data in a grid or table, along with sorting, paging, and the editing of a single row of data. The DetailsView displays only a single record at a time, but allows paging through multiple records, as well as the editing of those records. It is most often used in conjunction with a master control such as a GridView, in order to show a single selected record for editing.

We will add our FCKEditor control the same way we did in the `Default.aspx` page, this time as an `EditItemTemplate` in our FormView control, using the following code:

```
<EditItemTemplate>
  <FCKeditorV2:FCKeditor ID="FCKeditor1" runat="server"
    Value='<%# Bind("Content") %>'>
  </FCKeditorV2:FCKeditor>
</EditItemTemplate>
```

If you now open `Edit.aspx` in a browser window, you should see something similar to this:

Of course, editing the content won't do much good if we can't save it back to the database. For that, we need to do two things. First, we need to add an `UpdateCommand` to our SqlDataSource control so that we can update the content. This is quite simple, as we simply need to add the following line right below our `SelectCommand` in the code:

```
UpdateCommand="UPDATE [Content] SET Content=@Content">
```

This updates the `Content` table in our database by setting the `Content` field to the `Content` in our FCKEditor control. But it won't do it unless we invoke the `UpdateCommand`, which we'll do from a `LinkButton`. Add the following code below the FCKEditor control in the EditItemTemplate:

```
<asp:LinkButton ID="button1"
  runat="server"
  CommandName="Update"
  Text="Update"
/>
```

Your `Edit.aspx` page will now look something like:

Testing the new `Edit.aspx` page is simple—just change the content and click **Update**. If you type in **This is new content** over the top of the existing text and click **Update**, you should see the following if you open `Default.aspx`:

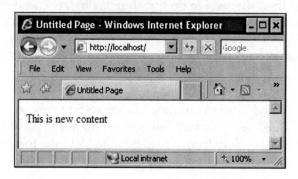

Creating multiple content pages

We've now replicated our file-based CMS in a database, but it's still just a single page you can update with new content. If this was all we were going to do, it would be much easier to have a static HTML page and just edit the content in it with a HTML editor, or even Notepad. The reason we've moved to a database is to create a dynamic site, with different content available in different pages, all easily changed by the user. No, a single page Content Management System won't do. Or will it?

We have had a single page for our content up to now because we only created one file and set it to use one piece of content, whether from a database or a text file. We could create a second page, call it `Page2.aspx`, duplicate the `Default.aspx` code and the `Edit.aspx` code, create a new table in our database for Page 2, and operate just like we have for the `Default.aspx` page. But that's a lot of work. And it defeats the purpose of a CMS, especially since creating new pages would mean creating everything over again. So, we will have a single page in our CMS.

Okay, that doesn't sound right, but you need to understand that a page could have different meaning in different contexts. A page in a web site, like that of a magazine, is different from every other page. We change pages by clicking links, often in a menu, just as we would turn a page in a magazine. But a web site is not a magazine. We have the ability to create that page on the fly as it's requested, piecing together data from multiple sources such as text, pictures, headlines, and so on. A page, in terms of ASP.NET code, is really just a file in our application. That file, such as `Default.aspx`, can display multiple web pages just by changing the content used to create the page in the web site.

Until now, we selected data only from a single location, based on no input from the user, just the developer's whims. That's not very useful to the user, and it's rather boring for the developer. It would also make for a very short book, as this would be the last chapter. The user wants more information and a better web experience. The developer wants a more challenging application to develop. The content providers want to be able to display more content in a more friendly manner. And the book publishers want a longer book. So let's keep going, shall we?

Altering the database table

Our database is currently set up to mirror our single file that we used in Chapter 1.
There is no provision for keeping track of the page that the content should appear
on, so we really can't store content for multiple pages in it. We need to modify the
table structure to accommodate pinning content to a page.

To do this, open SQL Server Management Studio and open the **SimpleCMS** database
from the **App_Data** folder. You may need to attach to the database in SQL Server
Management Studio. In **Object Explorer**, expand the **SimpleCMS** database, expand
Tables, and then the **dbo.Content** table. Right-click on **Columns** and choose **New
Column**. This will open the **dbo.Content** table with a new column ready for input.
Enter a column name of PageName, with a data type of nvarchar(50), and check to
allow nulls. We need to allow nulls because we already have a record in the table,
which will have a null entry in the new column when we create it. We'll populate it
later. Your new column should look something like this:

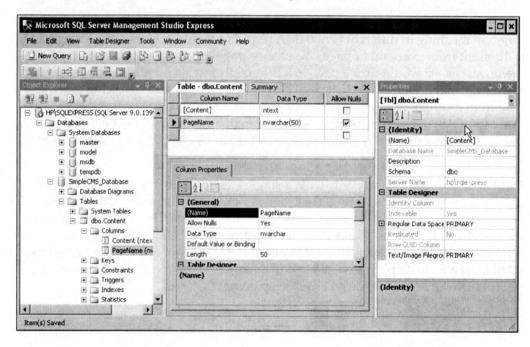

Adding data to the new column

We already have a record with data in the **Content** field of our new table, but it has a **NULL** entry for our new **PageName** field. We need to add the name of our page that will display the content we created and edited in the previous section. To do this, right-click on the **dbo.Content** table in **Object Explorer** and choose **Open Table**. This opens our table and allows us to enter data directly into the database fields.

Start by changing the **NULL** entry in the **PageName** field in the first record to Home. This will be the content displayed in our site's home page. You'll notice that the **Content** field is populated with **<p>This is new content</p>**, which is the data saved to our database from the FCKEditor control when we tested our Edit.aspx page.

While you're on this screen, add a new record by clicking in the empty field next to the asterisk and typing **Content for page two**. Add a **PageName** of **Page2** for the **PageName** field for this same record. Add a third record with **Content for page three** in the **Content** field and **Page3** in the **PageName** field. Your table should look like this:

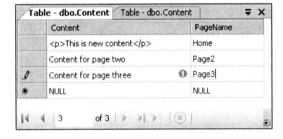

You'll notice the red exclamation point on the record until you move the cursor to another record. This indicates the record has not been saved to the table. As soon as you move off this record, it is saved to the database without needing to do anything special to save your data. SQL Server, as with all Microsoft databases, saves a record as soon as possible to prevent any loss of data in the case of a power failure or any other disruption. This is important both to maintain data security and to maintain integrity. The record is locked, as it is written to prevent two users from editing the same record, and only one user's changes are effected. Until you move off the record in the interface, you may still be editing it, so changes are unsaved and could be overwritten or lost. This is a good reason not to edit records directly in database tables unless there is no possibility of someone else being in the database at the same time.

We now have data for three separate pages in our database. If you were to run the SimpleCMS application in your browser, you would have unexpected results, as we have written code to deal with only a single record and we have done nothing to specify the specific record we want. To do that, we need to change the SqlDataSource to include a query for our data that will result in a single record.

Altering the SqlDataSource code

Our current SqlDataSource uses a `SelectCommand` in the `Default.aspx` file, and both a `SelectCommand` and an `UpdateCommand` in the `Edit.aspx` file. In all cases, this `SelectCommand` simply selects the `Content` field from the `Content` table, without selecting a specific record from which the `Content` field is read. This was fine when we had a single record, but now as we have three records, we need a way to select just the record we want and then the `Content` field from that record. We will use the PageName field to select the record.

SQL queries can have a WHERE clause to specify specific parameters to match in the query. We'll cover this more completely later in the chapter, but a simple example will make it easier to understand the concept. Suppose you had to select a specific person from a crowd of people. Each person has a number of attributes—some are male, some are old, and some have blonde hair. But to select a single unique person out of the crowd, you need an attribute that is unique to that person. Suppose every person had a different name. There was Jim, and John, and even Mary, but no two people had the same name. If you asked all the men to come forward, you might get dozens of people. If you asked everyone with blonde hair, maybe dozens more. Even if you asked for all the blonde males in the crowd, chances are you would have several step forward. But if you asked for Richard, only Richard would step forward.

Now, suppose everyone in the crowd has a sign, all with different words or symbols. If you wanted to know the sign a specific person had on him/her, you would ask for the sign that Armando is carrying. As there is only one Armando in the crowd, you get only one sign. And you've just created a query for a specific piece of data, the sign, carried in a specific record, Armando's. The query would be something like "Give me the sign that Armando has". Or in terms of our database and the Content field, "SELECT Content FROM Content WHERE PageName = Page2".

We just need to add that to our SqlDataSource. We don't want a specific record to always show when we use that SqlDataSource, we just want to change the SqlDataSource, so we can specify a `PageName` to select the `Content` from. We do that by using a variable. If you change the `SelectCommand` in the `Default.aspx`, and both the `SelectCommand` and the `UpdateCommand` in `Edit.aspx` to the code shown below, we'll have that ability:

```
SelectCommand="SELECT [Content] FROM [Content]
   WHERE PageName=@PageName"
UpdateCommand="UPDATE [Content] SET Content=@Content
   WHERE PageName=@PageName"
```

This allows us to specify the `PageName` variable when we use the SqlDataSource. We will do that by using a query string, which is appended to the URL to specify the page we want to view. To read the query string, we use a `QueryStringParameter` for both the `SelectCommand` and `UpdateCommand` in our SqlDataSource. To do this, add this code directly below the modified `SelectCommand` and `UpdateCommand` in the `Edit.aspx` file:

```
<SelectParameters>
   <asp:QueryStringParameter Name="PageName"
     QueryStringField="PageName" Type="string"
   />
</SelectParameters>
<UpdateParameters>
   <asp:Parameter Name="Content" Type="string" />
   <asp:QueryStringParameter Name="PageName"
     QueryStringField="PageName" Type="string"
   />
</UpdateParameters>
```

This code adds parameters to the `SelectCommand` and `UpdateCommand` in our SqlDataSource. The `QueryStringParameter` accepts a QueryString called `PageName` from the URL, and adds that QueryString value as a parameter to the SELECT and UPDATE queries that go to SQL Server Express in our WHERE clause. This query then matches the **PageName** field in the database to the `PageName` QueryString value, returning only that record having that **PageName** value in the **PageName** field.

The ASP.NET QueryString

A QueryString in ASP.NET, as well as other dynamic web languages such as Classic ASP, is a method for passing parameters between web pages, using the URL to pass the parameter. The URL with a query string attached takes the format of the page URL—a question mark followed by a parameter and value, or sometimes a series of parameter and value pairs. The code on the destination page then reads the query string from the URL. You probably recognize these query strings in many of your favorite web sites; they show up in the following format:

```
http://www.samples.com/Default.aspx?PageName=Home
```

To test your new SqlDataSource, browse to the following URL in a web browser:

`http://localhost/Default.aspx?PageName=Home`

You should see a page similar to this:

If you change the URL to `http://localhost/Default.aspx?PageName=Page2`, you should see the page change to:

Later on in the development of this application, we'll add more functionality such as menus to navigate between pages. But, for now, we have walked through the process of replacing our file-based CMS with a database version. We have also written the database and application to handle multiple pages, something we couldn't easily do with a single text file as our source of content. As we move further, you'll need to know some basic SQL Server commands and techniques.

Understanding SQL Server commands

The nice part about learning Microsoft SQL Server query language is that there really aren't a whole lot of commands to learn. When you're trying to look something up, you use a SELECT query. Adding data uses INSERT for a new record and UPDATE to change an existing record. And when you want to get rid of data, you use the appropriately named DELETE query. Other than commands that work with the database and table structure itself, the rest are simply commands used to modify the query.

Rows / Records and Columns / Fields

When databases were simple non-relational tables for storing data, the idea of rows and columns was used to describe the actual data in the database. As the database expanded, and became larger and more flexible, rows and columns didn't seem correct. Therefore, the terms records and fields were used instead. Through common use and the hold over of older definitions, rows and records are now used interchangeably as are columns and fields. This book will flip between them — don't let the different terms confuse you.

SQL query syntax

SQL query syntax is extremely simple, though it can get quite complex. At the most basic, it consists of a query type, the data you want to retrieve, and where to retrieve it from. There are some conventions to writing a query and some required information, but most of the query is optional, as long as the meaning of the query is not ambiguous. However, there are some best practices you should learn and obey, to ensure that the more complex queries you write are easily understood with no ambiguity.

Query notation generally has any SQL command in capital letters such as SELECT, FROM, WHERE, and so on. In addition, specific data values must be enclosed in single quotes and the semi colon terminates a query statement. A well-formed query might look like:

```
SELECT UserName FROM Users WHERE Email ='jsmith@aol.com';
```

White space and line breaks are generally ignored in SQL queries, and you will see queries broken across multiple lines to either make them more understandable or simply because they fit better on the page. A single line query will usually be understood without the semi colon terminator, but coding standards requiring the semi colon as a terminator in all cases make for better programs and easier-to-maintain code.

A best practice for writing any query is to always specify exactly the data you want, using the format of {TableName}.{ColumnName}, so there is no ambiguity in where the data resides. The above query would look more like the following one with table names specified:

```
SELECT Users.UserName
FROM Users
WHERE Users.Email ='jsmith@aol.com';
```

Now, this is a simple query from a single table, so it's unlikely you or the system will be confused about what table the Email column is in. But you might find a query that looks like:

```
SELECT Users.UserName, Roles.RoleName, Portals.PortalName
JOIN Users, Roles
ON Users.UserID = Roles.UserID
JOIN Users, Portals
ON Users.UserID, Portals.UserID
Where Users.Email LIKE'%@aol.com';
```

With that many tables with a UserID field, it's easier to get confused. By specifying the table name, along with the column name, the confusion is cleared up.

Out, out damned Asterisks!

The asterisk character, *, is used in simple queries to indicate all columns in a table. The query:

SELECT * FROM Users;

is a way of saying "Give me all fields in all records from the user's table". It's also sloppy. Very rarely will you want all the fields in a record. You will usually want pertinent information such as FirstName and LastName, not everything you track, including shoe size. Specifying the exact fields you want to be returned will help both eliminate mistakes and reduce the size of the data returned by the query. The more data you get back, the slower your application will run. After all, you would ask something like "Can you give me the names of everyone we hired in 1992?" rather than "Can you send me all the employment records for 1992?" Why dig through boxes and folders when you just want a list of names? Listing out all the specific columns you need to use is always a better alternative to the dreaded asterisk.

SELECT queries

The most used query is probably a SELECT query which, like it sounds, is used to select data from a database. The query returns data in the order of the fields listed in the query, and can be modified through the TOP and the ALL | DISTINCT options. Data can also be returned in a specific order or grouped by fields. A typical SELECT query would be:

```
SELECT StudentName, Grade FROM Gradebook;
```

WHERE clause

The most common clause added to a query is the WHERE clause, allowing a selection to be filtered to a specific value or range in a field. Typical WHERE clauses might be used to select all students who got an A, or any student who got a C or better:

```
SELECT StudentName, Grade FROM Gradebook WHERE Grade ='A';
SELECT StudentName, Grade FROM Gradebook WHERE Grade <'D';
```

LIKE

A modifier to the WHERE clause is LIKE, which can be used to select values where the exact value isn't known. A common situation would be looking for the grade of a student named "Peter Westin", but not knowing if he is listed as "Peter Westin", "Pete Westin", or even "Peter James Westin". This can be solved by using LIKE:

```
SELECT StudentName, Grade
FROM Gradebook
WHERE StudentName LIKE'Pete%';
```

This returns all records where the student name begins with "Pete", so it will match all the possibilities listed above. Unfortunately, it will also return "Pete Marshall", "Petersen Lowenstein", and "Peteya Russinovich"—a good reason to specify first name and last name as separate fields.

AND | OR

AND and OR can be used to add additional parameters to a WHERE clause, further narrowing the selection returned. An example to limit our results to only Seniors or Freshmen with a Grade of "A" might look like this:

```
SELECT StudentName, Grade, ClassLevel
FROM Gradebook
WHERE Grade ='A'
AND ClassLevel ='Senior'
OR ClassLevel ='Freshman';
```

TOP

SELECT queries can be modified using TOP to select only a specific range of data. TOP takes a number and returns that number of records based on the order of the data. The number may not actually be the number of records returned, as TOP treats all ties with the same priority. A query to select the TOP 10 ordered by grade could return 10 or more records. Suppose that five had a grade of 100 and nine had a grade of 99. TOP 10 would return 14 records, as it can't distinguish between the nine grades of 99 as to which is higher than the other. A typical TOP selection might look like the following:

```
SELECT StudentName, Grade FROM Gradebook ORDER by Grade DESC;
```

ALL | DISTINCT

ALL and DISTINCT are two options for modifying a selection to either all elements in a specific group or just a single element from each group. Suppose you had records in a table with a Grade of A, B, C, or D. A SELECT query that is grouped by grade using the ALL option would return all records with a grade of A, then all with a grade of B, and so on. DISTINCT would return only a single record for each grade. Therefore, if you had thirteen grade A, nine grade B, no grade C, and five grade D, it would return one record for A, one record for B, and one record for D. Typical ALL and DISTINCT selections might look like:

```
SELECT ALL Grade FROM Gradebook ORDER BY Grade;
SELECT DISTINCT Grade FROM Gradebook ORDER BY Grade;
```

COUNT

The COUNT option in a selection doesn't return data, it returns a count of the records matching that query. It requires a name and a field to count, and would return a numeric value by the name. A typical COUNT option, used to count the number of times each grade appeared in the Gradebook table, might look like:

```
SELECT Grade, Count(*) AS Students FROM Gradebook GROUP BY Grade;
```

and might return data that looks like the following:

Grade	Students
A	13
B	9
C	0
D	1

GROUP BY clause

The GROUP BY clause groups the data results by the field specified. It is used to combine records with similar values into smaller results. GROUP BY is often used in an aggregate function such as COUNT, or to prevent duplicate records from affecting the results of the query. A typical GROUP BY clause would be used as in the COUNT query above.

HAVING clause

HAVING is an option for the GROUP BY clause that uses a comparison to filter results from groups, similar to a WHERE clause. WHERE is applied to every record in a table, while HAVING is applied to the group. A typical use for the HAVING clause would be to select only those grades received by five or more students in our COUNT example above, as shown next:

```
SELECT Grade, Count(*) AS Students
FROM Gradebook
GROUP BY Grade
HAVING Students > 4;
```

ORDER BY clause

The ORDER BY clause is used to determine the order records are returned in — ascending (ASC) or descending (DESC). If left out of a query, records are returned in the order in which they appear in a database, and the order will be unpredictable. Therefore, it is recommended to specify the order, whenever it is desired to have the output in a particular order. A typical ORDER BY clause would be:

```
SELECT StudentName, Grade FROM Gradebook ORDER BY Grade ASC;
```

It may seem odd, but this query orders the student and grade, according to the grade, from highest grade to lowest. This is because while number grades descend from 100 to 99 to 98 and so on, letter grades ascend from A to B to C, and so on.

INSERT queries

INSERT, UPDATE, and DELETE queries are used to add, modify, and remove records in the database. An INSERT query will insert a new record with the data in the appropriate fields, and has a very specific format. When inserting a new record, all the fields are normally empty or null, unless the database was configured with a default value. Any field you do not provide a value for will remain null, and you must provide values if the database does not allow null entries for a specific field.

The format of an INSERT query is as follows:

```
INSERT INTO {Table Name} ({Field Names}) VALUES ({Field Values});
```

{Field Names} is a list of field names in which the values will be inserted, separated by commas, whereas {Field Values} is the list of values to be inserted into those fields, also separated by commas. The values are inserted into the fields, in the order in which the fields appear in the {Field Names} list, and there must be an equal number of values as there are field names. A typical INSERT query might look like the following:

```
INSERT INTO Gradebook (StudentName, Grade, ClassLevel)
VALUES ('Kurt VanGelder','B','Junior');
```

UPDATE queries

An UPDATE query is identical to an INSERT query, except that it operates on an existing record instead of inserting a new record. An UPDATE can be used on a single field in a record, or on any number of fields, simply by providing the appropriate field names and values. For instance, if our student from the INSERT query changes his grade to A, we can change his record with the following query:

```
UPDATE Gradebook SET Grade ='A'
WHERE StudentName ='Kurt VanGelder';
```

DELETE queries

A DELETE query is just want it sounds like, a query that deletes a record. DELETE queries operate only on the entire record. If you need to delete just the data in a field in a record, use an UPDATE query to change the field value to null. A typical DELETE query might be:

```
DELETE FROM Gradebook WHERE StudentName ='Kurt VanGelder';
```

Other queries

There are other types of queries, though they will be used less often. A MERGE query will combine data from two or more tables, sort of a combination INSERT and UPDATE in one. You will also see SQL commands that create a table, alter a table, or drop a table from the database, changing the structure of your database and tables as your application needs change.

One type of command you will see are transactions in SQL, especially in the manipulation of financial data, which protects data integrity when multiple queries are executed to process a transaction. A transaction in SQL might look something like this:

```
START TRANSACTION;
    UPDATE Credit.Account
    SET Credit.AccountTotal = Credit.AccountTotal - 10000.00
    WHERE Credit.AccountNumber = 61644871;
    UPDATE Debit.Account
    SET Debit.AccountTotal = Debit.AccountTotal + 10000.00
    WHERE Debit.AccountNumber = 41665790;
IF ERRORS = 0 COMMIT;
IF ERRORS <> 0 ROLLBACK;
```

This transaction first updates a `Credit.Account` record to take out $10,000, and then updates `Debit.Account` to add $10,000. If an application crashed or there was another failure during the transaction, and one of the UPDATE queries didn't complete, the financial records would be out of synch. The transaction solves this issue, as the transaction is not committed in the database until all parts of the transaction have completed successfully, otherwise all changes are rolled back and undone. Imagine a world where you wrote a check for rent and it was taken from your bank account, but never added to your landlord's bank account. Your bank says you don't have the money and your landlord says he doesn't either, so you're being evicted. We won't use transactions in our application for this book, but you might want them if you extend this Content Management System to include e-commerce functions.

It is well beyond the scope of this book to teach you SQL, but as we create our Content Management System, we may need to review some SQL statements again. You may want to look at `http://www.sqlcourse.com/` for a quick interactive introduction to SQL queries and syntax. You can install SQL books online (from the same web site you downloaded SQL Server 2005 Express) for a complete reference to SQL Server, especially command syntax.

Entities and relationships in brief

SQL Server works on the principle of RDBMS. This means that tables and data can be related to each other, and in fact should be. We'll work with some of these relationships in designing the architecture of our application in the next chapter. Also, it's important that you have an idea of what entities and relationships are, and how they work.

Entities

In database terms, an **entity** is a specific object having features, called attributes, which can be used to describe it. You are an entity. Your attributes include your first name, last name, email address, phone number, and shoe size. Some attributes are important—you would probably like your users' names and email addresses—while others are less important. Unless you run the web site of the International Association of Web Developers with Two Left Feet, probably you won't care about your users' shoe size. But the Nike retail web site may be very concerned about shoe size. The attributes in your database, called fields or columns, will be those that you choose to track. In your database, each entity is a table. So, the table for a person might look like:

PersonID	FirstName	LastName	EMail	Phone
1	Ron	Davis	rdavis@aol.com	212-547-1818
2	Betty	Randall-Smythe	betty@yahoo.com	813-484-5200
3	Sidhartha	Pandoori	sidp@gmail.com	11-435-537-8900

Each of the three people listed is a specific entity that can be identified by one of the attributes in the table. In this case, we used a unique identifier called `PersonID`, a number that is unique to only that record. After all, as we add people to the table, there is possibly another Ron Davis who could be entered, making both `FirstName` and `LastName`, as well as a combination of the two fields, non-unique. In a database, we always want a unique identifier, or **Primary Key**, which could be used to select a single record.

SQL Unique Identifier and IDENTITY column

In SQL Server, there are two ways to ensure a unique identifier in a database table. Perhaps the simplest is to create an IDENTITY column, which gets assigned a unique number as soon as the record is created. This ensures there will always be a unique identifier in the record that can be used as a key value, and which can be found in only one record in the table.

A problem with the IDENTITY column is that it is unique, but only within this table and database. If you were to merge a database (for example, merging your company's database with your competitor's when the companies are merged), this identifier may no longer be unique.

A **Unique Identifier** data type, normally called a **GUID**, is globally unique across everything. These can't be automatically created when the record is inserted into the table, and they are generally large, a 16-byte binary value. This makes indexing them take longer and be less efficient.

In our project, we'll be using the IDENTITY column approach—partly for ease, and partly because our application is for learning purposes and unlikely to be widely used for production. But if you are tasked with creating a unique identifier for your SQL records, remember that there is a difference between the two.

Entity relationships

Entities have relationships to each other as well, the principle behind an RDBMS. For example, take a student attending courses at a university. The student is an entity, and so is the course and the instructor. They relate to each other in different ways. A course will have only one instructor, a one-to-one relationship in the database. But each instructor may have many courses, a one-to-many relationship. And many students will have many courses, a many-to-many relationship. It is through these relationships that we can find the data that applies to a specific query. For example, we may want to find all the courses taught by an instructor. We query the database for all courses having a specific instructor. Simple enough, but the query needs to handle data from multiple tables. We do this by associating the identities, or creating relationships between them. Consider the following database tables:

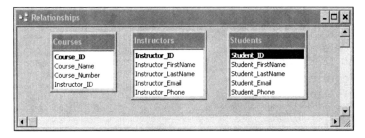

We have three entities, or tables—Courses, Instructors, and Students. We have a number of attributes that we track for each. Each table is all the attributes of a single entity, so we don't list Courses under Students, or under Instructors. Instead, we use keys to each entity, to define the relationship between tables, so that we can select from across multiple tables. Each table has a unique identity column, or primary key, which identifies a specific record in that table. No two records will have that unique value. In these tables, we arbitrarily assigned an automatic ID for each Course_ID, Instructor_ID, and Student_ID. This is called the Primary Key, or PK, as it is the primary means of identifying a unique record in this table.

Database normalization

Normalization of a database is a technique that is used to design a database to eliminate duplication of information and to help maintain data integrity. In our example, we had Students as a separate table. We could have had a single table for courses, and for each instance of a course taken by a student, we could enter the course information and the student information. This would be a database that isn't normalized because you might have four courses which have a record for "John Smith", along with his email and phone number. This amounts to four opportunities for data to be entered incorrectly.

Suppose one of the entries listed "Johnny Smith", as that's what his friends call him, and another had "John Michael Smith" because he gave his full name while registering for the course. A search of the database for all courses taken by "John Smith" would miss both these records, as that's not what was entered as his name. Now, suppose he changed his email address. Someone would have to search through every record in the database to change his email address.

Normalized, the database has Students as a table and all details about the student are kept in that table. There are still data entry errors possible, but the chances are lessened and the corrections are easier. Simple data entry checks and searches for similar names can allow an operator to enter data correctly, and with a fairly high confidence that the data is correct and cohesive across all databases.

You'll also notice that Instructor_ID appears in the Courses table too. This is because each course can have only a single instructor, so we can include this field as a key to the Instructors table, where we store the attributes of the instructors. This field is called a **Foreign Key**, or **FK**, as it identifies a unique record in another (or foreign) table. This foreign key also identifies the relationship between the Courses and Instructors tables. We use this relationship to create our query, looking for the courses taught by a given instructor for whom we know the email address is jsmith@sample-university.edu. The SQL query would look something like this:

```
SELECT Courses.CourseName, Courses.CourseNumber
FROM Courses INNER JOIN Instructors
ON Courses.Instructor_ID = Instructors.Instructor_ID
WHERE Instructors.Instructor_Email ='jsmith@sample-university.edu';
```

This query joins the two tables together using the `Courses.Instructor_ID` and `Instructors.Instructor_ID` fields as the common link between the tables. The results of this query will be the course name and number for the instructor with an email address of jsmith@sample-university.edu. An INNER JOIN simply indicates that only the records with the same value appearing in the `Instructor_ID` field of both tables will be selected. An OUTER JOIN would select all the records where the value appeared in neither record, or display every record that didn't match the given email address. That would be a query for all courses not taught by this instructor.

So, how about courses and students? What if you wanted to query all the courses for a student, or all the students for a course? There are no foreign key fields to link the tables. How do we query then? Well, the answer is, we can't. At least not without another table. We need a table that sits between the `Courses` table and the `Students` table, and maps the students to the courses and vice versa. Consider this table diagram, this time with the entity relationships shown:

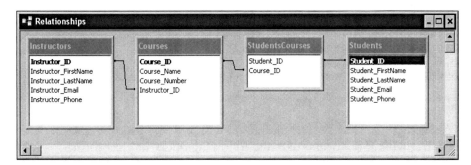

You'll see a new table here, `StudentsCourses`, with only the primary keys of the `Students` table and the `Courses` table listed. This is used in the SQL query with a double JOIN statement to link the `Courses` and `Students` tables through the `StudentsCourses` table, as shown next:

```
SELECT Courses.CourseName, Courses.Course_Number,
    Students.Student_FirstName, Students.Student_LastName
FROM Courses, Students
JOIN Courses, StudentsCourses
ON Courses.Course_ID, StudentsCourses.Course_ID
JOIN Students, StudentsCourses
ON Students.Student_ID, StudentsCourses.Student_ID
WHERE Courses.Course_ID = "3";
```

This query will list course name, course ID, and student names for all students in the course with a `Course_ID` of 3. Yes, SQL queries can get complicated, especially when you're unfamiliar with the query syntax. We'll get into database structures more in the next chapter where we work on the architecture of our application, and you might consider additional resources if you want to understand entity relationships better.

SQL injection

SQL injection is a hacking technique that attempts to gain access to the system by sending escape characters in a SQL command and injecting a rogue command into the SQL statement. It happens when a web site allows user inputs to pass directly to the command string, and be executed by SQL without any filtering for unwanted command characters. Needless to say, it's something we don't want happening in our Content Management System.

An example of SQL injection is where an input into a form contains an unexpected set of characters. Suppose you had an SQL statement that accepted a product name as input and searched for it in the Products table of your database. The SQL statement might look like this:

```
SQLstatement = "SELECT * FROM Products
WHERE ProductName ='" & ProductName & "';"
```

If a user entered `Chair`, the resulting statement would look like:

```
SELECT * FROM Products WHERE ProductName ='Chair';
```

This is perfectly fine. Your `SELECT` statement will find any product named `Chair` and display it. But what if the user enters the following query in your form:

```
Chair' or'x' ='x';DROP TABLE Products;SELECT * FROM Products WHERE
ProductName ='Chair
```

The resulting SQL command would look like:

```
SELECT * FROM Products WHERE ProductName ='Chair' or'x' ='x';DROP
TABLE Products;SELECT * FROM Products WHERE ProductName ='Chair';
```

This query would be evaluated to select any record with the product name of `Chair`, or where $x = x$. As x always is equal to x, the `WHERE` clause will evaluate true. The next statement following the semi colon would be followed, dropping the table `Products` from your database. The third statement after the next semi colon is simply there to make this a valid SQL query with the addition of the last single quote from your code. The end result is that the injected SQL just deleted the `Products` table, rendering your application useless.

Preventing SQL injection

There is no easy way to prevent all SQL injection attacks, so defense in depth
is appropriate. The first layer of defense is the input itself, which needs to have
malicious characters filtered out. In particular, not allowing the SQL query
terminator (;) or SQL comment characters (- and /* */) will prevent quite a few
automated injection attacks. Filtering out any inputs that begin with xp_ is also
a good idea, as these are the first three characters of SQL Server extended stored
procedures. You do not want the stored procedure xp_cmdshell to be run on your
system. Many production SQL servers will have this extended procedure removed
for this purpose, as well as any others that can be used malevolently. Using field
validation in input forms can help and, in your code, you can replace any of these
malicious input characters with harmless text, something like:

```
strFormInput = strFormInput.Replace(";","--")
SQLstatement = "SELECT * FROM Products WHERE ProductName ='" &
strFormInput & "';"
```

This takes the form input, and replaces the SQL query termination character (;) with
the comment characters (- -), effectively commenting out malicious code entered
into the form input. But relying on field validation or replacing character strings
won't prevent all SQL injection. Someday, someone will try a string of characters you
didn't think to filter on.

Parameterized queries are another line of defense against SQL injection. A
parameterized query is one where the user input is added to the SQL query as a
parameter, not as part of the original query statement. For example, our original
SQL statement:

```
SQLstatement = "SELECT * FROM Products
WHERE ProductName ='" & ProductName & "';"
```

could be rewritten something like this:

```
SELECT * FROM Products WHERE ProductName = @ProductName",
SQLConnection);
SQLCommand.SelectCommand.Parameters["ProductName"].Value ='Chair';
```

SQLConnection and SQLCommand would need to be defined somewhere of course, but the idea is that SQL Server allows query values to be substituted with parameters that are inserted into the SQL query by SQL Server. Parameterized queries are even more effective when used by stored procedures, especially when type-safe parameters are used. SQL Server allows the specification of the data type in the creation of the parameter, requiring the correct data type for the field. For example, if your field is an integer, a string entered as a parameter won't be accepted. Protecting your code from SQL injection is only one of the security issues you'll face in your development career, and it's unfortunately beyond the scope of this book. You will likely see some of the code in future chapters exposing potential security problems. Please remember that the code in this book is to teach a concept, not to be used immediately in a production environment.

Microsoft has more SQL injection suggestions online at http://msdn.microsoft.com/en-us/library/ms161953.aspx, and a section on SQL injection in the *Patterns and Practices Security Guidance* documents at http://msdn.microsoft.com/en-us/library/ms998271.aspx.

Changing the database user account

In this chapter, we used the sa account to connect to our database, even though earlier we created the SimpleCMSUser account for this purpose. There's nothing wrong with this for developing a site that will not be published on the Internet, but the sa account is the master account for your database and it's not a smart idea to use it on a production system. In addition, many hosts will not allow you to use it, and will make you create an account or use one they create for you. Fortunately, it's simple to change the account we use.

Assuming you created the account in SQL Server Management Studio, or by using your host's control panel, you simply need to change the connection string in the web.config file. In your web.config, you will find a line similar to:

```
<add name="SimpleCMS_DatabaseConnectionString"
  connectionString="Data Source=HP\SQLEXPRESS;
  Initial Catalog=SimpleCMS_Database;
  Persist Security Info=True;
  User ID=sa;Password=SimpleCMS"
providerName="System.Data.SqlClient" />
```

Simply change the `User ID` and `Password` to match the database user you or your host created. To use the SimpleCMSUser account we created earlier, you would change this line in the `web.config` as below, with the changes highlighted:

```
<add name="SimpleCMS_DatabaseConnectionString"
   connectionString="Data Source=HP\SQLEXPRESS;
   Initial Catalog=SimpleCMS_Database;
   Persist Security Info=True;
   User ID=SimpleCMSUser;Password=SimpleCMS"
providerName="System.Data.SqlClient" />
```

Summary

In this chapter, we replaced the file-based CMS from Chapter 1 with a database version. You should now have a basic understanding of working with SQL Server Express 2005 and ASP.NET, as well as a basic understanding of how SQL Server works. You should be able to create a database, create a table in that database, and add columns to that table within SQL Server Management Studio Express.

We also explored the SqlDataSource, and using SQL Server 2005 Express as a source for data in our application. We created both a `SelectCommand` and an `UpdateCommand` to be used in that SqlDataSource to select records and modify the data in specific fields. You should also understand the role of the `ConnectionString` in the `web.config` in providing a connection to the database. As you work with ASP.NET and databases, you will find that moving applications to new systems will require changes to the connection string to get the database connected to the application. The web site at `http://www.connectionstrings.com/` is a good source for example connection strings to many different data sources and databases.

In the next chapter, we'll work with the basic architecture of our application, including the database schema, along with the way tables, rows, and columns relate to each other and to our application. We'll discuss some methods of designing the application architecture, and we'll make some decisions that will provide the base for the entire application we create. A good part of this next chapter relies on a solid understanding of SQL Server basics. Therefore, if you feel a little shaky, feel free to review Chapter 2 again.

3
Content Management System Architecture

In the last chapter, we upgraded our Content Management System to use a database, pretty much without any real thought to the overall application we want to end up with. We created a table for our content, which originally had no provisions for multiple pages. While we did add a column to the table when we figured out that we wanted multiple pages worth of content, we had to go back and add data for the new column for those records we had already created. It wasn't hard; we added the name Home to our first record in the PageName column. However, what if we already had 100, or 500, or even a million records in the table? It would have been a lot smarter to plan the columns in the table before we started filling them with data.

And that's what architecture is. Just like architecture for a building, program architecture is a plan for the development of the program. It includes a foundation for the program to rest on, supporting structures for the various parts of the program and individual rooms, or functions, of the program. They are all spelled out in vast detail, so that the builder, or programmer, can work from the architectural plan and create the program. But they are also only lines on paper, which can be changed as needed such as when the client wants a three-car garage instead of two, or an event calendar on every page.

One of the basic standards of good development is to separate content from presentation. This means we want the content, the actual words, pictures, and so on, to be present in the system without being attached to any presentation specifics such as fonts, background colors, layout, or anything else. The advantage to this is that we don't need to edit the content to change the way our site looks. We will also stay away from using HTML for formatting, and instead use cascading style sheets (CSS), wherever possible. This allows us to change a few lines in a single CSS file to change the look of all of our web pages.

In this chapter, we'll look at all of these, as well as plan our database structure and lay out our data relationships. We'll look at ways to access the data, apply some simple business logic to it, and then present that data on a web page. This separation of the data, data access, business logic, and presentation is often referred to as **n-tier** programming. Although we won't get heavily into programming separate tiers for our Content Management System, we will walk through the process.

By the end of this chapter, you will have a better understanding of:

- Multi-tier architecture
- Interacting with the data store
- Creating sample articles to work with
- The fundamentals of a data access layer
- The fundamentals of a business logic layer
- Using typed datasets
- Creating your data access and business logic layer classes
- The beginnings of your presentation layer

Multi-tier architecture

In larger programming environments, where the entire application is not created by a single developer, many of the programming tasks are broken into separate tiers. Separation of these tiers makes maintenance and expansion of an application easier, and allows for the development of each tier to fall to a programmer who is expert in that programming arena. There is no way a modern application developer can be an expert, or even relatively fluent, in all aspects of development, so teams of developers are essential. There are often database programmers, network programmers, and graphic designers involved in a project, each of whom may have little or no idea about the other's job.

Another reason why n-tier architecture is so prevalent is that modern applications have to adapt to changing conditions. A corporate merger may mean a change of database, new business rules, or a new design for the end-user interface. It is far easier to change these aspects if they are separated from each other than if a developer has to sift through thousands of lines of code to find the needed changes.

The solution for these issues is separation of the application into tiers, usually four tiers that are often referred to as three. These tiers are:

- Data Layer: This tier represents the database itself and any programming within it. There may be specific programming involved such as stored SQL procedures to handle data retrieval or SQL triggers to update data when other data is changed.

- Data Access Layer (DAL): This layer accesses the data and exposes the data to the Business Logic Layer. This layer often includes some validation of data, constraints on the type of data that can be entered, and possibly some data formatting.

- Business Logic Layer (BLL): This layer is where business logic occurs. Business logic includes whatever might be specific to the business such as gross receipts always being reported before taxes, finances must be expressed in Euros and US dollars, or employees are always listed as last name, first name.

- Presentation Layer: This layer determines the actual presentation that is viewed by the user, the styles, themes, layout of pages, and so on. It is at this layer that all typographic settings occur, including font size, color, and so on.

These tiers are often referred to as three-tier architecture because the data layer (the data store itself) is often combined with the data access layer. In fact, for small applications, it makes little sense to abstract these layers when there is very little for a layer to do. In the case of our Content Management System, we will not be using SQL stored procedures, as this is a learning application and there aren't enough pages in this book to teach SQL database programming. We'll also tend to blur the lines in these layers because our application is small, but we'll make sure the concept of the separate tiers is still adhered to. Just because our application is small doesn't mean we should toss aside good programming techniques.

The data store

Our architecture starts at the foundation with the data store, in our case, with the SQL Server 2005 Express database. We created the database and the `Content` table in Chapter 2, but we need more than just a single table for a full Content Management System. While we'll create other new tables as we move deeper into the application, let's create a `Pages` table now to hold information about our web site pages. In Chapter 2, we had a single table with the content assigned to a page name, but that structure is entirely inflexible as we couldn't easily move content from one page to another. In addition, we may need to store additional information about pages such as page hierarchy. However, database normalization principles tell us that data about a single entity such as a page should be kept in the same table, excluding data about another entity such as content.

As we're also going to be adding additional tables as we add features to the application, we want a consistent naming scheme that won't confuse us as to what data we're asking for and receiving. Our Chapter 2 `Content` table had a column, which also was named `Content`, making the use of the word Content ambiguous—do we want the `Content` field or the entire `Content` table? SQL uses a dotted notation for specifying the database, user, table, and field, so the specific `Content` field would be specified as `SimpleCMS.sa.Content.Content`. However, we really want a better scheme for identifying data quickly and uniquely.

Specifying an SQL Server database

In Chapter 2, we referred to the `Content` field in the `Content` table as `Content.Content`, which is an acceptable notation. The full identification is actually `{Database}.{DatabaseUser}.{TableName}.{FieldName}`, which in this case would be `SimpleCMS.sa.Content.Content`. The database user in our case is also the database owner, so `dbo` can be substituted for `sa`. As we are connected to only a single database with a single user account, we can drop these specifications and still be specific because they cannot be misconstrued. We will never use a second database or username in our application. If we were working in a single table, we could drop the table name as well, but good practice is to always use the table name to avoid confusion for other developers. It also makes maintenance easier, as we might upgrade the application in the future to use two tables for the query, and as we could possibly have two tables with the same field names such as `employee.address` and `customer.address`, it's always safest to specify both.

To provide further uniqueness, we could name the fields `employee.employee_address` and `customer.customer_address` if we think there may ever be an issue. Remember, it's harder to change a field or table name later than it is when planning the layout.

We're going to modify our application into three parts that will make up a page when combined. The first will be an **article**, which is the part that displays the content. The second is a **pane**, which holds modules on a page. And the third is the **page** itself, which holds panes containing articles. The reason for this is that we want the overall look and feel to be governed at the page level, making every additional page fit into the same theme as the first. We will also want to organize multiple panes on a page to define the layout, and we want to have multiple articles that can display in panes. Now, we'll have three entities—named **Pages**, **Panes**, and, **Articles**—each being a table.

The Pages table

Each page will have a number of attributes that we want to manage. We'll want a name, an ID, and we'll need to determine where a page is in relation to other pages. To do this, we'll use the parent/child relationship and identify a parent page for every page. This way, if a page has no parent, it will be in the root of our page menu. On the other hand, if it has a parent, it will fall under the parent page on the menu.

To create the `Pages` table, open **SQL Server Management Studio** and expand **Tables** under the **SimpleCMS** database. Leave the `Content` table alone for now, we won't use it in this chapter. However, we don't have a reason to get rid of it yet, especially if we already have data we want to store in it. Right-click in the **Tables** pane and choose **New Table**. Create a `Pages` table with three columns, `PageID`, `PageName`, and `PageParentID`, set to data types of `int`, `nvarchar(50)`, and `int` respectively. Do not allow nulls in any field. In the **Properties** pane, set the name to **Pages** and the Identity Column to **PageID**. Your table should look something like this when you save it:

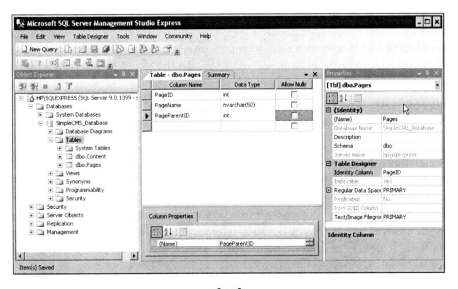

The Panes table

We need to create the `Panes` table in the same manner. Right-click on **Tables** in the **Object Explorer** pane and choose **New Table**. Create a `Panes` table, with columns of `PaneID`, `PaneName`, and `PanePageID`, set to the data types of `int`, `nvarchar(50)`, and `int` respectively. Allow nulls for the **PaneName** and **PanePageID** fields. You guessed it, **PaneID** will be the **Identity Column**. The table should look like this:

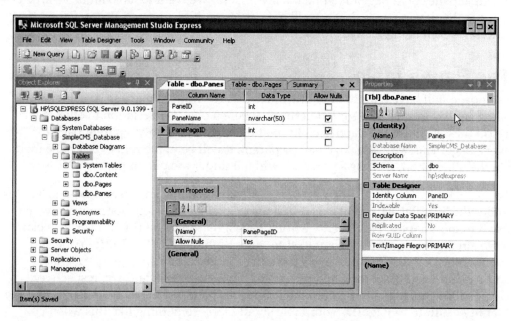

In this table, we left the **PageName** and **PageID** as null because we don't actually need them when we create a pane. We will assign them individually. In the case of `Pages`, we don't want a page without a name, or the identification of its parent page, as we wouldn't be able to add it to a menu. In later chapters, we'll expand these tables to accommodate other data, but we just need these fields for now.

The Articles table

Articles are what our content will be displayed with, along with the permission to edit that content. This table is essentially the heart of the application, with other tables controlling the display and positioning of the articles and the structure of the web site. To begin this table, we need four columns—`ArticleID`, `ArticleName`, `Article`, and `ArticlePaneID`. We need the `ArticlePaneID` column to define which pane this particular article will appear in. We will eventually want to describe this article with many other pieces of data such as an author, date, and expiration date, but the available columns would suffice for now. Create the `Articles` table with the following settings:

Column name	Data type	Can be null
ArticleID	int	No
ArticleName	nvarchar(50)	Yes
Article	nvarchar(max)	Yes
ArticlePaneID	int	Yes

Name this table `Articles` and use the **ArticleID** as the **Identity Column**. When you finish, it should look something like this:

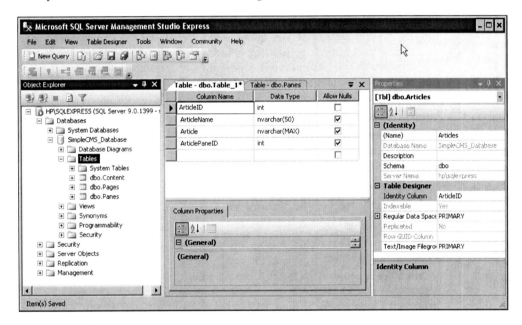

Sample data for the Articles table

We're going to use the `Articles` table, as we did the `Content` table in the previous chapter, and it helps to have some sample data in the table when we start working with it. In the previous chapter, we added data manually, by directly editing the table. However, that's not the most efficient way to add sample data to a table. Instead, we can use a simple SQL query to add the data.

Open SQL Server Management Studio Express if it's not already open, highlight the **SimpleCMS** database and click on the **New Query** button on the toolbar. This brings up the query window. Enter the following query into the window:

```
INSERT Into Articles
    (ArticleName, Article, ArticlePaneID)
VALUES
```

```
('Article 1','<p>Lorem ipsum dolor sit amet, consectetuer
adipiscing elit. Donec sodales luctus nisl. Duis fringilla felis
convallis magna. Nullam urna. Nulla ante. In eget tortor. Sed est
nibh, consectetuer ut, aliquet nec, euismod sit amet, odio. Nam nisl.
Morbi sapien dolor, consectetuer sit amet, condimentum non, lobortis
vitae, lorem. Sed consequat, erat vitae feugiat rutrum, ligula ipsum
pharetra dui, in dapibus nisi massa ut sem. Integer at nunc quis
lectus facilisis molestie. Vestibulum fermentum.</p>',1);
GO
```

SQL Note:

You will note that we haven't included the `ArticleID` parameter in the INSERT statement, any guess as to why? If you remember, the `ArticleID` column is an Identity column with an auto-numbering. This means that the column will automatically generate a new ID, so we don't have to insert is manually.

Click on the **Parse** button on the toolbar (the green check mark) or press *Ctrl+F5* to parse the query. If you have any errors, check the code and test with the **Parse** option until the code passes. Then click on the **Execute** button or press *F5* to execute the query and populate one record. Do this several more times, each time changing the article title, so you add multiple records to the `Articles` table. The code download includes a simple SQL query you may run to populate the table without entering this query if you wish.

Parsing SQL queries

When entering a query in the SQL Server Management Studio Express, it's always wise to parse the query before executing it. Parsing simply processes the query for SQL syntax errors without actually affecting the database, and is a safe way to ensure the code will work before it is executed. Remember that even code that is syntactically correct may be wrong, so double check any query before you execute it, to make sure it will do what you intend. Executed queries affect the data immediately, and the effect is irreversible. If in doubt, make sure you have a good backup before you start entering queries.

The data access layer

The purpose of the **Data Access Layer (DAL)** is to abstract the data source — in our case, to abstract the SimpleCMS database from the rest of the code. This allows us to change the data source (to maybe an Oracle or MySQL database) with minimum effort, which may be needed to move our application to a new client or company. The data access layer also allows us to handle database access more securely, as the actual page code doesn't touch the database and can't pass on security vulnerabilities.

We want to include anything related to accessing data in the DAL — the business logic layer and presentation layer should never access the data source directly. In addition, the DAL should use strongly typed datasets, which inherit from the ADO.NET DataSet class and provide all the methods and properties we will need to access the data source itself. In many cases, the DAL would also include SQL stored procedures to handle data manipulation, but we will not be using stored procedures for our application. There simply isn't enough space in the book to cover database programming in addition to our basic CMS application.

Creating the typed dataset

We'll start by creating a typed dataset using the Visual Web Developer wizard, which will also walk us through creating a table adapter to access the dataset. Open Visual Web Developer and open the **SimpleCMS** web site. In **Solution Explorer**, right-click the root of the site and choose **Add New Item**. Add a **DataSet**, using the default settings and name. When you are prompted, choose to save the dataset in the **App_Code** folder. After the dataset saves, you will be presented with the **DataSet Designer**.

Right-click in the designer pane and choose to **Add** a new **TableAdapter**. The **TableAdapter** wizard will open. Choose your existing **SimpleCMS** connection string and click **Next**, then choose **SQL Statements** and again click **Next**. You'll be presented with the SQL query window. We'll create this table adapter for use with the Articles table, and we'll start with a query that selects all the tables. Enter this in your query window:

```
SELECT ArticleID, ArticlePaneID, Article, ArticleName
FROM Articles
```

This selects all columns in our Articles table. We could simply use the code:

```
SELECT * FROM Articles
```

But this is a lazy programming method. In a query, we may not need every column and, even if we do, specifying the columns individually will let someone reading the code immediately know what we want.

Click the **Advanced Options** button, choose **Generate Insert, Update and Delete Statements**, and click **OK**. At this point, you may select **Next** until the **TableAdapter** is created, or simply choose **Finish** and the **TableAdapter** will be created, looking something like this:

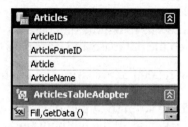

At this point, you have created the `DataSet` attached to the `Articles` table, along with a corresponding `ArticlesTableAdapter` that includes a `Fill` method and a `GetData()` method. These can be used in an ASP.NET form with simple programming and no data coding. Let's create a simple test page for the data adapter we have created.

Right-click the root of your site in **Solution Explorer** and choose **Add New Item**. Add a new web form, and name it `Test.aspx`. We'll just delete it after we test, so we don't need anything fancy. In the `Test.aspx` form, we'll use a `GridView` control to display the data from our table. You can either drag one from the toolbox to the page or add the following lines in the default `<div>` created with the new form:

```
<asp:GridView ID="GridView1" runat="server">
</asp:GridView>
```

This is all we'll do with the `Test.aspx` page itself. Open the code behind file, `Test.aspx.vb`, and add the following `Page_Load` subroutine:

```
Protected Sub Page_Load(ByVal sender As Object,
   ByVal e As System.EventArgs) Handles Me.Load
     Dim articlesAdapter As New DataSet1TableAdapters.
ArticlesTableAdapter
     GridView1.DataSource = articlesAdapter.GetData()
     GridView1.DataBind()
End Sub
```

As you add this code, you'll notice that Visual Web Developer's IntelliSense will pick up `DataSet1` and the methods we created for it. This is because of the strongly typed dataset, which allows IntelliSense to work with it. The `Test.aspx` form will then look like the following:

Okay, it's ugly. But this isn't the presentation layer, so we don't care. All this page does is show that a few simple lines in the `Page_Load` event allow us to work with the data access layer we created.

Filtering data from the dataset

The table adapter we created for our dataset has a `Fill` method and a `GetData()` method, both of which return the entire table. We will almost never want every article in the `Articles` table returned. We would want only the specific article we wanted to display. And we would normally want to retrieve our article by name, or maybe using the unique identifier, `ArticleID`. To make these retrievals possible, we simply set these methods up in our table adapter.

We know from the last chapter that we want a `WHERE` clause in our SQL query that specifies the data we want returned. The only thing we won't know until the user requests a specific article is the actual `WHERE` clause, so what we need to use is a parameterized query. This is simply a `WHERE` clause that uses a parameter in place of the specific `WHERE` details. Our current query that returns the entire table looks something like this:

```
SELECT ArticleID, ArticlePaneID, Article, ArticleName
FROM Articles
```

What we really want is something more like this:

```
SELECT ArticleID, ArticlePaneID, Article, ArticleName
FROM Articles
WHERE ArticleName = "Article 1"
```

But we don't know that we want `Article 1` every time, so we have to substitute a parameter for the article name and then provide that parameter, when we call for the table adapter to do its work.

To configure the table adapter to handle the `WHERE` clause, open `DataSet1.xsd` from the **App_Code** folder in Visual Web Developer. Right-click on the **ArticlesTableAdapter** and choose **Add Query**. Choose **Use SQL Statements** and click **Next**. Now, choose **SELECT**, which returns rows, and finally click **Next**, bringing up the query window. The original query should be in the query window, which you can modify using the **Query Builder**. Otherwise, simply type in your new query. Modify the query by adding the `WHERE` clause at the end, so the query now looks like:

```
SELECT ArticleID, ArticlePaneID, Article, ArticleName
FROM Articles
WHERE (ArticleName = @ArticleName)
```

Click **Next** and rename the `Fill` and `GetData` methods to `FillByArticleName` and `GetDataByArticleName`. Finish the wizard and you'll see two new methods added to the **ArticlesTableAdapter** — `FillByArticleName` and `GetDataByArticleName(@ArticleTitle)`.

Once these methods have been added to the **ArticlesTableAdapter**, you can test them by modifying the code-behind file for `Test.aspx` — `Test.aspx.vb`. Change the `Gridview1.DataSource` line to read:

```
GridView1.DataSource = articlesAdapter.GetDataByArticleName _
    ("Article 1")
```

Now, when you view `Test.aspx` in your browser, you should see only a single record, something like shown in the following screenshot:

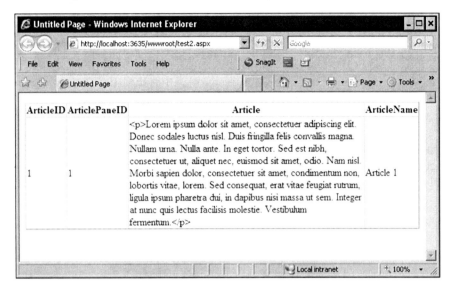

Add a second set of methods to the table adapter using the same process, this time to select by `ArticleID`, using this `WHERE` clause:

```
WHERE ArticleID = @ArticleID
```

As long as we pass the parameter required by the method to the table adapter, we no longer need to write SQL queries for this data. If you wish, you can modify the `Test.aspx.vb` file to display by `ArticleID`. Just remember that `ArticleID` is an integer, so the value doesn't need to be in quotes.

Insert method

Now we can retrieve a record based on the `ArticleName` or `ArticleID` field.
However, what if we want to add a new record—should we change an existing one or
delete one altogether? For those functions, we'll create custom methods for our table
adapter. In the designer screen, right-click on the **TableAdapter** and choose **Add |
Query**. Choose **Use SQL Statements** and click **Next**, then choose **Insert Query** and
Next. This will bring you to the query screen. Notice that the query is already created
for you in a very basic manner. However, we need to modify it because when we insert
a new article, we want to retrieve the automatically created `ArticleID`, so we can use
it in our code. To do this, we will use the `SELECT SCOPE_IDENTITY()` function that
returns the value of the last auto-generated Identity column in the scope of the query.
This is actually a second query to the database, so we end the first query with
a semicolon and then add this query to the code. Your query should look something
like this:

```
INSERT INTO [Articles]
   ([ArticlePaneID], [Article], [ArticleName])
VALUES
   (@ArticlePaneID, @Article, @ArticleName);
SELECT SCOPE_IDENTITY()
```

Name this function `InsertArticle` and save it. Insert methods normally return
the number of rows affected, but we want to return the new `ArticleID` instead. To
accomplish this, we have to change the **ExecuteMode** on our query. Click on the
InsertArticle method we just created in the **ArticlesTableAdapter** and change the
ExecuteMode to **Scalar** in the properties pane, as shown below:

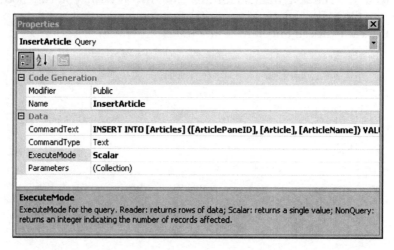

To test this function, open the `Test.aspx` file and edit the `Page_Load` subroutine in the code behind to look like the following:

```
Protected Sub Page_Load(ByVal sender As Object, ByVal e _
   As System.EventArgs) Handles Me.Load

  Dim ArticlesAdapter As New _
    DataSet1TableAdapters.ArticlesTableAdapter()
  Dim NewArticleID As Integer = (ArticlesAdapter.InsertArticle( _
    1, "This is a new article.", "New Article"))

  GridView1.DataSource = ArticlesAdapter.GetData()
  GridView1.DataBind()

End Sub
```

This test page will insert a new article on page load and then display the grid with all the articles. The newest article should be on the bottom, with an `ArticleName` of `New Article` and text reading: "This is a new article".

Update and delete methods

We also will need `update` and `delete` methods in our **ArticlesTableAdapter**. To create these, click on **ArticlesTableAdapter** to select it, and look at the **Properties Pane** for the **DeleteCommand** and **UpdateCommand** properties. Click the drop-down next to the **UpdateCommand** and select **(New)**. This will create a new **UpdateCommand** listed as **(UpdateCommand)**. In the **CommandText** property for the **UpdateCommand**, select the ellipses (**...**) to open the **Query Builder**. Here, we need to enter the query that will be executed when we update an article. Enter the following query:

```
UPDATE Articles
SET ArticleName = @ArticleName, Article = @Article,
   ArticlePaneID = @ArticlePaneID
WHERE (ArticleID = @Original_ArticleID)
```

This query simply updates the `ArticleName`, `Article`, and `ArticlePaneID` fields with the parameters passed to the query, when the `ArticleID` is the same as the `ArticleID` passed to the query. Save this query and then modify the **DeleteCommand** in the same way, but with this query:

```
DELETE FROM Articles
WHERE (ArticleID = @Orginal_ArticleID)
```

This query simply deletes the article which has the `ArticleID` passed to the query. Once you have finished these changes, right-click on your web site root in the **Solution Explorer** pane and choose **Build Web Site**. The site must build with no errors before we can create the business logic layer.

The business logic layer

The **Business Logic Layer** (BLL) is different from the data access layer in that it enforces business rules, those rules which are determined by business decisions and not by data restrictions or conditions. An example in our Content Management System would be if we had a mechanism to archive older articles, allowing retrieval but not editing. We might also want to restrict deletion of articles to a subset of users and not allow just anyone to delete an article. These would be business rules, as the only basis for the rule is how we wish to conduct our business.

For many rules, we could incorporate them into the table adapter code at the data access layer. We also might include them at the presentation layer. For example, we could disallow editing of archived articles in the data access layer code just as easily as anywhere else. We could also not allow archived articles to even get to the presentation layer for display by modifying code in the presentation layer. There are even some business rules that you will want to enforce at other layers such as corporate logos being displayed in the presentation layer, or the fact that dates and times are stored in the database as Date/Time fields so that we can perform calculations on them.

In our case, we won't have a lot of business logic, simply because this is a tutorial application. But if you were to extend this application for use in a business, good coding techniques mean we should plan for future code at this level now. So, let's create a business logic layer. To begin, let's clean up our project structure to make it easier to separate the DAL and BLL from each other, as we'll be creating BLL classes within the App_Code folder where our DataSet1.xsd file already is.

In **Solution Explorer**, right-click the **App_Code** folder and choose **New Folder**. Name this folder DAL. Create a second folder named BLL. You can now click and drag DataSet1.xsd into the **DAL** folder. One feature of the App_Code folder is that all files within that folder are compiled into the application at run-time (or during a command-line compile operation) without having to add code directories to the web.config file.

The ArticlesBLL class

Our business logic layer will use classes, each of which handles a specific table adapter. In these classes, we'll handle basic business rules and validation, and pass requests between the presentation layer and the data access layer. In some ways, the BLL behaves as a proxy between the layers, especially for those functions where all we will do is pass information without working with the information within our BLL. For our BLL class, we will have methods for SELECT, INSERT, UPDATE, and DELETE operations on our DAL. We'll also have two separate SELECT methods — one to select by ArticleName and the other by ArticleID.

In Visual Web Developer 2008, right-click on the new **BLL** folder you created under the **App_Data** folder and choose **New Item**. Select the **Class** template and name it `ArticlesBLL.vb`. We will give this class five methods:

- `GetArticles()`: Retrieves all articles in the database
- `GetArticleByArticleID(ArticleID)`: Retrieves a specific article when given the ArticleID
- `AddArticle(ArticleID, ArticleName, Article, ArticlePaneID)`: Adds a new article to the database
- `UpdateArticle(ArticleID, ArticleName, Article, ArticlePaneID)`: Updates an article already in the database
- `DeleteArticle(ArticleID)`: Deletes a specific article when given the ArticleID

The first three functions merely pass a query on to the data access layer, passing either an `ArticleID` or `ArticleName` to retrieve a specific article, or nothing at all to retrieve all articles. The code that does this in our class looks similar to this code for the first function in our list, retrieving a list of all articles:

```
<System.ComponentModel.DataObjectMethodAttribute( _
    System.ComponentModel.DataObjectMethodType.Select, True)> _
 Public Function GetArticles() As DataSet1.ArticlesDataTable
    Return Adapter.GetData()
 End Function
```

We are simply passing the request to return all records to the `GetData()` method in our `ArticlesTableAdapter` and returning the data as a typed dataset. We can add validation logic or other business rules into this function, but for now we'll leave it as is. For example, in future, we might want to retrieve only those articles that haven't been archived, in which case we could modify the business rule to handle this.

The `AddArticle` and `UpdateArticle` functions are somewhat different from the `GetArticle` functions, as both `AddArticle` and `UpdateArticle` need to pass new data to the database access layer. We do this by creating a `DataTable` with the data to be added or updated, and passing it as a new `DataRow` to the data access layer. For example, the `AddArticle` function code looks like this:

```
<System.ComponentModel.DataObjectMethodAttribute _
  (System.ComponentModel.DataObjectMethodType.Insert, True)> _
 Public Function AddArticle(ByVal ArticleName As String, ByVal _
 Article As String, ByVal ArticlePaneID As Nullable(Of Integer)) _
 As Boolean
 Dim Articles As New DataSet1.ArticlesDataTable()
 Dim ArticleRow As DataSet1.ArticlesRow = Articles.NewArticlesRow()
```

```
      If ArticleName Is Nothing Then ArticleRow.SetArticleNameNull() _
        Else ArticleRow.ArticleName = ArticleName
      If Article Is Nothing Then ArticleRow.SetArticleNull() _
        Else ArticleRow.Article = Article
      If Not ArticlePaneID.HasValue Then _
        ArticleRow.SetArticlePaneIDNull() Else _
        ArticleRow.ArticlePaneID = ArticlePaneID.Value

      Articles.AddArticlesRow(ArticleRow)
      Dim rowsAffected As Integer = Adapter.Update(Articles)

      Return rowsAffected = 1
    End Function
```

We first create the `ArticlesDataTable`, and then the `NewArticlesRow` to add the new row to the database. We populate this row with the `ArticleName`, `Article`, and `ArticlePaneID` by setting each to the data we pass into the function from the presentation layer. In this process, as these columns in our database are null, we must also check to see if the data passed in is null and, if it is, we should set that data as null in our data row too.

Finally, we add the new row to the database and test the addition to ensure that only a single row was affected by the function. If no rows are affected, or more than one row is affected, we return `False` from our function, which we can process to present an error message to the user.

The last type of function we use is the `DeleteArticle` function which, as its name suggests, simply deletes the article matching the `ArticleID` we pass in. The code for this is simple.

```
    <System.ComponentModel.DataObjectMethodAttribute _
      (System.ComponentModel.DataObjectMethodType.Delete, True)> _
      Public Function DeleteArticle(ByVal ArticleID As Integer) _
      As Boolean

      Dim rowsAffected As Integer = Adapter.Delete(ArticleID)
      Return rowsAffected = 1
    End Function
```

We simply delete the article matching the `ArticleID` and return a `True/False`, depending again on whether a single row was affected.

Testing the business logic layer

A quick test of the business logic layer can be made by modifying our Test.aspx application. Change the Page_Load subroutine in the code-behind file to the following:

```
Dim ArticlesLogic As New ArticlesBLL()
GridView1.DataSource = ArticlesLogic.GetArticles()
GridView1.DataBind()
```

This code uses the ArticlesBLL class that we created in our business logic layer to return all the articles in our database, through the GetArticles function in our business logic layer. It will actually look like the page we created to test the GetData() method from our ArticlesAdapter, and it should. While we are accessing that method through the intervening business logic layer, we aren't changing it in any way with our BLL. You'll see a more dramatic change, when we create the presentation layer.

The presentation layer

The ASP.NET framework gives us some very useful tools for developing a presentation layer for our application. The major tool we'll use here is Master Pages, a template system for ASP.NET pages that provides for dynamic data to be inserted into the content panes. Using Master Pages cleanly separates the overall site design from the content, essentially creating a site-wide look and feel that is independent of the dynamically generated content displayed.

Building the Master Page

We'll start our presentation layer for the application by building a Master Page, which will hold our content and provide some basic site-wide formatting. To begin, add a new file to the **SimpleCMS** application, choose the **Master Page** template and name the file SimpleCMS.master. You will notice that the default code added to the SimpleCMS.master file includes a new control—the ContentPlaceHolder control. This is a special control that takes all code and text from a related Content control in a content page and displays it as is in the Master Page. By default, the new Master Page has two ContentPlaceHolder controls—one named Head and the other named ContentPlaceHolder1. There cannot be two ContentPlaceHolder controls on a Master Page with the same name, as this is what is used to determine which content page is loaded.

Designing the Master Page

We are going to add some layout and some default design to our Master Page, which affects all pages that are built using this particular Master Page. To start, we'll do the layout for the Master Page with tables, an old HTML standby that still works. Tables have passed from favor, and CSS is the way you really want to handle this. However, for our first run-through, we'll stick with tables.

For our Master Page, we'll add a design table that has one column and three rows. The top row will be our site's logo, the middle row will be our ContentPlaceHolder, and the bottom row will be our copyright statement, so nobody tries to steal our brilliant design work. Open the SimpleCMS.master file and replace everything between the <form> tags with this code:

```
<table border="0" cellpadding="2" cellspacing="0">
  <tr>
    <td>
      <img src="Images/SimpleCMSLogo.jpg" alt="SimpleCMS" />
    </td>
  </tr>
  <tr>
    <td>
      <asp:ContentPlaceHolder id="ContentPlaceHolder1"
          runat="server">
      </asp:ContentPlaceHolder>
    </td>
  </tr>
  <tr>
    <td>
        <p><strong>Website design Copyright 2009
            by SimpleCMS</strong></p>
    </td>
  </tr>
</table>
```

You'll find the SimpleCMSLogo.jpg file in the file downloads for this chapter.

Creating the Default.aspx home page

Our Master Page isn't much use to us without a standard web page that implements this new Master Page. Master Pages are never requested on their own. They are combined with an ASP.NET page at compile time and served as part of the request for the ASP.NET page. This ASP.NET page is called the content page, as it contains the content displayed in the ContentPlaceHolders on the Master Page. This is easily demonstrated by creating a quick content page.

Add a new file to the SimpleCMS application, this time choosing the **Web Form** template. Name it `Default.aspx` and make sure the **Select Master Page** option is checked. Click on **Add** and select the **SimpleCMS.master** — the Master Page we just created. This will create the `Default.aspx` content page. If you look at the default code created, you'll see something like this:

```
<%@ Page Language="VB" MasterPageFile="~/SimpleCMS.master"
  AutoEventWireup="false" CodeFile="Default.aspx.vb"
  Inherits="_Default" title="Untitled Page" %>
<asp:Content ID="Head" ContentPlaceHolderID="head" Runat="Server">
</asp:Content>
<asp:Content ID="Content1" ContentPlaceHolderID="ContentPlaceHolder1"
Runat="Server">
</asp:Content>
```

You'll see first off that the `@Page` directive sets the `MasterPageFile` to the Master Page we selected. You'll also see that a title method has been added to the directive as well. Beyond that, the page is really just content controls with `ContentPlaceHolderID`s that match those found in the `SimpleCMS.master` Master Page. Before we test it, let's add some static content to the `Content1` Content control. Change this section of code to read:

```
<asp:Content ID="Content1" ContentPlaceHolderID="ContentPlaceHolder1"
Runat="Server">
<h2>----]  Content for ContentPlaceHolder1 goes here  [----</h2>
</asp:Content>
```

This addition of a single line of content will provide some content for our Master Page to display in the matching ContentPlaceHolder control. If you view the `Default.aspx` page in a browser, it should look something like this:

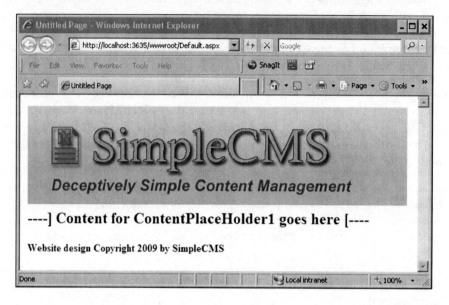

Notice that the logo and the copyright statement that show for the `Default.aspx` page are not part of the `Default.aspx` page code; they exist only in the `SimpleCMS.master` Master Page.

Adding dynamic content

A Content Management System is pretty useless if you need to create a new page for every piece of content you might want to serve. Plus, we didn't go through the first two thirds of this chapter building application layers just to abandon them now. We need to add the dynamic content functions that we created to our content page, in order to retrieve the content from the database. To do this, we'll use some of the code we already created earlier in the chapter.

Edit the `Content1` content control in `Default.aspx` to the following code:

```
<asp:Content ID="Content1" ContentPlaceHolderID="ContentPlaceHolder1"
Runat="Server">
  <asp:GridView ID="GridView1" runat="server">
  </asp:GridView>
</asp:Content>
```

The GridView control is the same one we have been using while testing the rest of our code in this chapter. Add this `Page_Load` subroutine in the `Default.aspx.vb` code behind file:

```
Protected Sub Page_Load(ByVal sender As Object, ByVal e As
    System.EventArgs) Handles Me.Load

  Dim ArticlesLogic As New ArticlesBLL()

  GridView1.DataSource = ArticlesLogic.GetDataByArticleID(1)
  GridView1.DataBind()

End Sub
```

This calls our `GetDataByArticleID` function in our business logic layer and passes it the `ArticleID` of 1. The GridView is then bound to the results of this function, and displays the record matching the `ArticleID` parameter we passed. The end result is similar to past test pages, except that it now uses our Master Page because this is the `Default.aspx` page we created. If you choose to view `Default.aspx` in your browser, it should look something like this:

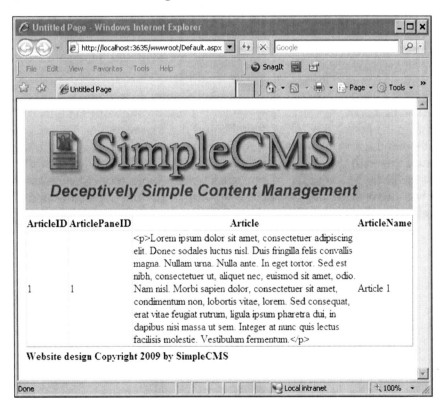

Okay, it's not pretty. We really don't want the entire row displayed, and we don't want it in a grid format either. The secret is to pull a trick from Chapter 2 and use a FormView control with an ItemTemplate that displays only what we want. To do this, first edit the `Default.aspx.vb` code behind, in order to change the GridView to a FormView using the following code:

```
FormView1.DataSource = ArticlesLogic.GetDataByArticleID(1)
FormView1.DataBind()
```

That's right, we're really changing only the GridView1 to FormView1 — the rest is already handled by our BLL and DAL. Now, change the `Default.aspx` code to remove the GridView control and replace it with the FormView control, using this code:

```
<asp:FormView ID="FormView1" runat="server">
  <ItemTemplate>
    <h2><asp:Label ID="Label1" runat="server"
        Text='<%# Bind("ArticleName") %>'></asp:Label></h2>
    <asp:Label ID="Label2" runat="server"
        Text='<%# Bind("Article") %>'></asp:Label>
    <hr />
  </ItemTemplate>
</asp:FormView>
```

This code uses a FormView control with an ItemTemplate to display two Label controls. The first is the `ArticleName` field retrieved through our DAL by the BLL, and bound to the FormView in the code-behind file. The second is the `Article` field. We also format the first label, the `ArticleName`, with a `<h2>` HTML tag, and we add a horizontal line with the `<hr />` tag before we close the FormView control. When you view the `Default.aspx` file in a browser, it now looks more like a web page, with the logo, an article title, an article, and a copyright line at the bottom of the page. Something like shown in the next screenshot:

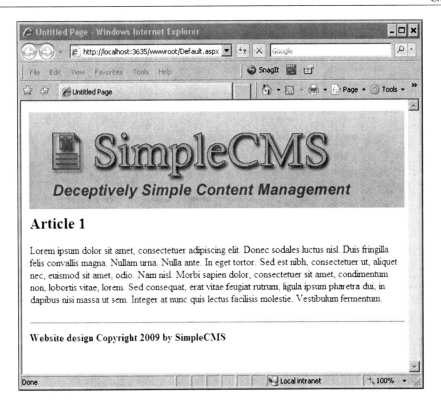

Finally, something that isn't truly lame. We have a lot more to add to our application, but by now you should be starting to understand the background concepts of our SimpleCMS application.

Summary

In this chapter, we built the database, a data access layer, a business logic layer, and a presentation layer for our Content Management System. We've only built a small part of the eventual application, and we'll need to add to all four of these architectural tiers as we continue the book. However, you should have a working knowledge of the basic architecture we are working with.

We first defined a table structure for our database, which we will expand upon in future chapters. A major reason for using a relational database management system such as Microsoft's SQL Server is the ability to grow the database as your application grows. We also created a data access layer to abstract access to the database. This allows us to write code to use other types of database engines without changing the rest of the application to match. It also allows us to access the database with minimal additional code from other layers in our architecture.

The business logic layer we created is extremely simple at this point. In fact, we have no business logic running in it at all. But it acts to further abstract the data storage from the presentation to the end user, and gives us a location to add future business rules. One reason to use a BLL for business logic is that these business rules are secure from being inadvertently changed by a designer working on the presentation layer. They can also be secured from prying eyes who might find ways to modify the request from the client to circumvent business logic in the presentation layer.

Finally, we built a rudimentary presentation layer based on Master Pages. The use of Master Pages, along with Themes, allows us to quickly change the look and feel of a site without affecting the underlying code; that is, it makes abstracting the layers from each other quite easier. We'll cover advanced use of Themes and Master Pages in Chapter 6.

The process we have used to build this architecture here is along the same lines as the tutorials at Microsoft's ASP.NET web site — http://www.asp.net. We have simplified much of the process in this chapter, but you are encouraged to continue learning through the tutorials and videos available online. This is also the first chapter, where full code has not been included in the book due to space. The code files are available from the project web site.

In the next chapter, we're going to add a security layer to our application, restricting functions to only certain accounts. After all, we don't want the general public changing the content of our web site at random, do we?

4
Adding Security and Membership to a Content Management System

Security is a concern in any web application, but the security this chapter deals with is that of user accounts, membership and roles. We'll be using the ASP.NET membership and roles functions to allow certain users such as administrators to perform specific tasks. These tasks may include managing the application, while other users such as content editors, may be restricted to the specific tasks we want them to manage such as adding or changing content. User account management can be handled either by the application (in our case, our Content Management System) or by Windows itself, using standard Windows authentication functions, as well as file and folder permissions.

The advantage of an application-based user authentication system is primarily in cost. To use Windows authentication, we need to purchase **Client Access Licenses (CALs)** for each user that will access our application. This is practical in an intranet, where users would have these licenses to perform other functions in the network. However, for an Internet application, with potentially thousands of users, licensing could be extremely expensive.

The drawback to an application-based system is that there is a lot more work to do in designing and using it. The Windows authentication process has been around for years, continually improved by Microsoft with each Windows release. It scales extremely well, and with Active Directory, can be extended to manage just about anything you can think of.

In this chapter, we will discuss:

- Membership—what it is and how it works
- Authentication—what it is and how to incorporate it into your application
- Setting up a basic application
- Creating the membership/authentication database pieces
- Adding a membership provider to the application
- Creating a login page and the controls associated with it
- Using the ASP.NET configuration tool and creating a login
- Forms authentication
- Membership roles

ASP.NET membership

Fortunately, Microsoft has provided relief for application-based authentication drawbacks in the 2.0 version of the ASP.NET framework, with the ASP.NET membership functions, and in our case, the `SqlMembershipProvider`. The membership API makes it simple for us to use forms authentication in our application, retrieving authentication and membership information from a membership provider. Similar to the classes we created in the last chapter for our data access layer and business logic layer, the membership provider abstracts the membership details from the membership storage source. Microsoft provides two providers—the `ActiveDirectoryMembershipProvider` that uses Active Directory and the `SqlMembershipProvider` that uses an SQL server database for the user data store.

By default, ASP.NET authentication uses cookies—small text files stored on the user's system—to maintain authentication status throughout the application. These cookies normally have an expiration time and date, which requires users to log in again after the cookie has expired. It is possible to use cookies to allow the client system to authenticate the application without a user login, commonly seen as a "Remember Me" checkbox in many web site login pages. There is naturally a downside to cookies in that a client system may not accept cookies. ASP.NET can encode the authentication information into the URL to bypass this restriction on cookies. Although in the case of our application, we will stick with the cookie method.

Forms authentication secures only ASP.NET pages. Unless you are using IIS7, and the integrated pipeline, where ASP.NET processes all file requests, the ASP.NET DLL won't be called for non-ASP.NET pages. This means that you cannot easily secure HTML pages, PDF files, or anything other than ASP.NET through forms authentication.

Configuring and using forms authentication

Let's start learning ASP.NET forms authentication by walking through a brand new application. We'll then add it to our Content Management System application. Forms authentication is actually quite simple, both in concept and execution, and a simple application can explain it better than adopting our current CMS application. Of course, we eventually need to integrate authentication into our CMS application, but this is also easier once you understand the principles and techniques we'll be using.

Creating a new application

Start by opening Visual Web Developer 2008 Express and creating a new web site by clicking on **File** | **New Web Site**. Use the **ASP.NET Website** template, choose **File System**, and name the folder FormsDemo.

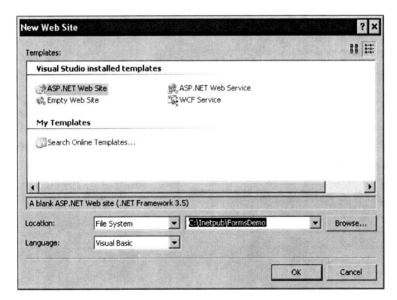

When the site is created, you are presented with a `Default.aspx` page created with generic code. We will use this as our home page for the new site, although we need to modify it for our needs.

Creating the home page

Visual Web Developer 2008 Express creates a generic `Default.aspx` file whenever you create a new site. Unfortunately, the generic file is not what we want and will need modification. The first thing we want to do is make sure our site uses a Master Page, just as our Content Management System application will. To do this, we could delete the page, create our Master Page, and then add a new `Default.aspx` page that uses our Master Page. In the case of a brand new site, it's pretty easy, but what if you have developed an extensive site that you want to convert to Master Pages? You would want to add a Master Page to an existing site, so let's go ahead and do that.

Create the Master Page

We will create a Master Page just as we did in the previous chapter. Leave the `Default.aspx` file open and press *Ctrl+Shift+A* to add a new item to the solution. Choose the **Master Page** template and leave the name as `MasterPage.Master`. Place the code in a separate file and click **Add** to create the Master Page. You will notice that this creates the same generic code as in the previous chapter. Unfortunately, our `Default.aspx` file is not a content page and won't use the `MasterPage.Master` we just created, unless we tell it to.

To tell our `Default.aspx` page to use the `MasterPage.Master`, we need to add the `MasterPageFile` declaration, in the @ **Page** declaration, at the top of the file. Add the following code between the **Language** and **AutoEventWireup** declarations:

```
MasterPageFile="~/MasterPage.master"
```

This adds the Master Page to our `Default.aspx` page. However, content pages include only those Content controls that match the Master Page, not the full page code as our `Default.aspx` page currently does. To fix this, replace the remaining code outside the @ **Page** declaration with the following two Content controls:

```
<asp:Content ID="Content1" ContentPlaceHolderID="head" Runat="Server">
</asp:Content>
<asp:Content ID="Content2" ContentPlaceHolderID="ContentPlaceHolder1"
Runat="Server">
   <h1>This is where the content goes.</h1>
</asp:Content>
```

We've left the `Content1` control empty for the moment, and we've added a simple text statement to the `Content2` control so that it can be tested. If you view the `Default.aspx` page in a browser, you should see the relatively uninteresting web page below:

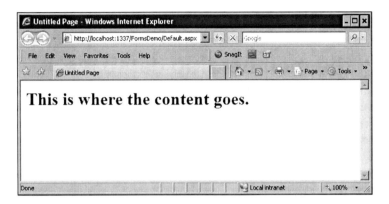

Enabling forms authentication

Okay, we have a boring home page for our new site. Let's leave it for a moment and enable forms authentication for the site, so we can restrict who can access our home page. The process of enabling forms authentication is simply adding a few lines to our `web.config` file. Or in the case of the generic `web.config` file, which we created while creating our new site, we simply need to alter a single line.

Open the `web.config` file in the new site and look for the line that says:

```
<authentication mode="Windows" />
```

Edit it to read:

```
<authentication mode="Forms" />
```

Save the `web.config` file and you have now enabled forms authentication for this site.

The default authentication mode for ASP.NET applications is Windows, which is fine if you're working in an intranet environment where every user probably has a Windows login for use in the corporate network anyway. Using Windows authentication, Windows itself handles all the security and authentication, and you can use the myriad of Windows utilities and functions such as Active Directory, to manage your users.

On the other hand, with forms authentication, ASP.NET is expected to handle all the details of authentication and security. While ASP.NET 2.0 and later have sophisticated membership and profile capabilities (which we'll take advantage of later), there is no ASP.NET mechanism for protecting files and folders from direct access, outside of the application. You will still need to secure the physical server and operating system from outside of your application.

Creating the membership database

To use forms authentication and the `SqlMembershipProvider`, we need to create a database to authenticate against. This database will hold our user information, as well as membership information, so we can both authenticate the user and provide access based on membership in specific roles. For our demonstration, we will create a new database for this function, but later on we will incorporate the membership schema into our Content Management System database.

As we did in Chapter 2, we'll create a database with SQL Server Management Express, so open it and right-click **Databases** in the **Object Explorer** pane. Choose **New Database** and name it `FormsDemo`. Change the location of the database path to the **App_Data** folder of your FormsDemo web application—the default is **C:\Inetpub\FormsDemo\App_Data** as shown below. Click **OK** and the new database will be created.

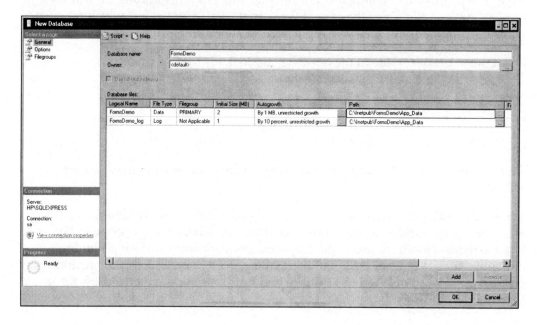

If you look at this database, you will see that it is empty. We haven't added any tables to it, and we haven't set up any fields in those non-existent tables. The database is pretty much useless at this stage. We need to create the database layout, or schema, to hold all the authentication and membership details. Fortunately, Microsoft provides a simple utility to accomplish this task for the 2.0 version of the ASP.NET framework – `aspnet_regsql.exe`. We'll use this too, in order to create the schema for us, and make our database ready for authentication and membership in our application.

To use `aspnet_regsql.exe`, we need to provide the SQL Server name and login information. This is the same information we set up SQL Server 2005 Express with in Chapter 2, and the same as shown in the login dialog when we open the database in SQL Server Management Studio Express, as shown below:

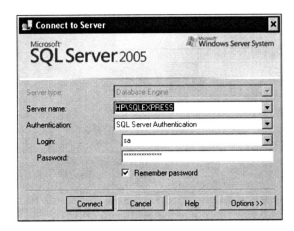

Note the server name, it will usually be `{SystemName}/SQLEXPRESS`, but it may be different depending on how you set it up. We used **SQL Server Authentication** with the **sa** account and a password of **SimpleCMS** when we set up SQL Server Express 2005, and that's what we'll use when we run the `aspnet_regsql.exe` tool.

To run `aspnet_regsql.exe`, you may browse to it in Windows Explorer, or enter the path into the **Run** dialog when you click on **Start** and then **Run**. The default path is `C:\WINDOWS\Microsoft.NET\Framework\v2.0.50727\aspnet_regsql.exe`. The utility may be run with command-line arguments, useful when scripting the tool or using it in a batch file, but simply running it with no parameters brings it up in a GUI mode. When the **ASP.NET SQL Server Setup Wizard** launches, click **Next**. Make sure that the **Configure SQL Server for application services** is selected and click on **Next**.

The **ASP.NET SQL Server Setup Wizard** will ask for the server, authentication, and database. You should enter these according to the information from above.

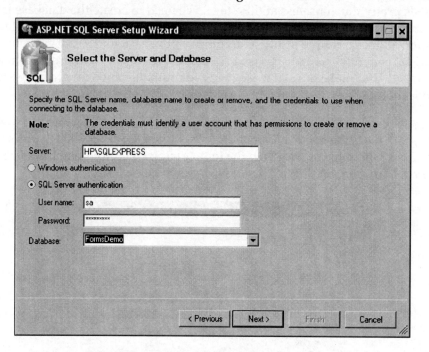

Click **Next** to confirm the settings. Click **Next** again to configure the database with the ASP.NET users and membership schema. Continue and exit the wizard, and the database is ready for us to use for authentication. If you were to open the FormsDemo database in SQL Server Management Studio Express, you would find that new tables, views, and stored procedures have been added to the database during this configuration process.

Configuring the SqlMembershipProvider

Our database is ready to use, but our application is not—at least not yet. We need to add a connection string in our `web.config` file so that we can connect to the database. We also need to add the `SqlMembershipProvider` information so that our application can access the database and use the new functions provided in our schema.

Open the `web.config` file in Visual Web Developer 2008 and find the default section that looks like:

```
<connectionStrings />
```

Replace it with:

```
<connectionStrings>
  <add name="FormsDemoConnectionString"
    connectionString="Data Source=.\SQLEXPRESS;
    AttachDbFilename=C:\Inetpub\FormsDemo\App_Data\FormsDemo.mdf;
    Initial Catalog=FormsDemo.mdf;
    User ID=sa;
    Password=SimpleCMS"
  />
</connectionStrings>
```

This will configure the database connection string so that we can use the database, as we did in Chapter 2.

To configure the `SqlMembershipProvider`, we need to add the `AspNetSqlMembershipProvider` to the Providers section of the Membership section, none of which we have in the default `web.config`. Immediately below the line that reads:

```
<authentication mode="Forms" />
```

add the following code:

```
<membership defaultProvider="FormsDemoSqlMembershipProvider">
  <providers>
    <add name="FormsDemoSqlMembershipProvider"
        type="System.Web.Security.SqlMembershipProvider,
        System.Web, Version=2.0.0.0, Culture=neutral,
        PublicKeyToken=b03f5f7f11d50a3a"
      connectionStringName="FormsDemoConnectionString"
      enablePasswordRetrieval="false"
      enablePasswordReset="true"
      requiresQuestionAndAnswer="true"
      applicationName="/"
      requiresUniqueEmail="false"
      passwordFormat="Hashed"
      maxInvalidPasswordAttempts="5"
      minRequiredPasswordLength="7"
      minRequiredNonalphanumericCharacters="1"
      passwordAttemptWindow="10"
      passwordStrengthRegularExpression=""
    />
  </providers>
</membership>
```

This provides the basic settings we need for our application. There are a few settings to take note of though:

- `defaultProvider`: We have designated a default provider for our application, as the `machine.config` file on our server uses `AspNetSqlMembershipProvider` as the default and expects a database named `aspnet.mdb` in the `App_Data` folder. Had we not created our own database and added the schema to it, `aspnet.mdb` would be the auto-created database. We do not want this for two reasons. The first is that every automatically configured application on the server would have the same database name. Also, it's easy to mix up database backups and maintenance schemes. More important though is that we have complete control and flexibility by creating our own database. The ASP.NET membership framework allows multiple providers so that we could split providers between databases for example. By specifically naming and creating our own database, and using it as the default for this application, we maintain explicit control.

- `applicationName`: We have set the `applicationName` to the root of the web application, which is what we want in this case. But this may not be where our application is located in a more complex application, and specifying the `applicationName` here would again provide us more explicit functionality. If we had not configured this, it would be set to the application root anyway. However, here we maintain control over it, as in the future, we may move the application.

- `enablePasswordRetrieval`, `enablePasswordReset`, `requiresQuestionAndAnswer`: These three are related, and set to the defaults. They determine whether a user can retrieve their password, reset their password, and whether or not answering a security question is required to perform either of those two functions. The default setting for these providers doesn't allow a user to retrieve his/her password because those would be sent to the user and could already be stolen by a hacker, but it allows a user to reset his/her password to a temporary one that can immediately be changed to the one known only by the user.

You also need to understand that these are defaults only in the `SqlMembershipProvider` we used, not the auto-created `AspNetSqlMembershipProvider`.

Password complexity in ASP.NET applications

ASP.NET password complexity often confuses both users and programmers. It is in the `SqlMembershipProvider` that the complexity is controlled. The default is a password with a minimum of seven characters, one of which must be non-alphanumeric, or not a number or letter. This means the password `Passw0rd`—which has eight characters, has both upper and lower case, and contains a zero—doesn't meet the default requirements because it doesn't contain a non-alphanumeric character. The password `password!` does meet the requirements, even though it has only lower case letters and no numbers. This is because the password has seven or more characters, and one of them, the exclamation point, is non-alphanumeric. You must decide on how complex you will require user passwords to be. More complex is more secure, but harder for users to deal with. At some point, security requirements become annoyances to the user and they will stop using your site. You may also use the `passwordStrengthRegularExpression` parameter to further refine your password strength, although the default is not to use it, leaving the expression blank. For example, the following code would require a password of at least seven characters, including one number and one non-alphanumeric character:
`passwordStrengthRegularExpression="@\"(?=.{6,})(?=(.*\d){1,})(?=(.*\W){1,})"`

You can find more about these, along with other `SqlmembershipProvider` properties, at `http://msdn.microsoft.com/en-us/library/system.web.security.sqlmembershipprovider_properties.aspx`.

Creating the login page

The first step to providing an authentication for users is creating a page for them to use to log into our application. The default name of this page for ASP.NET forms authentication is `Login.aspx` and we will stick to the defaults for this demonstration. So, start by adding a new item to our application in Visual Web Developer 2008 Express and choosing the **Web Form** template, naming it `Login.aspx` and selecting the **MasterPage.master** as your Master Page.

To add the login control to the page, enter the following code inside the `Content2` ContentPlaceHolder control:

```
<asp:Login ID="Login1" runat="server">
</asp:Login>
```

If you save the `Login.aspx` file and run it in a web browser, you should see a page similar to this:

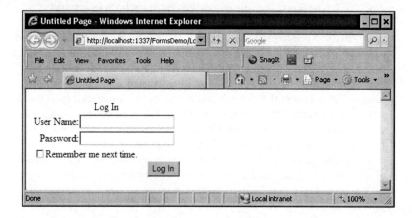

Changing the default login page

ASP.NET uses a default login page `Login.aspx`, and this is the URL that an unauthenticated user is redirected to when they try to access a page that requires authentication. To change this page name, we simply need to alter the authentication section of the `web.config`. The default `web.config`, and the one we used here, has a line similar to this:

<authentication mode="Forms" />

If we change this to:

<authentication mode="Forms">

<forms loginUrl="UserLogin.aspx" />

</authentication>

Our application will then expect a page file named `UserLogin.aspx` and will use that as the login page for this application. We could also change the URL that logged in users are sent to if none is specified by using the `defaultUrl` parameter, similar to:

<authentication mode="Forms">

<forms loginUrl="UserLogin.aspx"

DefaultUrl="MembersPage.aspx" />

</authentication>

Although we have ignored these settings for this demo, good programming practices would include specifying these in the `web.config` for an application so that application doesn't accidentally inherit incorrect settings after deployment to a server with other applications on it.

Of course, if you try to log in using the `Login.aspx` page we just created, nothing will happen. We don't have a user account to log in with, so, let's create a quick one to test our logins.

Creating a user account with the ASP.NET configuration tool

Visual Web Developer 2008 Express has a built-in tool to help configure several different aspects of your application and IIS installation. We're going to use it to manage security by creating a new user account for accessing our web site. In Visual Web Developer, click on **Website**, and then **ASP.NET Configuration**. When the utility opens, click on the **Security** tab and you'll see a screen like this:

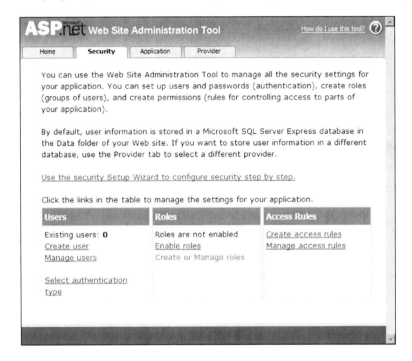

We have already created the database to store our user accounts in and we just need to create a user, so click on **Create user** and fill in the form on the following page, as shown below. Enter a **User Name** of User1, with a **Password** of Password!. Enter a valid email address, a **Security Question** of First Pet, and a pet's name such as Goldie. Click **Create User**, and after a couple of moments, you should get a confirmation that the user was created.

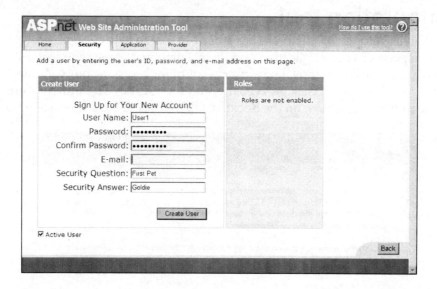

Windows authentication

In our application, we are using forms authentication to provide the security we need. We could use Windows authentication in a similar manner, for example in an intranet where users would normally already have Windows accounts. In Windows authentication, Windows users and groups take the place of user accounts and roles in forms authentication. You would create users and groups in Windows to be used to grant access to the application. Assigning user accounts to the groups would allow those users the access provided by group membership. Note that the **Web Site Administration Tool** cannot be used to manage users and groups in a Windows authentication application. You need to use the tools provided by Windows such as Active Directory. The advantage of Windows authentication is obvious—we have a single directory of users and access groups for all functions within your network. The disadvantage is the licensing costs of all those user accounts, if the only function they are needed for is to provide access to a single application.

Creating a login

Okay, we've created a user and we have a login page to log that user in. But why would a user log into our application? That's right, to reach pages or content that are restricted to logged in users. In our application, we will be restricting access to content based on whether a user has logged in or not. To do this, we make use of a LoginStatus control. This control will let us know the current status of the page viewer and also provide a way for that viewer to log into our application for further access.

Open the home page `Default.aspx` in Visual Web Developer, and locate the `Content2` ContentPlaceHolder control. Immediately before the `<h1>` tag, enter the following code:

```
<asp:LoginStatus ID="LoginStatus1" runat="server" />
```

That's it, just one line of code. Doesn't ASP.NET make this simple? When you save the file and run it in a browser, you should see a page like this:

Click on that little **Login** link and you'll see the `Login.aspx` page displayed, as that is the default login page for the ASP.NET login control. It will look similar to this:

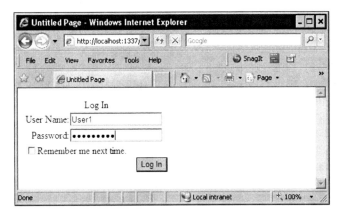

Enter a user name of **User1** and a password of **Password!**, as we used when creating our user account. You will then be authenticated and returned to the home page, where the login link has now become a **Logout** link, as shown below:

So, with a few lines of ASP.NET code, we have created an authentication system for our application. Of course, it's not really our application, just a demonstration, so let's move on and add these functions to our SimpleCMS application. We'll also need to extend this a bit more.

Adding forms authentication to our CMS

Now that you understand the process behind forms authentication, we need to add it to our application. The process will be slightly different because we already have a database to use, but without the ASP.NET membership schema. We'll add that to the database and then create some user accounts and membership roles to handle the security for our application. We'll also secure some of our content and add a menu to our Master Page to navigate between the pages of our Content Management System.

Preparing an existing SQL database

As we have an existing database, we can't create a new database for our membership and authentication system. Well, actually we could, but using a second database is problematic when we upload the application to a host because many web hosting companies allow only a single database under the hosting plan. Besides, we can easily add the membership schema the same way we did earlier in the chapter with our empty database, using `aspnet_regsql.exe`. Previously we used the wizard; this time we'll use the command line. If you take a look at the database in SQL Server Management Studio Express now, before we execute the command to add the schemas, you should see the few tables we created in earlier chapters, as shown in the following figure:

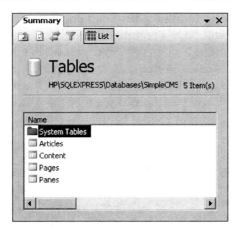

The aspnet_regsql.exe tool

Using the command line, the executable is simple, as long as you know the command-line arguments. The syntax and command arguments for `aspnet_regsql.exe` are available online at `http://msdn.microsoft.com/en-us/library/x28wfk74.aspx`. The following table shows the arguments we will use:

Argument	Description	What we use
-S	The server name	\SQLEXPRESS
-U	The database username	sa
-P	The database password	SimpleCMS
-d	The database name	SimpleCMS_Database
-A	The schema functions to install	All functions

Our command line will look like this (all one line):

```
aspnet_regsql.exe -S .\SQLEXPRESS -U sa -P SimpleCMS -d SimpleCMS_
Database -A all
```

To run the command line, go to **Start | Run** and enter cmd in the **Run** dialog box. Press *Enter* and you will be at a command prompt. Type cd\ C:\WINDOWS\ Microsoft.NET\Framework\v2.0.50727\ and press *Enter* again, and you will be in the correct folder to find aspnet_regsql.exe. Note that you may need to change the path if your ASP.NET framework files are in a different location. Type the command line above and press *Enter*, and you should see that the command completed successfully, with a dialog similar to that below:

```
C:\WINDOWS\system32\cmd.exe

C:\WINDOWS\Microsoft.NET\Framework\v2.0.50727>aspnet_regsql.exe -S .\SQLEXPRESS
-U sa -P SimpleCMS -d SimpleCMS_Database -A all

Start adding the following features:
Membership
Profile
RoleManager
Personalization
SqlWebEventProvider

..........

Finished.

C:\WINDOWS\Microsoft.NET\Framework\v2.0.50727>
```

Now that we have executed the aspnet_regsql.exe command line, if you look at the database tables in SQL Server Management Studio Express, you should see the added table for the users, membership, and roles we will use in our application.

User accounts

Earlier in the chapter, we created a single user account for accessing protected content. In a real-world environment, we would normally have many user accounts, way too many to add each account to each page we wanted to protect. Fortunately, the ASP.NET framework provides us with membership roles that we can place user accounts in, allowing us to define our access by role, not by user account. But first, we need some user accounts.

Let's start by creating three accounts in our application — User1, User2, and Administrator. Open the SimpleCMS web site in Visual Web Developer 2008 Express. Use the downloadable code provided for Chapter 4 of this book, it has the web.config file modified similar to what we did when we walked through the forms authentication demo earlier in the chapter. Open the **Web Site Administration Tool** by clicking on **Website** and then **ASP.NET Configuration**.

If you click on the **Security** tab, you will see that we have no users configured for this application. As you did earlier in the chapter, click on **Create User** and create the three users with user names of User1, User2, and Administrator. Use Passw0rd! as the password for each, and provide a valid email address for each (they can have the same email for testing). Also, provide a question and answer such as Favorite Color? and Blue. You can use the same question and answer for all three accounts if you wish. Each user entry should look something like the following:

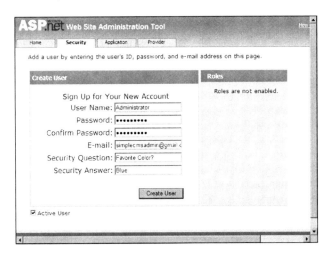

If you return to the **Security** tab, you will notice that we have three user accounts, but no roles for those accounts. Let's add them next.

Membership roles

ASP.NET membership roles provide the ability to group many individual accounts into a single role to provide access to a resource such as a page or application. Changing access for an individual user then becomes a simple task of assigning them to or removing them from the appropriate role. A single user account can belong to multiple roles to provide extremely granular access to the application resources if your security demands are extensive.

To add roles to our application, we first need to enable roles. On the **Security** tab of the **Web Site Administration Tool**, under **Roles**, you should see a link to enable roles. Enabling roles consists of simply adding the following line to the `web.config` file in the **system.web** section:

```
<roleManager enabled="true" />
```

Similar to the membership provider we created earlier, roles require a role provider. We need to add this provider to the role manager, so edit the `web.config` **roleManager** section to read:

```
<roleManager enabled="true">
  <providers>
  <clear/>
    <add name="AspNetSqlRoleProvider"
      connectionStringName="SimpleCMS_DatabaseConnectionString"
      applicationName="/"
      type="System.Web.Security.SqlRoleProvider, System.Web,
      Version=2.0.0.0,
      Culture=neutral, PublicKeyToken=b03f5f7f11d50a3a" />
  </providers>
</roleManager>
```

This adds an `AspNetSqlRoleProvider` that uses our connection string to the SimpleCMS database. At this point we have no roles defined, so let's create a few. Open the **Web Site Administration Tool**. If it's already open, you may need to close and reopen it because we modified the `web.config` file to add the role provider. Now, open the **Security** tab. In the **Roles** section, click on **Create or manage roles**.

Let's create an administration role first. We'll need it to secure areas to just administrative access. Simply enter `Administrator`, click on **Add Role**, and you'll see the new role in the list. Add roles for Author, Editor, and Registered User in the same manner. The roles list should look something like the following figure when you finish:

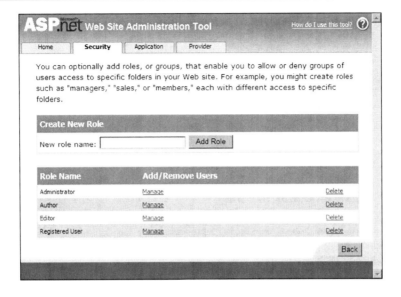

Adding users to roles

Once we have users and roles created, we need to assign users to roles. To do this, use the **Security** tab of the **Web Site Administration Tool**, under the **Users** section, to manage users. You'll see a list of user accounts, in our case all three of them, along with the ability to edit the user, delete the user, and edit the user's roles. Click on **Edit roles** next to the **Administrator** user and you'll see a checkbox list of user roles this account can be added to. Any roles currently assigned to the user will be checked. As there are currently none, check the **Administrator** role, and the Administrator user will be immediately added to the Administrator role, as shown below:

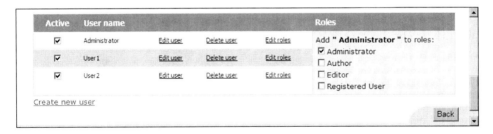

If you were to look at the database tables that hold the user accounts and roles, you would see something like this for the users:

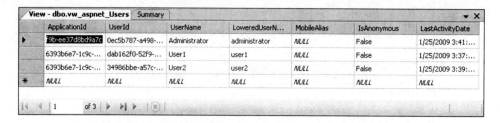

Similarly, the roles would look like this:

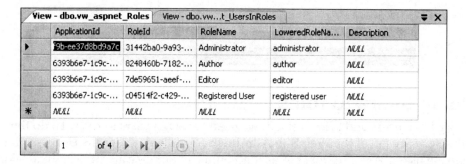

You'll note that both the users and the roles contain an `ApplicationID` that defines what application these users and roles belong to, and that each user or role is identified by a `UserID` or `RoleID`. These are automatically created by the ASP.NET membership framework and are globally unique identifiers (GUIDs), which ensure that the specific user or role is unique across all possible applications and uses of this specific database store.

You would also find in the database a table that identifies users in roles, looking something like this:

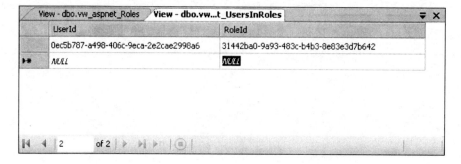

You'll notice that this is a joining table, used in a database when there is a many-to-many relationship. Many users can belong to a role and a user can belong to many roles, thus the use of this table. You'll also notice that the database table uses the `UserID` and `RoleID`, making it very hard to simply look at this table directly to find what users are assigned to what roles. Fortunately, with the ASP.NET framework, you're isolated from having to work directly with the database, as well as relieved from having to create it and the code needed to access it.

Login page

We'll create the login page the same way we did with our demo application. Open the site in Visual Web Developer 2008 Express and add a new item to the application. Choose **Web Form** as the template and name it `Login.aspx`. Select the **SimpleCMS.master** as your Master Page and add the login code to the `Content2` ContentPlaceHolder control as done before. Your login page should look very similar to our demo application.

New user registration

Previously, we added user accounts to the database through the Web Site Administration Tool. This becomes impractical in our application for two reasons. The first reason is that the Web Site Administration Tool is not designed to work outside of the same system the site is hosted on. This makes using our application on a web host problematic. The second is that we really don't want to manually enter every user into the system, that's too much work. The ASP.NET framework makes life easy for us through the CreateUserWizard control, allowing users to add their own information to the user database and thus sign up for accounts on our system.

To add the CreateUserWizard to our login page, add the following code inside the `Content2` ContentPlaceHolder control, immediately below the login control we added:

```
<asp:CreateUserWizard ID="CreateUserWizard1" runat="server">
  <WizardSteps>
    <asp:CreateUserWizardStep ID="CreateUserWizardStep1"
runat="server">
    </asp:CreateUserWizardStep>
    <asp:CompleteWizardStep ID="CompleteWizardStep1" runat="server">
    </asp:CompleteWizardStep>
  </WizardSteps>
</asp:CreateUserWizard>
```

If you run the page in your browser, you should see something like:

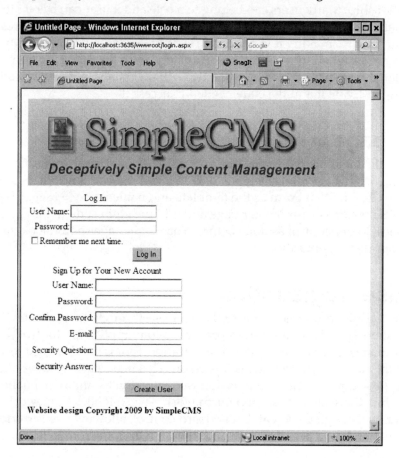

You'll notice the same login control we used in our demonstration application, plus a new control that allows a user to sign up for an account. The CreateUserWizard control reads the Membership settings from our `web.config` file and populates the control accordingly. In our case, it asks for the user name, password, email, and both the security question and answer. This control also provides client side validation of the entries, requiring that each text box have an entry before submitting the form, and validating that the password entered meets the password requirements for our application.

Go ahead and sign up a new user, entering all the required fields and clicking on **Create User**. You should get a page similar to the one shown next, indicating that the user account has been successfully created.

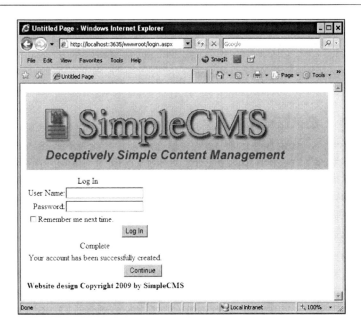

Naturally, we want to create a more appropriate design for this page and these controls. It would help them look better and be more intuitive for users who want to register a new account, versus those who already have an account and wish to login. One of the simplest ways to do this is to open the **Design View** of the `login.aspx` page in Visual Web Developer 2008 Express, right-click on the **Login** control, and then choose **Autoformat**. Pick a format such as **Classic**, and your control will automatically take on that format. Doing the same with the **CreateNewUser** control should look similar to:

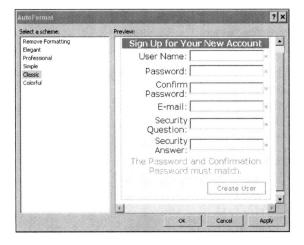

If you open the code for the login.aspx page, you'll see the formatting for the controls has been added automatically. In a later chapter, we will work on formatting and layout options, along with the layout techniques. However, for now, let's get back to securing the content on our important pages.

Securing content

Okay, our application now has user accounts and roles for those users, but just how do we use them to secure the content in our Content Management System? In our demonstration, we secured entire pages and restricted access to those pages to specific accounts. But in our Content Management System, we want to secure the content itself, not the page. And if content is secure, we want to let our users know that they need to create an account and log in to see the content.

Let's begin by requiring users to have an active account to view an article from our database. Open the Default.aspx file in Visual Web Developer 2008 Express, and look at the **FormView** control that displays our article using the ArticlesBLL class, which in turn uses the DataSet1TableAdapters class. We don't want to change the functionality of that code, we just want that code to be available only to those users who have logged into our application. To do this, we'll use a LoginView control.

Change the **FormView** control section to the following code:

```
<asp:FormView ID="FormView1" runat="server">
  <ItemTemplate>
    <asp:LoginView ID="LoginView1" runat="server">
      <AnonymousTemplate>
        <p>We're sorry, this article requires you to have an
          account and be logged in to view the article.
        </p>
        <p><a href="login.aspx">Register or Login</a><br /></p>
      </AnonymousTemplate>
      <LoggedInTemplate>
        <h2>
        <asp:Label ID="Label1" runat="server"
          Text='<%# Bind("ArticleName") %>'>
        </asp:Label>
        </h2>
        <asp:Label ID="Label2" runat="server"
          Text='<%# Bind("Article") %>'>
        </asp:Label>
        <hr />
      </LoggedInTemplate>
    </asp:LoginView>
  </ItemTemplate>
</asp:FormView>
```

The **LoginView** control shown here has two templates—an **AnonymousTemplate** and a **LoggedInTemplate**. These do just what they indicate, provide the user with the information that is laid out in the appropriate template, either Anonymous or LoggedIn Template, based on their current login status. If you run the page in your browser, you should see the following:

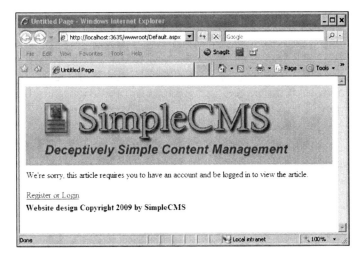

If you then click on the **Register or Login** link, and log in as a registered user, you should see the Default.aspx page, complete with the article from the database.

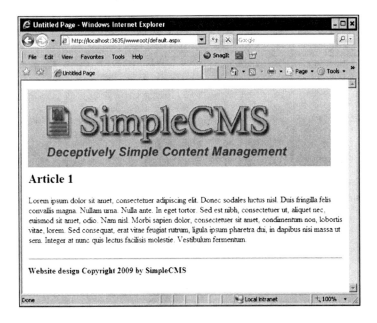

Login status

There is an even more elegant way to handle login requirements in the ASP.NET 2.0 framework via the LoginStatus control, similar to what we did in our demo application. We can use it to add a login link to every page, so we don't have to build a login link into all the LoginView controls we might add to our application. This control displays a login or logout link, according to the logged in status of a user. This means if a user is not logged in, we will automatically show them a link to do so. That link will take them to the login page we created earlier.

Open the `SimpleCMS.master` Master Page file in Visual Web Developer 2008 Express. At the bottom of the page, you will find the copyright statement we added earlier. Immediately below that line, add this code of the LoginStatus control:

```
<asp:LoginStatus ID="LoginStatus1" runat="server" />
```

That's it, everything we need to add a login link on every page in our application. We can go back and delete the line from our `Default.aspx` LoginView that reads:

```
<p><a href="login.aspx">Register or Login</a><br /></p>
```

If you then view the `Default.aspx` page in a browser, it should look like the following figure when you are not logged in:

The **Login** link is automatically displayed on any page where the user is not logged in because it is part of our Master Page. If a user is already logged in, the link simply changes to a **Logout** link.

Password recovery

A major headache with almost any web site on the Internet that requires registration is that you often do not want to, or even cannot, use the same password as you do on other sites. This results in most users having multiple passwords, and most users forgetting at least some of those passwords. The ASP.NET 2.0 framework has a PasswordRecovery control for just this purpose. Let's go ahead and add it to our application.

In Visual Web Developer 2008 Express, add a new web form with the name `ForgotPassword.aspx` and then select the `SimpleCMS.master` page Master Page file. In the `Content2` ContentPlaceholder control, add the following code:

```
<asp:PasswordRecovery ID="PasswordRecovery1" Runat="server">
</asp:PasswordRecovery>
```

Open the **Design View** for this page, and **AutoFormat** the control to the same **Classic** format we used in the other login controls.

To link to this page, we'll use a LinkButton control on the `login.aspx` page. Open the page and add this code after the Login control:

```
<asp:LinkButton ID="LinkButton1" runat="server"
 PostBackUrl="~/ForgotPassword.aspx">
 Forgot Password?
</asp:LinkButton>
```

Save these files and when you run the `login.aspx` page in the browser, you should see the **Forgot Password?** link below the login control. Clicking on that link will show our `ForgotPassword.aspx` page, which looks like this:

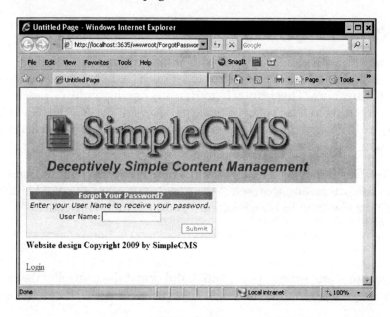

A user entering their login name will then be presented with their challenge question and must answer it to receive their password. A correct answer results in the user receiving an email, containing his/her password, to his/her account. At this point, you will receive an error if you try to recover your password because we have not set up any email capability in our application. We'll take care of that in a later chapter.

Summary

In this chapter, you learned how to configure ASP.NET forms authentication, along with how to provide controls for users to log in, as well as ways to secure the content displayed on the pages. We used the `aspnet_regsql.exe` utility to create the database for membership and authentication. We also used the ASP.NET Configuration utility to configure some authentication parameters for our web application, add users and roles, and assign users to roles. We also created pages that were secured from access by unauthorized users.

When we added these features to our application, we expanded our login page to allow users to register a new account and even to recover a password if they forgot it. We used the Login and CreateNewUser controls, which are built into the ASP.NET 2.0 framework, and we used the AutoFormat option to format these controls as the user will see them. We also used the LoginView control to restrict access to an article on our page, as well as the LoginStatus control to add a login link to all of our pages through our Master Page.

If you are interested in more depth on the ASP.NET membership controls, you should check out the MSDN Patterns and Practices information at `http://msdn.microsoft.com/en-us/library/ms998347.aspx`. You will also find more information in the online tutorials at `http://www.asp.net/learn/security/`.

As we move through future chapters, we'll add a few more features to our application related to users and user management. In Chapter 9, we'll build a control panel that allows us to manage user accounts and role memberships without using the ASP.NET Configuration utility. We'll also do some advanced formatting of our pages and controls in Chapter 8 and work more with Master Pages in Chapter 6.

In the next chapter, we'll build our first complete module for our application, an Articles module that will allow us to create and manage the articles in our database. This module is the basis for our dynamic content in the Content Management system, although we'll deal with static content such as existing documents, pictures, and other files in a later chapter.

Creating the Articles Module

Over the past chapters, we have worked through some basic instructions for parts of our Content Management System. In this chapter, we will build the first major module of our application—the Articles module. This module will allow us to edit content in our application without having to use any developer tools or have any programming knowledge. General users will be able to use the module for most of their functions of adding content to the system.

This module will make use of the techniques you have learned until now. We will provide data access methods through the multi-tier structure we developed, and we will use the user accounts and access groups we covered in the last chapter to control access to specific functions of our application. Let's get started by creating a set of specifications for this module.

In this chapter, you will learn about:

- The way Articles will be published in our application
- How to implement and use user controls
- Building an Articles module
- Building your DAL and BLL classes for the Articles
- Beginning to see how roles will be used in the application

Application specifications

The basic idea of this module is for a user with no programming knowledge to be able to add, edit, and delete content from our Content Management System. We also want to work through a publication process, allowing for users with different levels of access to control the stages of content production. If you are used to working alone in publishing a web site, or even with a few others, the process we'll use may be foreign to you. But you'll see that the process we develop here can be expanded to many users, or simplified to a single content publisher, without rewriting the application.

The Article publication process

For the publication process, think about a newspaper or magazine. After all, these printed materials are simply Content Management Systems that are extremely inflexible once the content has been published, though before publication, content management is a key to their business success. Publishing the wrong or inaccurate content can cause them to lose subscribers and force them out of business. Ensuring content is correct before publishing is vital to these publications, and it's just as vital in our Content Management System.

In the magazine or newspaper world, you generally have a writer or author, along with an editor and a publisher, for each Article or story that is printed. The author creates the content, the editor reviews the content and changes or corrects it as needed, and the publisher controls what is finally published. We'll replicate this process in our application, allowing for author, editor, and publisher roles in our Content Management System.

In our Articles module, think of the Author, Editor, and Publisher roles as increasing levels of authority. An Author can only create a new Article or change their Articles. They cannot change anyone else's Article, nor can they change or delete an Article after publication. They also cannot publish an Article, or make it live and visible on the web site. An Editor can perform all of the functions of an Author, plus they can perform these functions on other Author's work. This way, an Editor could change any Author's or Editor's Article, but cannot publish it to the web site.

A publisher has all the functions of an Author and an Editor, plus one additional set of functions that only the Publisher role has available. This role can publish Articles, so they are live on the web site. This role also has permission to delete Articles that have been published. A publisher can also change the publication status, or "unpublish" an Article, allowing it to be changed by the original Author or an Editor. This role has full control over what is or is not published on the web site.

User controls

ASP.NET 2.0 provides the ability to store code in a user control, and then simply load this control in a page, to make use of the functions of that control. Think of a user control as reusable code snippets, similar to the controls you find in the toolbox of your Visual Studio 2008 Express Edition. For our module, we will build a number of user controls to simplify the use of our module, as well as deployment. Although we won't cover compiling an application or user control in detail, one advantage to user controls is that you can compile them and make them extremely simple for other developers to use in their applications, as well as protect any code in your deployed application.

Building a user control

The easiest way to understand user controls is if we build a quick one, so you can see how easy it is. A user control is really just another ASP.NET page, but one that can only be used within an existing page. In fact, the code is the same, only a few things are different from building a regular web form.

Consider the following web form and code behind:

- **ImageRotator.aspx**:

```
<%@ Page Language="VB" AutoEventWireup="false"
    CodeFile="ImageRotator.aspx.vb" Inherits="ImageRotator" %>

<html xmlns="http://www.w3.org/1999/xhtml">
<head runat="server">
    <title>Image Rotator</title>
</head>
<body>
    <form id="form1" runat="server">
    <div>
        <asp:Image ID="RandomImage" runat="server" />
    </div>
    </form>
</body>
</html>
```

- **ImageRotator.aspx.vb**:

```
Imports System.IO

Partial Class ImageRotator
    Inherits System.Web.UI.Page

    Protected Sub Page_Load(ByVal sender As Object, _
        ByVal e As System.EventArgs) Handles Me.Load
```

```
        If Not Page.IsPostBack Then
             RandomImage.ImageUrl = ImageFromDirectory("~/
RotatorImages")
        End If
    End Sub

    Private Function ImageFromDirectory(ByVal directoryPath _
        As String) As String

        Dim dirInfo As New DirectoryInfo(Server.
MapPath(directoryPath))
        Dim fileList() As FileInfo = dirInfo.GetFiles()
        Dim numberOfFiles As Integer = fileList.Length

        Dim rnd As New Random
        Dim randomFileIndex As Integer = rnd.Next(numberOfFiles)

        Dim imageFileName As String = fileList(randomFileIndex).
Name
        Dim fullImageFileName As String = _
            Path.Combine(directoryPath, imageFileName)

        Return fullImageFileName
    End Function
End Class
```

This page simply reads a list of image files in a folder named `RotatorImages` and randomly displays one of them whenever the page is loaded. The `If Not Page.IsPostBack` line ensures that any postbacks to the page leave the image as it was, so the random image displays only when a page is first loaded or refreshed without a postback occurring. This is a very simple web form, but one that easily lends itself to creating a user control. If you wanted to display a random image on a page, you would need to add this code to every page you wanted a random image on. You could put it into the Master Page of course, but that would limit the use of the Master Page to only those pages you wanted a random image on. But if we turn this into a user control, you can just add the user control on any page where you want a random image.

To create a user control, open Visual Studio 2008 Express Edition and open our CMS web site. Right-click the root of the web site, choose **New Folder**, and then create a folder named `Controls`. Repeat this and create a folder named `RotatorImages`. You may copy your own images into this folder or use the images in the downloadable code files. While you're setting this up, create the `ImageRotator.aspx` and `ImageRotator.aspx.vb` files above, or add them from the downloadable code files.

Why the controls folder

You don't need to use a separate folder for your user controls; it just makes managing them easier. Using a single folder for controls is an indicator that the files in that folder are user controls for your application, and it allows you to easily copy the folder of controls to a new application. Segregating controls in this manner, or even further using subfolders, is simply a good programming practice to get used to.

Open the `ImageRotator.aspx` and `ImageRotator.aspx.vb` files. Save them as `ImageRotatorControl.ascx` and `ImageRotatorControl.ascx.vb` in the `Controls` folder we created earlier. You'll notice the `aspx` extension for web forms has been changed to the `ascx` extension for user controls. Modify the two new files as follows:

- `ImageRotatorControl.ascx`:

```
<%@ Control Language="VB" AutoEventWireup="false"
    CodeFile="ImageRotatorControl.ascx.vb"
Inherits="ImageRotatorControl" %>
<asp:Image ID="RandomImage" runat="server" />
```

- `ImageRotatorControl.ascx.vb`:

```
Imports System.IO
Partial Class ImageRotatorControl
    Inherits System.Web.UI.UserControl

    Protected Sub Page_Load(ByVal sender As Object, _
        ByVal e As System.EventArgs) Handles Me.Load

        If Not Page.IsPostBack Then
            RandomImage.ImageUrl = ImageFromDirectory("~/
RotatorImages")
        End If
    End Sub

    Private Function ImageFromDirectory(ByVal directoryPath _
        As String) As String

        Dim dirInfo As New DirectoryInfo(Server.
MapPath(directoryPath))
        Dim fileList() As FileInfo = dirInfo.GetFiles()
        Dim numberOfFiles As Integer = fileList.Length

        Dim rnd As New Random
        Dim randomFileIndex As Integer = rnd.Next(numberOfFiles)

        Dim imageFileName As String = fileList(randomFileIndex).
Name
        Dim fullImageFileName As String = _
```

```
            Path.Combine(directoryPath, imageFileName)
        Return fullImageFileName
      End Function
   End Class
```

Besides the fact that we changed the class name to more appropriately indicate what the class does, the only change to the code-behind file is that we inherit `System.Web.UI.UserControl` instead of `System.Web.UI.Page`. This is because we are no longer modifying the `Page` class, but only the `UserControl` class in the ASP.NET 2.0 framework.

On the other hand, the control itself has changed quite a bit. We've stripped out all of the page markup, that is, the HTML, as that will be in the page we add this control to. We have also changed the `@ Page` directive on the first line to `@ Control`, to indicate that this is a control, not an entire page. Beyond the names changing to reflect the new filenames, the only real code we have in the control file is the ASP.NET Image control from our original page.

However, we can't use this control directly because it has to be in a page to be functional. Let's create a simple web page to use this control. Create a new web form `ImageRotatorControlTest.aspx`, using the following code:

```
<%@ Page Language="VB" %>
<%@ Register Src="~/Controls/ImageRotatorControl.ascx"
    TagName="ImageRotator" TagPrefix="cms" %>

<html xmlns="http://www.w3.org/1999/xhtml">
<head runat="server">
    <title>Image Rotator Control Test</title>
</head>
<body>
    <form id="form1" runat="server">
    <div>
    <cms:ImageRotator ID="ImageRotator1" runat="server" />
    </div>
    </form>
</body>
</html>
```

You'll notice that there are only two differences between this page and our original image rotator page, and those differences are highlighted in the code. The first line you haven't seen before is used to register our user control so that we can use it elsewhere on the page. It provides the source of the control, the tag name, and the tag prefix. You can use tag prefixes to identify controls as being from a specific group, application, or developer, or simply use a generic tag name such as `uc1` that is automatically assigned by the Visual Studio.

The second highlighted line is our new control being invoked on our page. It uses the tag name and prefix we assigned, as opposed to the built-in controls we have used with the asp prefix. It must also have a unique ID on the page, as with any other control. If you now run this page in a browser, it should display a random image each time the page is refreshed, just like the original aspx page did. Except that we can now use this user control anywhere we like, just by registering it on the page and invoking it as any other control.

Registering controls in the web.config file

User controls may also be registered in the web.config file, eliminating the need to register them on each page where they will be used. You need to have a <pages> section in your web.config's <system.web> section, and add a <controls> section inside the <pages> section with your control definition. A sample web.config for our ImageRotator control might look like:

```
<configuration>
  <system.web>
    <pages>
      <controls>
        <add tagPrefix="cms" src="~/Controls/
ImageRotatorControl.ascx"
          tagName="ImageRotator"/>
      </controls>
    </pages>
  </system.web>
</configuration>
```

Once the control is registered in the web.config file, you can use it on any page by just invoking the control, without registering it. The disadvantage to this method is that the control will always be loaded, reducing resources on your system.

We will need to create a number of user controls for our module, including controls to create a new Article or edit an existing one, display an Article, and display lists of Articles.

Additional specifications

We want our module to meet some other goals as well. The Articles must be stored in the database, so we can dynamically retrieve Articles and display them as selected by the user. We should be able to display a list of Articles, and have that list sorted in various ways such as Article name, publish date, and so on. We want to be able to display the Article title with only a few lines of the Article and include a "read more" link, and we don't want to display Articles that have passed their expiration date. We want to work within our three-tier architecture, and integrate security into both the Article creation process, as well as the viewing process. This all is fairly simple to explain, but some of the coding can get complicated, so let's get started.

Building the Articles module

You've been walked through most of the code creation in previous chapters. However, in some of this chapter, we'll load existing code and use it without a complete explanation. Some of this will happen because you have already learned how to create the code, and we don't want to double the size of the book by repeating it. Some of it is outside the scope of this book, so we'll load it with a brief explanation and you can dig deeper into it when you're ready. But most of the time, the code is just too tedious to type, so we'll load it from already existing code and will walk through its explanation.

Database layout

In order to build the Articles module, we need to know what data we are going to store and where we are going to store it. We also need to configure the appropriate business logic layers for the various methods we will use to manipulate the data. In a full-fledged Content Management System, we might use stored procedures within the database to manage some of the functions, but that is beyond the scope of this book. We'll start by building the database for our Article module and then add the functionality as we need it.

For each of our Articles, we need to track the title, the full body, the summary, the author, the date the Article was authored, and whether or not the Article is published. We also need to know an expiration date for the Article. And as we did in Chapter 3, we'll use an ID as a primary key to our database table. Once created, the `Articles` table looks something like this:

Column Name	Data Type	Allow Nulls
ArticleID	int	☐
ArticleTitle	nvarchar(50)	☑
ArticleBody	nvarchar(MAX)	☑
ArticleSummary	nvarchar(MAX)	☑
ArticleCreatedBy	nvarchar(50)	☑
ArticleCreatedDate	datetime	☑
ArticlePublished	bit	☑
ArticleExpirationDate	datetime	☑
		☐

 In this new table, you will want to set the `ArticleID` column as an Identity column. By doing this, the server will automatically insert this ID and track what the next number will be, saving us the additional work.

You'll notice this is very similar to our database in Chapter 3, although some of the columns have been renamed and more added. You'll also notice that each column name begins with the word "Article", indicating the function of the column, as well as the table it is in. This isn't necessary because we can refer to a column by the `{TableName}.{ColumnName}` syntax, but using the table name helps keep names straight between tables with similar column names. We might also have a foreign key in a table, creating a relationship with another table, and having that key use the original table's name will help identify the relationship. Establishing naming practices such as this is a good programming technique.

Data access layer

As we did in Chapter 3, we will create a data access layer for our Articles module. We have created an `ArticlesTableAdapter` in an `ArticlesDataSet` with a number of methods, as shown in the following figure:

FillAllArticles,GetAllArticles ()
DeleteArticleByArticleID (@Original_ArticleID)
FillAllCurrentArticles,GetAllCurrentArticles ()
FillAllCurrentPublishedArticles,GetAllCurrentPublishedArticles ()
FillByArticleCreatedBy,GetDataByArticleCreatedBy (@ArticleCreatedBy)
FillByArticleID,GetDataByArticleID (@ArticleID)
FillByArticleTitle,GetDataByArticleTitle (@ArticleTitle)
InsertNewArticle (@ArticleTitle, @ArticleBody, @ArticleSummary, @Articl...
UpdateArticleByArticleID (@ArticleTitle, @ArticleBody, @ArticleSummary,...

You'll notice that we have INSERT, UPDATE, and DELETE queries to handle inserting a new Article, as well as updating or deleting an existing one. We also have a number of selection methods for these Articles—selecting all Articles, all Articles that are current or have not passed their expiration date, and all current Articles that have been published. These queries will return a number of Articles that meet the query parameters. We also have queries to return a specific Article by the `ArticleID`, all Articles with the same title, and all Articles created by the same user. These will come into play in our module, to provide alternate ways of finding and displaying Articles.

We also have a second data adapter, the `ArticleSummariesTableAdapter`, in the same dataset. This adapter has similar methods to our `ArticlesTableAdapter`, except that the methods return only summary information on Articles, including the `ArticleID`, `ArticleTitle`, and `ArticleSummary`. After all, why should we return the contents of an Article's body if we'll be displaying only the summary?

If you look at the individual queries within the two table adapters, you will find the difference between the queries. For example, the query for `ArticlesTableAdapter.FillByArticleID` looks like this:

```
SELECT
   ArticleID, ArticleTitle, ArticleBody, ArticleSummary,
   ArticleCreatedBy, ArticleCreatedDate, ArticlePublished,
   ArticleExpirationDate
FROM
   Articles
WHERE
   ArticleID = @ArticleID
```

On the other hand, the `ArticleSummariesTableAdapter.GetCurrentPublishedArticleSummaries` query looks like the following:

```
SELECT
   ArticleID, ArticleTitle, ArticleSummary,
   ArticleCreatedBy, ArticleCreatedDate
FROM
   Articles
WHERE
   (ArticlePublished = 1) AND (ArticleExpirationDate > { fn NOW() })
```

You'll notice the latter query returns only the `ArticleID`, `ArticleTitle`, `ArticleSummary`, `ArticleCreatedBy`, and `ArticleCreatedDate`, not even returning the body of the Article. This is because we will use this query to list all current published Articles, along with their title and a summary of the Article. We will provide a link from this to the complete Article, to be displayed only if the user wants to read the complete Article and selects the link.

Business logic layer

You'll find the business logic layer code to be very close to the code we created in Chapter 3. Some naming changes have been made, but the biggest difference is the inclusion of two adapter properties — the original `Adapter` we used in Chapter 3 and a second `SummariesAdapter` that handles the second table adapter in our dataset. We also have similar functions for the two different table adapters, although we have no INSERT, UPDATE, or DELETE functions for the `SummariesAdapter`. All of our insertions, updates, and deletions will affect all data in a table row, not just those fields exposed in the `SummariesAdapter`, so we needn't duplicate these in the second table adapter.

User controls

We will build a few user controls to list, read, create, and edit Articles, as well as managing them. We'll use the controls in our page to provide functionality, without having to mix a large amount of code into our individual pages, and we'll have the individual controls available for separate parts of this and other applications. Let's start with the ListArticles control.

Listing Articles

In our application, we need to provide a listing of Articles in various states — Articles visible to all users, Articles restricted to specific roles, Articles that haven't been published, and Articles that have expired. We don't need separate controls for each of these. We can use a single control and manage the display by working with the roles in our application. We'll begin with a simple list of the Articles, using a repeater control to list the Articles.

First, using Visual Web Developer 2008 Express, add a new item to the web site and choose **Web User Control** for the template. Name it `ListArticles.ascx` and choose to put the code in a separate file, as shown below:

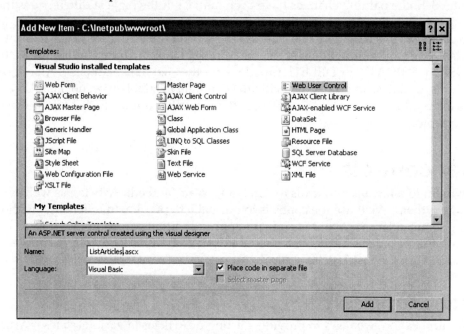

Drag the new control into the `Controls` folder we created for our `ImageRotatorControl` earlier in the chapter. You should open the `ListArticles.ascx` and `ListArticles.ascx.vb` in Visual Web Developer if they aren't open already.

As we did in Chapter 2, we'll create a page with a repeater control, only this time it will be our ListArticles control. Add the following code to the `ListArticles.ascx` file after the auto-created line:

```
<asp:Repeater ID="ListArticlesRepeater" runat="server">
  <ItemTemplate>
    <h2>
      <asp:Label ID="ArticleTitle" runat="server" _
    Text='<%# Eval("ArticleTitle") %>' />
    </h2>
      <asp:Label ID="ArticleSummary" runat="server" _
    Text='<%# Eval("ArticleSummary") %>' />
    <hr />
  </ItemTemplate>
</asp:Repeater>
```

This is essentially the code from Chapter 2, except this time we are evaluating both the `ArticleTitle` field and the `ArticleSummary` field from our database. We have also added some HTML formatting to our ItemTemplate, in order to separate our records.

In the `ListArticles.ascx.vb` file, add the following code in the ListArticles partial class that was created automatically when we created the file:

```
Protected Sub Page_Load(ByVal sender As Object, _
    ByVal e As System.EventArgs) Handles Me.Load
  Dim ArticlesLogic As New ArticlesBLL()
  ListArticlesRepeater.DataSource = _
    ArticlesLogic.GetCurrentPublishedArticleSummaries()
  ListArticlesRepeater.DataBind()
End Sub
```

You'll notice our code is using the `ArticlesBLL` we created earlier, but that otherwise, it's very similar to the repeater from Chapter 2. We are getting the summaries of Articles that have been published and that are not expired here, using the query we created for the DAL.

```
SELECT
    ArticleID, ArticleTitle, ArticleSummary,
    ArticleCreatedBy, ArticleCreatedDate
FROM
    Articles
WHERE (ArticleExpirationDate > { fn NOW() })
```

You'll notice we displayed only the `ArticleTitle` and `ArticleSummary` from this query. Just because we returned the data doesn't mean we have to display it, but it is available if we later decide to change the ListArticles control to display it. If we never intended to display this information, it would be more efficient not to return it in the query. However, at this point in the design, we really don't know what we may use. In a later phase of the project, we could optimize the code when we have a better idea of what we are using.

Create a new **Web Form** named `Articles.aspx` and use the `SimpleCMS.Master` Master Page. Add the following code immediately below the `@ Page` declaration, so we can register the ListArticles control as we did earlier in the chapter:

```
<%@ Register Src="~/Controls/ListArticles.ascx"
    TagName="ListArticles" TagPrefix="cms" %>
```

In the Content2 placeholder control, add the following line of code:

```
<cms:ListArticles ID="ListArticles1" runat="server" />
```

This is all we need on the `Articles.aspx` page to display our ListArticles control as we designed it. If you run this page in a browser, you should see something like this:

The page displays two Articles with titles and summaries from the database—in this case, the two Articles that were published and had not expired.

Now that we have a way to display the Articles to the users of the site, we need to make a way for us to create them. This process is something that's more complex than a simple listing of the Articles and is also a piece that is unlikely to ever need to be reused within the site, so for this we'll opt for creating it as a Page instead of a UserControl. Let's begin by adding a new page to the site and call it `AddArticle.aspx`. Be sure that when you create the new **Web Form** that you choose the option to use a **Master Page** and that you select the **SimpleCMS.master** for your Master Page. We'll need to add some input controls on the page to allow us to enter the data. Go ahead and add the controls so that yours looks similar to this:

```
<asp:Content ID="Content2" ContentPlaceHolderID="ContentPlaceHolder1"
Runat="Server">
<table>
  <tr>
   <td valign="top" align="right">Title:</td>
   <td><asp:TextBox ID="txtTitle" runat="server"></asp:TextBox></td>
```

```
  </tr>
  <tr>
    <td valign="top" align="right">Body:</td>
    <td></td>
  </tr>
  <tr>
    <td valign="top" align="right">Summary:</td>
    <td></td>
  </tr>
  <tr>
    <td valign="top" align="right">Expiration:</td>
    <td><asp:TextBox ID="txtExpDate" runat="server"></asp:TextBox></td>
  </tr>
  <tr>
    <td colspan="2">
      <asp:Button id="btnSave" runat="server" text="Save" />
    </td>
  </tr>
</table>
</asp:Content>
```

There are a couple of things to notice at this point. The first thing is that a few of the fields didn't contain any input. These are the `ArticleID`, `ArticleCreatedBy`, `ArticleCreatedDate`, and `ArticlePublished`, all of which we will take care of with code. Also notice that when we made out inputs, we didn't add controls to create the `ArticleBody` or `ArticleSummary` yet. For this, we're going to use FCKEditor, which was discussed in Chapter 1. Add that control so that it looks similar to this:

```
<tr>
  <td valign="top" align="right">Body:</td>
  <td><FCKeditorV2:FCKeditor ID="fckEditorBody" runat="server"></
FCKeditorV2:FCKeditor></td>
</tr>
<tr>
    <td valign="top" align="right">Summary:</td>
    <td><FCKeditorV2:FCKeditor ID="fckEditorSummary" runat="server"></
FCKeditorV2:FCKeditor></td>
</tr>
```

Once you've added the controls to your page, the end result should look something like this:

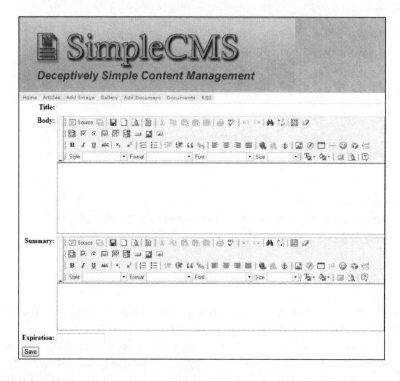

The next thing we need to do is to put in the code for saving the new Article when we enter the information, as well as creating some validations to ensure what we need is filled in. First thing is the validations. There are a number of ways, or combinations of ways, to accomplish this. However, for this site, we'll opt for a simple "code" approach. By that I mean we'll handle the validations within our code to save the data, but we could easily handle it with ASP.NET validator controls. We'll build our validations into a simple method in our code for the page. Let's start with the actual function. Let's call it `ArticleValid`. The method would look similar to this:

```
Private Function ArticleIsValid() As Boolean
   Dim _isValid As Boolean = True
   ' validation code goes here
   Return _isValid
End Function
```

As you can see, it's pretty simplistic at this point. But it's a simple "stub" for us to use within our page to ensure that when we are ready to save the Article, we have everything in place. As a note, remember that we don't want to validate any business rules here—that will be handled in our `ArticlesBLL` class. We're validating only the physical inputs from the UI and then passing the business validations call to the `ArticlesBLL`. Here is a sample of the simple input control validations:

```
If DateTime.TryParse(txtExpirationDate.Text, Nothing) = False Then
  _isValid = False
If txtTitle.Text.Trim.Length = 0 Then _isValid = False
If fckEditorBody.Value.Trim.Length = 0 Then _isValid = False
If fckEditorSummary.Value.Trim.Length = 0 Then _isValid = False
```

Now, we need to check the business rules, and come up with them for our Articles. For the purpose of this section, we'll keep the rules simple and say that the expiration date must be at least one day out from today. For this, we will need to first create a `Validate` function in our `ArticlesBLL`. The code for that, put within the `ArticlesBLL.vb` file, would look similar to this:

```
Public Shared Function Validate(ByVal _expDate as Date) As Boolean
    Dim _isValid As Boolean = True
    If Not _expDate > Today.AddDays(1) Then _isValid = False
    Return _isValid
End Function
```

You could easily add more validations to this as you see necessary. However, the basic premise is that you pass in the Article we've created and the method determines if it matches all the criteria. Our next step is to call this new method from within the `ArticleIsValid()` method we wrote in the code for the page. To do this, we need to add the following to the method:

```
If ArticlesBLL.Validate(CDate(txtExpirationDate.Text)) = False Then
  _isValid = False
```

Now that we've got a way to verify that all the Article information passes our tests, we need to actually create the Article object and see about calling our new method and, if it passes, calling the Save to commit it to our database. We have a Save button on our page, "btnSave", so now we need to create the event that happens when you click it. The code for that would look similar to this:

```
Protected Sub btnSave_Click(ByVal sender As Object, _
  ByVal e As System.EventArgs) Handles btnSave.Click
End Sub
```

Once the event has been created, we just need to go and put our call to the `ArticleIsValid()` method and determine the result. To do this, we place the following code into our `btnSave_Click()` event:

```
If ArticleIsValid() Then
  ' Everything is OK
Else
  ' Article Failed Validation
End If
```

If everything was OK, we will want to call our `ArticlesBLL`, passing in all the necessary data, and commit the Article to the database. To accomplish this, we put the following code into the above `If/Then` check so that it looks similar to this:

```
Dim _ArticlesBLL As New ArticlesBLL()
If _ArticlesBLL.CreateArticle( _
  txtTitle.Text, _
  fckEditorBody.Value, _
  fckEditorSummary.Value, _
  Page.User.Identity.Name, _
  Today, _
  0, _
  CDate(txtExpDate.Text)) Then
  ' Article Was Saved.
Else
  ' Article Was Not Saved.
End If
```

As you can see in the call to the `CreateArticle()`, we've hardcoded a few values and pulled a few from outside of the user inputs on the page. The `ArticleCreatedBy` we are pulling from part of the login information that is required on the site. We set the `ArticleCreatedDate` as "Today", meaning that the system will automatically use the current date retrieved from the Server. The last item is the `ArticlePublished`, which can be a 1 or a 0, with 0 being unpublished. For this, we always set it to 0 when the Article is created so that (as you will see later in this chapter, as well as being covered in Chapter 9) we can put the Article through an approval process.

I'm sure that in your usage of the code presented here, you will want to do a number of things beyond the simple approach such as adding friendly error messages, handling what to do when the Article saves (messages, redirect to another page, and so on). However, for the purposes here, we'll keep it simple.

Author, Editor, and Publisher roles

Now that we have a way to actually create the Articles for our CMS system, we should revisit the security and roles we want to be able to use. We said earlier that we would have four distinct Roles in our CMS—Author, Editor, Publisher (Administrator), and Registered User. As far as creating Articles within our site, we will want to limit this ability to just the Author, Editor, and Administrator roles, making sure to disallow the users who are only registered, along with any Unregistered Users. ASP.NET has a very simple way for us to handle these scenarios. First, let's take a look at any Unregistered (or Anonymous) Users and force them to log in before they can access the page to create Articles. Within the `Page_Load()` method of the `AddArticles.aspx.vb`, we will want to add the following code:

```
If Not Page.User.Identity.IsAuthenticated Then
   Response.Redirect("login.aspx")
End If
```

This code will check if the user is logged in and redirect them to the `Login.aspx` page if they are not properly authenticated. Next, we will want to extend our check so that only those roles mentioned above have access. To do this, we will take the `IF` check we just wrote and add a second part to it, as shown next:

```
If Not Page.User.Identity.IsAuthenticated Then
   Response.Redirect("login.aspx")
Else
   If Not Page.User.IsInRole("Author") _
   AndAlso Not Page.User.IsInRole("Editor") _
   AndAlso Not Page.User.IsInRole("Administrator") Then
      ' User Does Not have Access
      Response.Redirect("default.aspx")
   End If
End If
```

The page should now be limited to only those users whom we wish to have access to create new Articles within our site. We will be delving into these roles a little more in Chapter 9. This will involve going into the specifics of how they can interact beyond creating the Articles, but this should suffice for now.

Additional features

From the basic setup we've laid out in this chapter, you could extend it in any number of ways depending on the requirements you may have for your CMS. We've added an expiration date, but you could also add a start date if you wanted. This would allow you to determine when the Article would start appearing, giving you the ability to create your content ahead of time. You could also add additional tracking information such as views to count the number of times your Article has been pulled up. Perhaps you would like detailed publishing information. For this, you may want to look at adding the `PublishedBy` and `PublishedDate` columns to your database, DAL, and BLL. All of these items are things that you could add, most with very little work, which could improve the way you use your CMS. With some additional work, you could extend the Articles to include versioning, saving all the edits to the Article. Perhaps you would like to extend the Articles to include a "blog-like" feel. To achieve this, you could add some additional tables to your database to store the comments.

The base concept of a CMS Article is really just that—a base. It's meant to be a starting point for your site—a way for you to provide content quickly and easily to your users. Beyond this simple approach, there is really no limit to what you could provide.

Summary

In this chapter, we've gone over the basics of how to display your Articles, how to create them, and touched briefly on how you may want to extend them. With all these pieces in mind, it's easy to get carried away and try to do too much, too quickly. With that in mind, I suggest you start simple and always keep the user in mind.

6
Pages and Zones

In this chapter, we will discuss a number of the visual aspects of a site design. Many of these topics are not specific to a CMS, but are great concepts to remember for any site you may be designing.

In this chapter, you will learn about implementing and using:

- Master Pages
- Themes
- Menus and navigation
- Page hierarchy
- Regions and Zones

Master Pages

Earlier you were introduced to a feature called Master Pages, but what exactly are they? The idea behind them is the one that's been around since the early days of development. The idea that you can inherit the layout of one page for use in another is the one that has kept many developers scrambling with Includes and User Controls. This is where Master Pages come into play. They allow you to lay out a page once and use it over and over. By doing this, you can save yourself countless hours of time, as well as being able to maintain the look and feel of your site from a single place. By implementing a Master Page and using ContentPlaceHolders, your page is able to keep its continuity throughout.

In Chapter 4, you saw a simple implementation of a Master Page that contained two ContentPlaceHolder controls (ContentPlaceholder1 and Head, identified by their IDs). The `Default.aspx` page was set up to use the Master Page that was created. We'll expand upon all of this in a bit more detail. Although let's first review the pieces that were already put in place. You'll see on the Master Page (`SimpleCMS.master`) that it looks similar to a standard `.aspx` page from ASP.NET, but with some slight differences. The `<@...>` declaration has had the page identifier changed for a Master declaration. Here is a standard web page declaration:

```
<%@ Page Language="VB" MasterPageFile="~/SimpleCMS.master"
   AutoEventWireup="false" CodeFile="Default.aspx.vb"
   Inherits="_Default" Title="Untitled Page" %>
```

Here is the declaration for a Master Page

```
<%@ Master Language="VB" CodeFile="SimpleCMS.master.vb"
   Inherits="SimpleCMS" %>
```

This tells the underlying ASP.NET framework how to handle this special page. If you look at the code for the page, you will also see that it inherits from `System.Web.UI.MasterPage` instead of the standard `System.Web.UI.Page`. They function similarly but, as we will cover in more detail later, they have a few distinct differences.

Now, back to the Master Page. Let's take a closer look at the two existing ContentPlaceHolders. The first one you see on the page is the one with the ID of "Head". This is a default item that is added automatically to a new Master Page and its location is also standard. The system is setting up your page so that any "child" page later on will be able to put things such as Javascript and style tags into this location. It's within the HTML `<head>` tag, and is handled by the client's browser specially. The control's tag contains a minimal amount of properties—in reality only four, along with a basic set of events you can tie to. The reason for this is actually pretty straightforward—it doesn't need anything more. The ContentPlaceHolder controls aren't really meant to do much, from a programming standpoint. They are meant to be placeholders where other code is injected, from the child pages, and this injected code is where all the "real work" is meant to take place. With that in mind, the system acts more as a pass-through to allow the ContentPlaceHolders to have as little impact on the rest of the site as possible.

Now, back to the existing page, you will see the second preloaded ContentPlaceHolder (ContentPlaceHolder1). Again, this one will be automatically added to the new Master Page when it's initially added. Its position is really more of just being "thrown on the page" when you start out. The idea is that you will position this one, as well as any others you add to the page, in such a way as to complement the design of your site. You will typically have one for every zone or region (see Chapter 8) of your layout, to allow you to update the contents within. For simplicity sake, we'll keep with the one zone approach to the site, and will only use the two existing preloaded ContentPlaceHolders for now at least.

The positioning of ContentPlaceHolder1 in the current layout is one where it encapsulates the main "body" for the site. All the child pages will render their content up into this section. With that, you will notice the fact that the areas outside this control are really important to the way the site will not only look but also act. Setting up your site headers (images, menus, and so on) will be of the utmost importance. Also, things such as footers, borders, and all the other pieces you will interact with on each page are typically laid out on your Master Page. In the existing example, you will also see the LoginStatus1 control placed directly on the Master Page. This is a great way to share that control and any code/events you may have tied to it, on every page, without having to duplicate your code.

There are a few things to keep in mind when putting things together on your Master Page. The biggest of which is that your child/content page will inherit aspects of your Master Page. Styles, attributes, and layout are just a few of the pieces you need to keep in mind. Think of the end resulting page as more of a merger of the Master Page and child/content page. With that in mind, you can begin to understand that when you add something such as a width to the Master Page, which would be consumed by the children, the Child Page will be bound by that.

 For example, when many people set up their Master Page, they will often use a `<table>` as their defining container. This is a great way to do this and, in fact, is exactly what's done in the example we are working with. Look at the HTML for the Master Page. You will see that the whole page, in essence, is wrapped in a `<table>` tag and the ContentPlaceHolder is within a `<td>`. If you were to happen to apply a style attribute to that table and set its width, the children that fill the ContentPlaceHolder are going to be restricted to working within the confines of that predetermined size. This is not necessarily a bad thing. It will make it easier to work with the child pages in that you don't have to worry about defining their sizes—it's already done for you, and at the same time, it lets you handle all the children from this one location. It can also restrict you for those exact same reasons. You may want a more dynamic approach, and hard setting these attributes on the Master Page may not be what you are after. These are factors you need to think about before you get too far into the designing of your site.

Now that you've got a basic understanding of what Master Pages are and how they can function on a simple scale, let's take a look at the way they are used from the child/content page. Look at the Default.aspx (HTML view). You will notice that this page looks distinctly different from a standard (with no Master Page) page. Here you have what a page looks like when you first add it, with no Master Page:

```
<%@ Page Language="VB" AutoEventWireup="false"
  CodeFile="Default2.aspx.vb" Inherits="Default2" %>

<!DOCTYPE html
  PUBLIC "-//W3C//DTD XHTML 1.0 Transitional//EN"
  "http://www.w3.org/TR/xhtml1/DTD/xhtml1-transitional.dtd">

<html xmlns="http://www.w3.org/1999/xhtml">
<head runat="server">
    <title>Untitled Page</title>
</head>
<body>
    <form id="form1" runat="server">
    <div>

    </div>
    </form>
</body>
</html>
```

Compare this to a new Web Form when you select a Master Page.

```
<%@ Page Language="VB" MasterPageFile="~/SimpleCMS.master"
    AutoEventWireup="false" CodeFile="Default2.aspx.vb"
    Inherits="Default2" title="Untitled Page" %>

<asp:Content ID="Content1" ContentPlaceHolderID="head"
    Runat="Server">
</asp:Content>
<asp:Content ID="Content2"
    ContentPlaceHolderID="ContentPlaceHolder1"
    Runat="Server">
</asp:Content>
```

You will see right away that all the common HTML tags are missing from the page with a Master Page selected. That's because all of these common pieces are being handled in the Master Page and will be rendered from the Master Page. You will also notice that the page with a Master Page also has an additional default attribute added to its page declaration. The `title` attribute is added so that, when merged and rendered with the Master Page, the page will get the proper title displayed. In addition to the declaration tag differences and the lack of the common HTML tags being absent, the two ContentPlaceHolder tags we defined on the Master Page are automatically referenced through the use of a Content control. These Content controls tie directly to the ContentPlaceHolder tags on the Master Page through the `ContentPlaceHolderID` attribute. This tells the system where to put the pieces when rendering. The basic idea is that anything between the opening and closing tags of the Content control will be rendered out to the page when being called from a browser.

Themes

Themes are an extension of another idea, like Master Pages, that has kept developers working long hours. How do you quickly change the look and feel of your site for different users or usages? This is where Themes come in. Themes can be thought of as a container where you store your style sheets, images, and anything else that you may want to interchange in the visual pieces of your site. Themes are folders where you put all of these pieces to group them together. While one user may be visiting your site and seeing it one way, another user can be viewing the exact same site, but get a completely different experience.

Let's start off by enabling our site to include the use of Themes. To do this, right-click on the project in the **Solutions Explorer**, select **Add ASP.NET Folder**, and then choose **Theme** from the submenu:

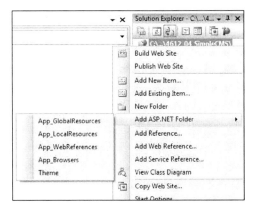

The folder will default to `Theme1` as its name. I'd suggest that you name this something friendlier though. For now, we will call the Theme as "SimpleCMSTheme". However, later on you may want to add another Theme and give your folders descriptive names, which will really help you keep your work organized.

You will see that a Theme is really nothing more than a folder for organizing all the pieces. Let's take a look at what options are available to us. Right-click on the **SimpleCMSTheme** folder we just created, select **Add New Item,** and you should see a list similar to this one:

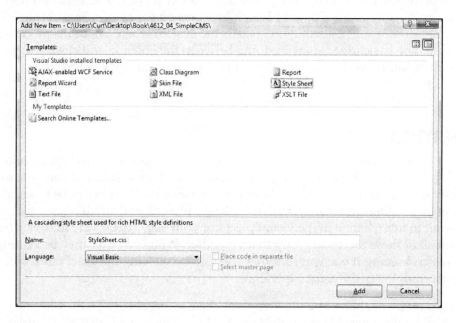

Your items may vary depending on your installation, but the key items here are **Skin File** and **Style Sheet**. You may already be familiar with stylesheets if you've done any web design work, but let's do a little refresher just in case. Stylesheets, among other uses, are a way to organize all the attributes for your HTML tags. This is really the key feature of stylesheets. You will often see them referenced and called CSS, which stands for Cascading Style Sheets that I'll explain in more detail shortly, but it's also the file extension used when adding a stylesheet to your application. Let's go ahead and add **Style Sheet** to our site just like the example above. For our example, we'll use the default name `StyleSheet.css` that the system selects. The system will preload your new stylesheet with one element — the `body{}` element. Let's go ahead and add a simple attribute to this element. Put your cursor between the open "{" and close "}" brackets and press *Ctrl+space* and you should get the IntelliSense menu. This is a list of the attributes that the system acknowledges for addition to your element tag. For our testing, let's select the `background-color` attribute and give it a value of `Blue`. It should look like this when you are completed:

```
body {
background-color: Blue;
}
```

Go ahead, save your stylesheet, run the site, and see what happens. If you didn't notice any difference, that's because even though we've now created a Theme for the site and added an attribute to the body element, we've never actually told the site to use this new Theme. Open your `web.config` and find the `<pages...>` element. It should be located in the `<configuration><system.web>` section, as shown next:

Go ahead, select the `<pages>` element, and put your cursor right after the "s". Press the spacebar and the IntelliSense menu should show up like this:

You will see a long list of available items, but the item we are interested in for now is the `theme`. Select this and you will be prompted to enter a value. Put in the name of the Theme we created earlier.

```
<pages theme="SimpleCMSTheme">
```

We've now assigned this Theme to our site with one simple line of text. Save your changes and let's run the site again and see what happens. The body element we added to our stylesheet is now read by the system and applied appropriately. View the source on your page and look at how this code was applied. The following line is now part of your rendered code:

```
<link href="App_Themes/SimpleCMSTheme/StyleSheet.css"
    type="text/css" rel="stylesheet" />
```

Now that we've seen how to apply a Theme and how to use a stylesheet within it, let's look at one of the other key features of the Theme, the `Skin` file. A `Skin` file can be thought of as pre-setting a set of parameters for your controls in your site. This will let you configure multiple attributes, in order to give a certain look and feel to a control so that you can quickly reuse it at any time. Let's jump right in and take a look at how it works, to give you a better understanding. Right-click on the **SimpleCMSTheme** folder we created and select the **Skin File** option. Go ahead and use the defaulted name of `SkinFile.skin` for this example. You should get an example like this:

```
<%--
Default skin template. The following skins are provided as examples
only.

1. Named control skin. The SkinId should be uniquely defined because
    duplicate SkinId's per control type are not allowed in the same
theme.

<asp:GridView runat="server" SkinId="gridviewSkin" BackColor="White" >
    <AlternatingRowStyle BackColor="Blue" />
</asp:GridView>

2. Default skin. The SkinId is not defined. Only one default
    control skin per control type is allowed in the same theme.

<asp:Image runat="server" ImageUrl="~/images/image1.jpg" />
--%>
```

We now have the default Skin file for our site. Microsoft even provided a great sample here for us. What you see in the example could be translated to say that any GridView added to the site, with either no SkinID specified or with a SkinID of gridviewSkin, will use this skin. In doing so, these GridViews will all use a BackColor of White and AlternatingRowsStyle BackColor of Blue. By putting this in a Skin file as part of our Theme, we could apply these attributes, along with many others, to all like controls at one time. This can really save you a lot of development time. As we go through designing the rest of the CMS site, we will continue to revisit these Theme principles and expand the contents of them, so it is good to keep their functionality in mind as we go along.

Menus

Navigation is the heart of any web site. It's your direct interface to your customers and allows you to guide them to all of the content that you've spent hours on putting together. A poorly laid out navigation menu can destroy the usability of your site, and can also transform your site into one that your customers/users will enjoy using. There are two common ways that menus are done within most ASP.NET web sites. The first is what I would consider the "old" way of doing it. That would be the manual method of making menus. By using simple HTML <a href..> tags, you could easily place a series of links on your page and, in reality, you have a menu. This will work great in certain circumstances. If your site has a very limited number of items you wish to display on the menu, if your menu is something that is likely to seldom change, and if you don't really have the need to dynamically enable or hide your menu items, then you may find that this simple menu system is one that will fit your needs nicely. It's still a commonly used option and is very fast and easy to set up. It could be as simple as the following code:

```
<td>
      <a href="Somepage1.aspx" title="Some Page 1">Click Me</a>
      <a href="Somepage2.aspx" title="Some Page 2">Click Me</a>
      <a href="Somepage3.aspx" title="Some Page 3">Click Me</a>
      <a href="Somepage4.aspx" title="Some Page 4">Click Me</a>
      <a href="Somepage5.aspx" title="Some Page 5">Click Me</a>
   </td>
```

With the above approach, you really could do a lot more than just this simple list of links, but it would involve doing a great deal of CSS and Javascript, not to mention really involving a time commitment to develop and lots of potential cross-browser issues. This is where the ASP.NET tools can really come into play and save you a great deal of time. Microsoft has taken most of the things you may want to do with your series of links, and done the work for you. Visual effects, drop-down sub-menus, and permissions are just a few of these pre-designed features. For this example, let's go ahead and put a Menu control on our Master Page. Open up the `SimpleCMS.master` page in the designer and drag a Menu control from the toolbox on to our page right below our logo.

As you can see, it has a set of default values; but for our needs, let's go ahead and replace these right away, and make this a horizontal menu instead of a vertical (the default) one. Doing this is as simple as going to the **Menu** Properties, looking in the **Layout** section, and changing its **Orientation**.

Another quick and easy thing we can do is change the look and feel of the menu. We could tweak all the little settings on the menu or we could take advantage of a number of pre-built themes that Microsoft has provided for us. Click the **Menu Tasks** button to extend them.

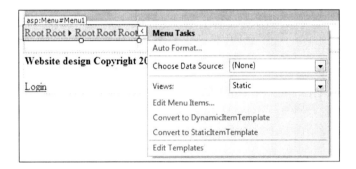

Then select the **AutoFormat** option.

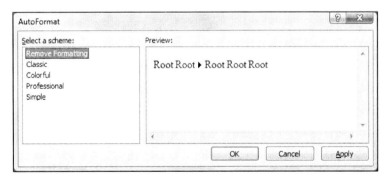

Here you will see a list of four pre-built options, as well as a handy option, to remove all the formatting. These formats are made to be used not only as they are, but also as a great starting point for your own design. Let's choose the **Simple** option for our site. If you were to run the site right now, you would notice that our menu doesn't show up. This is not because we've done anything incorrectly; it's because even though we've added a menu to the site, we haven't yet added any items to the menu. For this, you again have two common ways of doing it. The first, again, is the more straightforward and simplistic approach. We can simply click the **Menu Tasks** button and choose **Edit Menu Items**. You will see an empty editor screen.

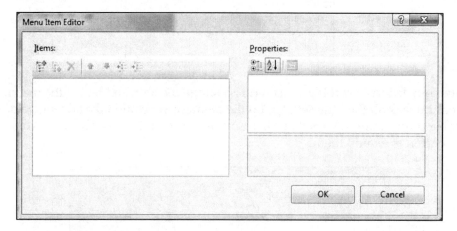

From here, simply choose **Add Root Item**.

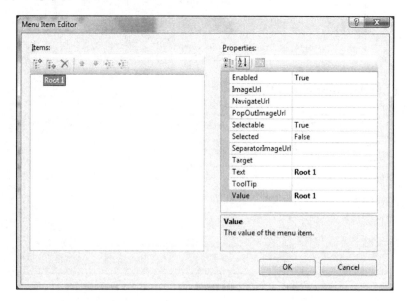

Then go ahead and give it some **Text** and a **Value**. Click **Save** and run your site once. You will see that the following screen will show up:

We really don't want a menu with just one item on it, so let's stop the site and go back in to the menu editor. Go ahead and add three more Root menu Items to your menu. When you are done with that, select your third Root menu item and choose the **Add Child Menu Item** from the editor.

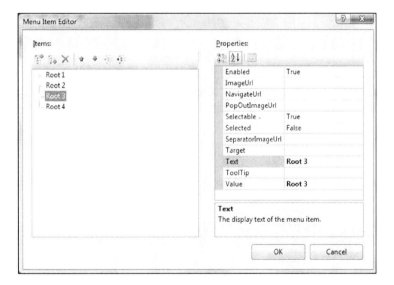

Add a couple of child items to your third Root menu Item. Be sure that you always highlight the Root menu item when you choose the **Add Child**, or you may find yourself adding child items in places you didn't intend them to be. When you are done, you should have a menu that looks something like this:

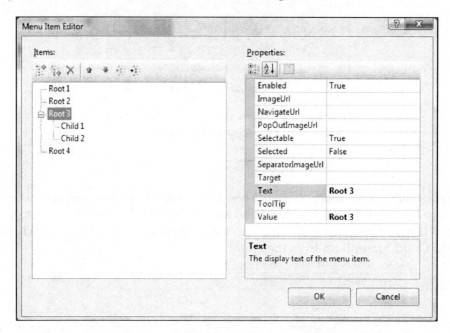

Go ahead and click the **OK** button and then run your site. You will see that it will display your new menu, as shown in the following figure:

Now as you can see, this would work perfectly well and you could easily create your menu items like this, but there is another way. If you still have the site running, go ahead and stop it. In your **Solutions Explorer**, select the root of your site. Then, from the menu, choose **File | New File**. Choose the **Site Map** option from the list.

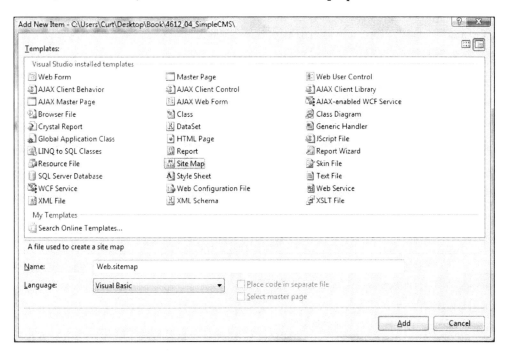

As always, you could leave the name of the file to the defaulted name, but in this case, we will use the defaulted name of web.sitemap. By keeping the default name, it will save us some configuration work later. It will create a set of default entries and take us immediately into the editor when we click **OK**.

```xml
<?xml version="1.0" encoding="utf-8" ?>
<siteMap
xmlns="http://schemas.microsoft.com/AspNet/SiteMap-File-1.0" >
  <siteMapNode url="" title="">
        <siteMapNode url="" title="" description="" />
        <siteMapNode url="" title="" description="" />
    </siteMapNode>
</sitemap>
```

As you can see, the site map is really nothing more than an XML file with some special tag names. Let's go ahead and create some simple entries in our file so that the end result looks something like this:

```
<?xml version="1.0" encoding="utf-8" ?>
<siteMap
xmlns="http://schemas.microsoft.com/AspNet/SiteMap-File-1.0" >
  <siteMapNode url="" title="">
          <siteMapNode url="~/Default.aspx" title="Link 1"
description="Link 1" />
          <siteMapNode url="~/Default.aspx" title="Link 2"
description="Link 2" />
          <siteMapNode url="~/Default.aspx" title="Link 3"
description="Link 3" />
          <siteMapNode url="~/Default.aspx" title="Link 4"
description="Link 4" />
    </siteMapNode>
</sitemap>
```

Now, let's go back to the Menu control we added to our Master Page. From that menu, choose the **Tasks** button, and then select **Choose Data Source**.

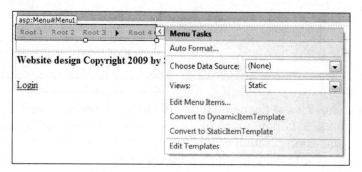

Select **New Data Source** from the menu and you will get a screen like this.

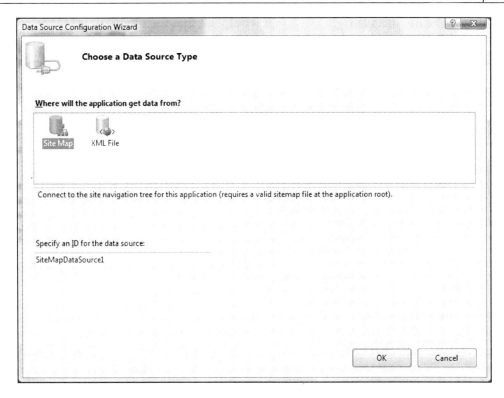

Click **OK** and you will now see that our page has a new control placed on it. This new **SiteMapDataSource1** control has been automatically created for us.

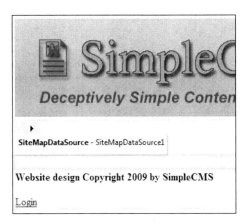

If you were to run the site right now, you would see that the menu we added is now populated, but odds are that it's not quite laid out as you would have expected. Stop the running of the site and let's go to the properties on the SiteMapDataSource.

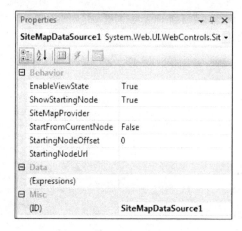

Our current sitemap file contains a "root" tag. This is simply the container that must exist to group all the other menu items together. However, in this case, we don't want that to actually show on the page, so we will set the **ShowStartingNode** property to **False**. This will tell the menu control to skip that first item and display the next level of items as the root of the menu. Run the site again and you should see a much different look for the menu on the site.

From here out, anytime you want to add a menu item, it's simply a matter of editing the `web.sitemap` file and instantly that menu change will be displayed throughout the site.

Page hierarchy

Page hierarchy can be thought of in two ways. There is the programmatic version of the hierarchy and then there is the logical hierarchy. First, let's discuss this from the consumer's side, that is, the logical side. When a person visits your site and goes to a page, let's say **About** page, and this page contains bios of your staff. If these bios link off to details on these individual people, your visitors will consider these pages to be child pages of the "About" page. While they could physically be in the same location (or possibly on the programmatically same page), the visitors will feel like they are on a child page, as they would expect these bio pages to be listed on **Site Maps** and **Menus** as children of the **About** page. They would also expect navigation to allow them to return to the "About" page. These are conventions that have been taught to the Internet users since the early days and are conventions that we can take advantage of. This logical flow allows us to help guide the users to pieces of content within the site. Whether it's simply going from a list to more details, or navigating a product catalog or narrowing search results, this logical progression through the site is something you need to maintain awareness of when deciding how you lay out your site.

The second Page hierarchy concept that needs mentioning is that of programmatic aspect. With ASP.NET, you are allowed to use what's called **inheritance**. This literally means that Page B can absorb and use Page A as part of itself. This allows us to share pieces across pages without having to rewrite them, as well as helping us maintain consistency. Master Pages, which we've already delved into earlier in this chapter, are a perfect example. Your child pages can be thought of as the merging of the Master Page and the content from within itself. This is a very powerful concept and one that can really save you a lot of time. This is not the same thing as the `Inherits` that you see in the page declaration, but rather it is one of usage.

```
<%@ Page Language="VB" MasterPageFile="~/SimpleCMS.master"
    AutoEventWireup="false" CodeFile="Default.aspx.vb"
    Inherits="_Default" Title="Untitled Page" %>
```

The `Inherits` declaration above is an even more powerful version of this same concept though. The `Inherits` declaration is the merging of two pieces again, but this time it's done at a much lower level, from within the .NET Framework. The `Inherits` declaration here is used to tell the site what class the page will use when it's compiled. In our current site sample, you will see that the `Default.aspx` page has an `Inherits=_default`. This means that when the application is compiled by the .NET Framework, it will find a class named `_default`, and will tie that to this page so that all its controls, methods, and events will be driven from that class. If we look at the `Default.aspx.vb` file, we will see the `_default` class declared there. It's the tying of these two pieces together that gives us the ability to program against it. Now, take a closer look at the `_default` class. Notice that it is also inheriting a class:

```
Partial Class _Default
    Inherits System.Web.UI.Page
```

By inheriting from the `System.Web.UI.Page` class, we are telling the .NET framework that the code we write should be merged with the code from that class. This means that anything that's exposed in that class is available to us. Take a moment now to delve into the `System.Web.UI.Page` class (either online or in the Help Files) and you will see that Microsoft has taken a great deal of time to give us a lot of functionality within this class and has already provided us with quite a bit. As we add functionality to the site, we will be utilizing these pieces frequently, so it pays to take the time to see what's available to us now.

Regions and Zones

The concept of a "Zone" or "Region" within a site is one that's been around since web sites were first created. Logically separating your site into pieces helps you keep a consistent feel to your site, as well as making sure your visitors know what to expect. If you've ever created a site, you have probably already implemented this concept, possibly without even realizing it. Let us take a look at a common layout used in many sites, and the same layout we currently have in our sample site. Here is how the site breaks down:

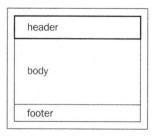

With this layout, we've already declared three Zones for our site—**header**, **body**, and **footer**. Each Zone serves a specific purpose and, when done well, the visitor will know easily what to expect from each. By understanding the functionality of each of your Zones, you will be able to spend less time on things such as your site layout and more time on getting the pieces your have within your site just the way you want them. In addition to the layout we are already using on our sample site—often referred to as "one column"—you will often see one of the two layouts:

The "two column" layout:

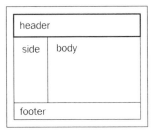

and the "three column layout":

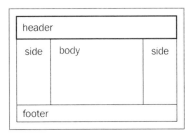

Take a look at the sites you visit and you will see that most will fall into one of these three layout styles. There has been a great number of research studies and usability discussions over the years, trying to determine what works "best", and that's the reason that you will find these three layouts most often because they work. Web site consumers have come to understand these layouts and are typically comfortable with them.

From a web site owner perspective, the "header" Zone is probably the most important Zone on the site. This Zone is where you will typically define who you are and what you are all about. Your logo and company name are often in this Zone. You will also find the site navigation, quick links, and search functionality here. These items are spanned across multiple pages—often your entire site—and are probably the most highly used (clicked on) pieces. Ensuring this Zone is well laid out can be the deciding factor on how your visitor's user experience will be. A poorly done header can drive your visitors away quickly, and may result in the users not returning again to your site and also passing the experience on to others. On the other hand though, a well done header will make your site easier to use, and let your visitors quickly get where they need to go, find what they are looking for, and always know where they are and who you are.

The "footer" Zone is often an overlooked, or at least barely considered area, and yet it can be a really vital piece. Simple things such as copyright information are usually held here, but it can also be a great place for other items. Page counters, company links, and product/site versions are often placed here so that they can be maintained and kept handy for all the pages in your site without detracting from your user's site experience. The footer is one of those great pieces that your user can always find, but at the same time, it's down out of their typical eye-line, so it won't draw their attention from rest of the site.

Before I talk about the main or "body" Zone, I do want to give a little explanation of the other common Zone(s)—the "side" Zone. Whether you are using the two or three column layout, you will have some side areas where you will want content displayed. These side Zones can be an extremely handy area for interacting with your visitor. The items that are contained in these Zones are typically consistent across your pages, but that isn't to say they are the same. The use will be the same, but the individual content within it will be dynamic and often directly tied to what's being used in the main body section of your site. As an example, if your site was designed around a blog, you may be displaying the latest entries in your body Zone, and at the same time, your side Zone may be displaying a list of top read entries, newest entries, or even a calendar of entries. These two zones are closely tied in this use, and may change as you browse through the content of the entries to be lists of other entries in a matching category or comments made on the current entry.

However, as you see by these examples, the side panels are very important to the body Zone. Without the side Zone, you aren't getting the complete picture, but only an isolated piece of it. The side Zone isn't just limited to the above-mentioned use either and can serve a number of additional functions. Advertisements, if you were to use them in your site, are often located in these side Zones, as they can be presented to the visitors without detracting from the main content in an overt fashion. Submenus, additional quick links, and search boxes can also often be found in these side Zones because you may want them always available to your user, again without detracting too much from the main content. The last common use of the side Zone would be what I call the "everything else" items. Sometimes you may have some small pieces of information you want to provide to your users, which is either not large enough to require its own page or is simply a convenience item, and the side Zone is a great place to stash these items.

The main body of the site is typically the largest and most dominant Zone on the site. This is where you will provide the majority of the information you want your visitors to see, and yet it is often the most simplistic piece of the site. The reason for this simplicity is really one of convenience. You want your visitors to quickly find what they need, and you don't want them to be inundated with too much extra that may distract them.

With all this information on the different Zones and what purposes they may serve, let's look at setting up our site Zones and how to use them within the code of our site. As we discussed earlier in this chapter, the use of a Master Page and ContentPlaceHolders is the starting point. This design uses an HTML table to define the areas we will use and the visible aspects of them (heights, colors, fonts, and so on) through the use of the stylesheets and Themes we've already started. From here, it's just a matter of making the individual pages, deriving them from the Master Page we created, and filling in the ContentPlaceHolders with the appropriate content. We've already begun to do this with the pages we've added to our site, although the pieces may make a bit more sense now.

Summary

In this chapter, we covered the concepts of why you lay out your site in a particular way, as well as beginning to help you understand all the pieces involved in this process. All of these pieces—Master Pages, Themes, CSS, Skins, Sitemaps, and Menus—combine together to make your site work. A solid understanding of these pieces will help you as you put together all the individual components. However, more importantly, it will aid you as you continue to expand your site, giving you the ability to quickly update it with as little work as possible.

7
Images, Files, and RSS

This chapter will discuss ways to use and save files, documents, and images to the CMS. We will cover not only the implementation of these features, but will also give you a firm background to help you understand how these features work, as well as other suggestions on implementing them.

This chapter will cover the following topics:

- Images and files on the Web
- Using the FileUpload control
- Creating a database table for the images and files
- Creating an image gallery and all classes associated with it
- Creating a document repository and all classes associated with it
- RSS feeds

How images and files work on the Web

Images are a key aspect for nearly any web site. They are the pieces that can let you be expressive and give your web site users a great experience, but that's not all they are good for. Images, and documents for that matter, can be provided to your users as usable content. In order to take advantage of all these pieces, you really need to understand how they work and why they act the way they do. If you've worked with HTML before, you have almost certainly used the `<img />` tag. That tag is universally understood and processed by browsers. This control uses an `src=` attribute to tell the browser where the file is located. However, there is more to it than just a pointer—it can also be used more intricately. For starters, the `src` attribute can not only be a "relative path" (`/folder/image.jpg`) and a "fully qualified URL" (`http://www.foo.com/folder/image.jpg`), but it can actually be a dynamically generated image (I'll cover that in more detail later). The key to take away from this is that the `<img />` tag is the root of imaging when it comes to the Web. Every web programming language has some sort of custom image control, but if you look at what is rendered out to the user's browser, it is almost always an `<img />` tag, simply because this is what the browser "knows" how to use. In reality, if you know the path directly to the image, you can put the image path into your browser most of the times, and point right to the image and display it. There are some limitations with the `<img />` tag, which you need to keep in mind when using the control. The biggest, or at least the most common hindrance, is the type(s) of images that are usable. Different browsers will accept and interpret some different image types, but in general, you will see that nearly every browser will accept `*.jpg`, `*.gif` and `*.png` image types, along with many also accepting `*.bmp` and `*.tif`. Now, there is also one other special case—the *.ico. However, that will be covered at another point.

File upload control and beyond

When building a CMS, one of the most important features you can have on your site is the ability to allow users to upload and view documents, images, files, and so on. For getting these files on to the web server—where they need to be for everyone to access them—you really have two basic choices. The first is a manual way where the file is delivered to someone (through email or disc) and then that person directly copies the files on to the server. The second way is to allow the users to upload these files directly to the server from their own computer. For reasons that are pretty obvious, you will usually opt for the second choice. For doing these direct uploads, one of the most common ways is to use the `<asp:FileUpload />`. The heart/core of this control is really nothing new, and has been around for quite a while. If you look at the control and what the rendered HTML is for this control, you will see that it's an `<input type="file" />` tag. This has been around for many versions of the HTML standards and is accepted by nearly every browser out there today. With that in mind, Microsoft took this fairly basic control, and extended it to allow you to do more with it, or at least more with the resulting file.

Before we get into too much detail of what you can do with the `<asp:FileUpload />` control, let's talk about what, and how, it does what it does. To put it simply, it allows you to browse to a file on your computer, select it, and then transfer it to the server. It breaks the files down into their binary components and starts sending them to the server where they are being waited for. All of the contents of the file are sent to the server and stored in memory (RAM) on the server until all the pieces are there, then recombined and saved on the server. This entire process is subject to a number of influencing factors, which you need to take into account while using this powerful control.

The first is you need a steady connection to the server throughout the uploading process. While you may think this sounds like no big deal, it wasn't always, and still isn't the case in many areas. The Internet can be thought of as a large ocean of data with waves rolling in and out. Your connection speed and even the actual connectivity can go up and down, sometimes drastically. When you are looking at web pages, it's not typically as noticeable because you aren't maintaining a constant connection to the site, but rather you are connecting, getting your data, and then disconnecting. If the connection fluctuates, you don't often notice because you aren't actually requesting any data at that moment, but when it comes to uploading a file, you need a steady connection. The speed can vary. But if the actual connection between you and the server is momentarily lost, for whatever reason, you will probably have to re-do the upload, as the pieces are no longer going anywhere and you've probably lost a few along the way.

The second factor you need to keep in mind, and this partially ties to the first, is the file size. The larger the file, the longer it will take to get all the pieces to the server. That leaves more opportunity and time for a connection to falter. This also means, if you remember that the entire file needs to be loaded into the server's memory before it's saved, that this can be resource intensive on the server. Trying to upload a large file can take a lot of memory away from the other things that the server may need to do. It's for this reason that ASP.NET has the ability to limit the file size when transferring a file. Within the web.config file, there is sometimes a setting called the HttpRuntime that explicitly sets the value, but there is also an inherited default value of approximately 4MB. This tells the site to not allow transfers larger than 4MB. This value is actually a default value that's inherited. Besides being just a site setting, which is defined in the `web.config`, it can also be set at a server level and enforced on all sites on that server. These values are typically stored in the `machine.config`. They work the exact same way, just on a larger scale. I'd suggest reading up on the different config files available to you, but for now, we will be working with just the `web.config`. However, you do need to keep in mind that your settings may be overridden by settings in another config file elsewhere. For now, we will use this 4MB file limit.

The third and last thing I want to mention in regards to how the `<asp:FileUpload />` control and it's use can be impacted is the security aspect of it. As this control is one of the few things that can have access to the user's computer, the security around it is vital. There is very little that you can do to adjust the way it interacts with the client's computer. The control has limited interactive capabilities from the developer's perspective just to help ensure the users' security—where the user selects the file from, what file type, and even the file sizes cannot be easily limited within the context of the control. This is all purposely excluded from the abilities of the control to ensure someone isn't extracting a file from the user's computer without their express consent.

Now that we've covered some of the background on the control, let's dig into how to use it. For our CMS, we know we are going to need the ability to upload documents and images, and make them available to a site user. So, let's look at our options on how we can do this. Firstly we need to make a decision on how we want to store these items within our site. For this, we have two common options.

The first is simply to stick them into a folder on the server when the user uploads them. This is a great approach and can work very smoothly, but there are a couple of distinct limitations. The first is that every item would need to have a unique name, otherwise files would be overwritten when a new one with the same name is added. This approach can also cause limitations within the security of these items. If you want to allow access to certain users to access only certain items, you could find yourself with some real difficulties. The last potential limitation that I wanted to mention was that of "versioning". By that I mean you have no way of maintaining multiple copies of the same file, at least not easily, as each new version would simply overwrite the previous. Although this approach of directly saving the files on the server does have some advantages. The most important advantage is that the items can be directly accessed through your links within the site. This can really increase performance of the site in that there is no processing that needs to be done when you want to access the files.

The other common option we have when it comes to saving the files on the server is that of using a database to store the binary data for the file, and then recombine it and provide it back to the user when they request it. This method was considered a far less preferred method, as it affected the performance of database servers. However, with current computing capabilities of database servers, I've found there to be little, if any, performance impact with this method. First, let's look at the potential negative aspects of this approach, the biggest of which is that we must do additional work to get the file back out of the database when you want to use it. The positive aspects of this method are much more numerous though, and due to these, it has become a very well accepted method for storing your files. The "pros" of this method are really all the same as the negatives from the previous method of directly storing your files—ability to reuse the same filename, ability to easily secure individual files, and a way to easily store multiple versions of the same file for future reference if needed. With all these factors taken into account, let's go with the database-stored files method for our CMS.

We'll need to start off by modifying our database to allow us to store the documents. We will need a new table, and since we can use this to contain both our images and documents, or really just about any file, let's call our table `SiteFiles`. Now we need to decide what columns our new table will need. We'll have to have an ID column for referencing the items, we'll need a column to store the actual binary data for the file, and technically that's all we'd need, but for ease of use we'll add a few more columns. We'll start with a column to hold the file's name, so we can present it to the user more easily. We will also want to add a column to hold a simple description of the file that the user can enter when they upload the file, again to make it clearer when presenting the file back to users. We should also add columns to track which user uploaded the file and when it was uploaded, as well as a column for us to tell what type of file it is that we are storing. If we want, we could extend the table and add columns to track things such as version numbers and an approval indicator, but for our CMS, we'll stick with a less complicated approach. Taking into account the columns mentioned, our new table should look like this in our SL manager:

Column Name	Data Type	Allow Nulls
🔑 FileID	int	☐
FileData	varbinary(MAX)	☐
FileName	varchar(250)	☐
FileDescription	varchar(500)	☐
FileType	int	☐
FileCreated	datetime	☐
FileCreatedBy	nvarchar(256)	☐

FileID in our new table is an Identity column with the autonumbering turned on. This means it will automatically generate a new identifier every time a record is inserted into the table, saving us all the hassle and time of doing it ourselves.

Now that we've created the database table, we will need to write the code to access the documents. We'll need to start by creating a new dataset, like we did earlier. Open your project, expand your **app_code** folder, and then right-click on your **DAL** folder. Select **Add New Item** from the menu. You should get a selection screen like this:

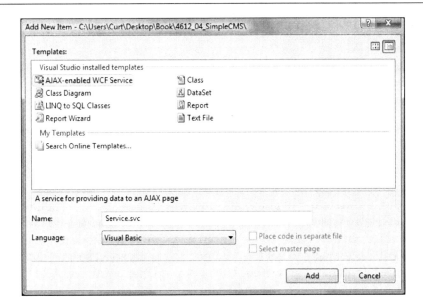

From this, select **DataSet** and give it a name of `SiteFilesDS.xsd` so that we can quickly find it again when we need it. You now have an empty dataset. Let's open the project's **Solution Explorer** and navigate to our database. Expand the **Tables** folder and you should get a listing similar to this:

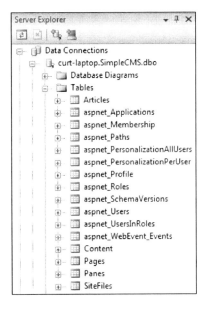

Drag the **SiteFiles** table from the list onto our new dataset and you should see this:

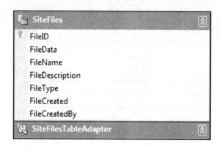

As you can see, the system will automatically create the GetData() method for us, and if all we ever wanted to do was retrieve a list of all the files, this would be sufficient. But for obvious reasons, we'll need a few more methods to get us going. First off we will need a way to get the data into the table, so let's right-click on the **SiteFilesTableAdapter** and you should get a pop up menu. Choose **Add Query** from the list and you will get a screen like this:

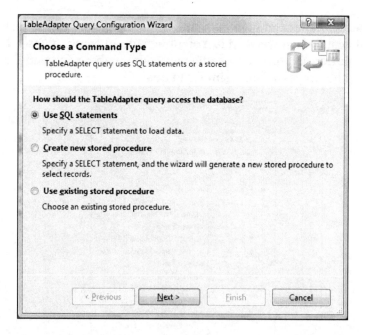

We will be using an SQL Statement, so choose that option. You will then go to another selection screen that looks like this:

As we will be wanting to insert a record into our table with the method, go ahead and choose the **INSERT** option, and click **Next**. The query it automatically builds is typically sufficient for the process and, in this case, it's exactly what we need. Yours should look like this:

Click the **Next** button and let's name our method `InsertSiteFile`. Once again by giving it a friendly, easy to remember name, we will be able to quickly find it when we need it. From here you can click either **Next** or **Finish**, and you should see that our dataset now looks like this:

The other methods that we will need right away will be one where we can retrieve an item from the table by an ID, one where we can retrieve a list of all the images, and one where we can retrieve a list of all the documents. We'll worry about those last two in a little bit. The existing `GetData()` method gets us the entire list, but we will also be able to retrieve a single record. Let's right-click on the **SiteFilesTableAdapter** and select **Add Query** just like before. Again we will choose the **Use SQL** option. But on the next screen, rather than selecting the **INSERT** option, we will choose the **SELECT** (the one which returns a row). We will be presented with an SQL statement that looks like this:

We will want to modify this statement to include the ID as parameter, like this:

Click **Next** and let's give some friendlier names to our methods, something like this:

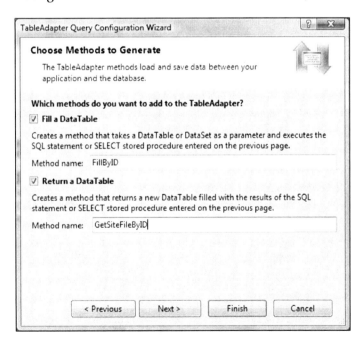

We should be ready to start working with our database table now. We'll come back and add some more functionality to this dataset at a later time in this chapter, but for now we should be able to insert records, retrieve lists, and retrieve a single item. Our next step will be to create our Business Logic Layer (BLL) that corresponds with the DAL we just created. Our BLL, just like the one we created earlier for the Articles, will need a number of methods to call out to our DAL layer. Here is an example of these methods as they could be written:

```
Imports SiteFilesDSTableAdapters
<System.ComponentModel.DataObject()> _
Public Class SiteFilesBLL
    Private _SiteFilesTableAdapter As SiteFilesTableAdapter = Nothing
    Protected ReadOnly Property Adapter() As SiteFilesTableAdapter
        Get
            If _SiteFilesTableAdapter Is Nothing Then
                _SiteFilesTableAdapter = New SiteFilesTableAdapter()
            End If
            Return _SiteFilesTableAdapter
        End Get
    End Property

    ' Get All Site Files Function
    <System.ComponentModel.DataObjectMethodAttribute(System.
ComponentModel.DataObjectMethodType.Select, True)> _
    Public Function GetFiles() As SiteFilesDS.SiteFilesDataTable
        Return Adapter.GetData()
    End Function
    ' Update File Function
    <System.ComponentModel.DataObjectMethodAttribute(System.
ComponentModel.DataObjectMethodType.Update, True)> _
    Public Function UpdateSiteFile(ByVal FileID As Integer, ByVal
FileData As Byte(), ByVal FileName As String, ByVal FileDescription
As String, ByVal FileType As Integer, ByVal FileCreated As DateTime,
ByVal FileCreatedBy As String) As Boolean
        Dim SiteFiles As SiteFilesDS.SiteFilesDataTable = Adapter.
GetSiteFileByID(FileID)
        If SiteFiles.Count = 0 Then
            ' If no matching record is found, return false
            Return False
        End If
        Dim SiteFilesRow As SiteFilesDS.SiteFilesRow = SiteFiles(0)
        SiteFilesRow.FileCreated = FileCreated
        SiteFilesRow.FileCreatedBy = FileCreatedBy
        SiteFilesRow.FileData = FileData
        SiteFilesRow.FileDescription = FileDescription
        SiteFilesRow.FileName = FileName
```

```
            SiteFilesRow.FileType = FileType
            ' Update the Article record
            Dim rowsAffected As Integer = Adapter.Update(SiteFilesRow)
            ' Return true if precisely one row was updated, otherwise
false
            Return rowsAffected = 1
    End Function
    ' Delete File Function
    <System.ComponentModel.DataObjectMethodAttribute(System.
ComponentModel.DataObjectMethodType.Delete, True)> _
    Public Function DeleteSiteFile(ByVal FileID As Integer) As Boolean
            Dim rowsAffected As Integer = Adapter.Delete(FileID)
            ' Return true if precisely one row was deleted, otherwise
false
            Return rowsAffected = 1
    End Function
End Class
```

Now that we have our DAL and BLL, we need the frontend pieces for the user to put the files in and retrieve them. In our CMS, we can break these down into two basic areas—Image galleries and document repositories.

Image gallery

An **Image gallery** can be thought of as a digital version of your home photo album. It's simply a listing of images that the user can browse through. In most galleries, you are displayed a listing of the images, often with a smaller version or thumbnail image as a representation, and then you have the ability to click on it and are presented with a larger image for easier viewing. This basic concept has been around since the early days of the Internet when people realized that they could easily allow a vast number of people to view their photos, images, or whatever. Galleries have come a long way since then, but the basic premise is still the same. For our CMS, we'll keep our gallery fairly simple, but we'll also point out the areas where you could further enhance it, should the need arise.

First thing we'll need to do is create a page to display our gallery. From the **Solution Explorer,** right-click on the **Website** and select **Add New Item**. You should get a selection screen like this:

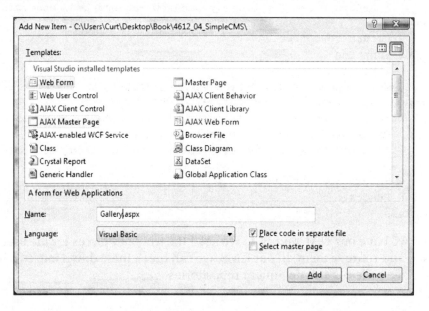

Choose **Web Form** from the list of options and name it **Gallery.aspx**. Be sure to check both options—**Place code in separate file** and **Select master page**. Then click **Add**. You should now get another selection screen asking you to choose the Master Page you want to use.

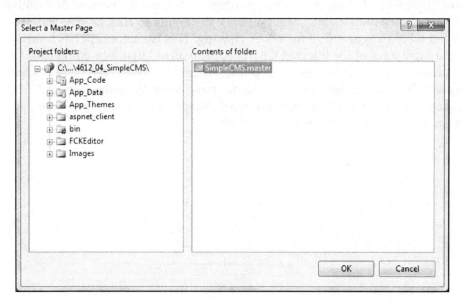

Browse to the **SimpleCMS.master** file that we created earlier and click **OK**. We now have a page to use for our gallery, but now we need to add some controls to our page, in order to allow us to actually display the list of images. We could do this any number of ways—from tables, grids, repeaters, or even just simple lists, all of which would work for our needs. However, if we want to make things easy on ourselves (and who doesn't want to), I'd suggest we stick with one of the great grids that are provided to us. From the **Toolbox**, select **Gridview** and drag it onto your page into the ContentPlaceHolder1 section that should be highlighted. You should end up with a page that looks like this:

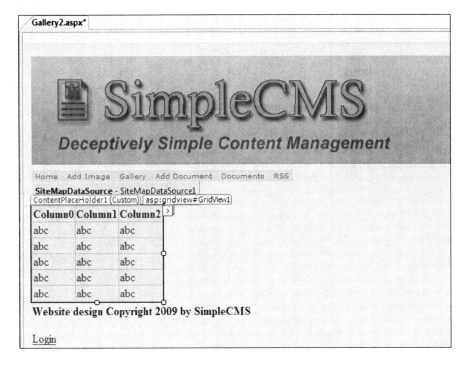

We now need to set up a few properties on our new Gridview so that it will work for us. First off, let's change the ID of the Gridview to something friendlier—"GalleryView". While we are in the **Properties** view, let's go ahead and set a few other items:

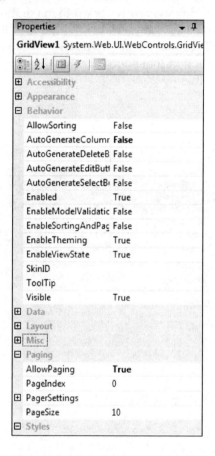

Now we need to set up the connection to our data. Earlier we created our SiteFilesDS with only a couple of simple methods. We'll need to add one to retrieve a list of images from the database. So, let's open up the **SiteFilesDS** and, like earlier, right-click on the **SiteFilesTableAdapter** and select **Add Query**. Again we will use the **SELECT** option and **SELECT** which returns rows. We will then be given the SQL statement that it prefilled for us, but we will add a little to it. Change the SQL so that it looks like this:

We will want to name the methods something friendlier again, so let's name them
FillImages and **GetImages**.

Click **Next** and then **Finish**. We should now have a dataset that looks like this:

We'll now need to add this new method to our BLL:

```
' Get Images Function
    <System.ComponentModel.DataObjectMethodAttribute( _
        System.ComponentModel.DataObjectMethodType.Select, True)> _
    Public Function GetImages() As SiteFilesDS.SiteFilesDataTable
        Return Adapter.GetImages()
    End Function
```

Okay, now that we have our methods in place, let's go back to our Gallery page. Open the **Tasks** menu for the Gridview we added earlier, and select **Choose Data Source** and then **New Data Source** from the menu options. You will get a selection screen like this:

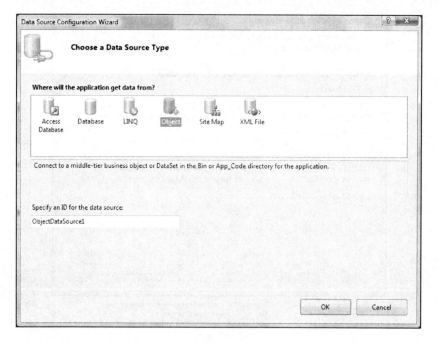

Select the **Object** option available and click **OK**. You will get another selection screen that looks like this:

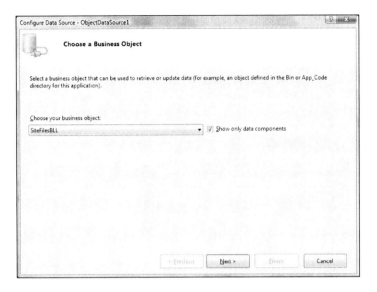

Choose the **SiteFilesBLL** option from the menu and click **Next**. As we will be retrieving a list from the database, we'll stay on the **SELECT** tab and then select the **GetImages()** method from the selection list. Click **Finish** and you should see some updates to your grid:

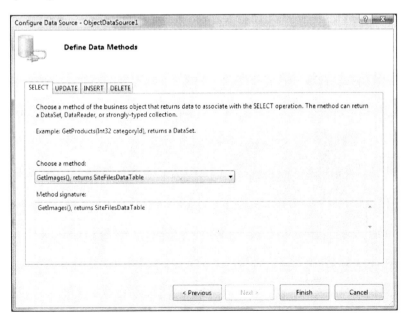

Ideally we could run the site now, but we're still missing one key component—a way to add images to the site. For this we'll want to create another new page. Just like before, let's right-click on the **Website** in the **Solution Explorer** and select **Add Item**. Choose **Web Form** from the options and name it **AddImage.aspx**, again selecting the **Place code in separate file** and **Select master page** options, as shown in the following screenshot:

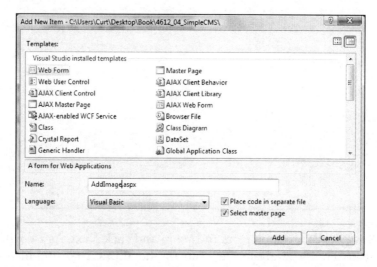

We'll choose the **SimpleCMS.master** once again and click **OK**. We've now got our new page. Let's go ahead and add a label and text box for us to enter the description for the file we want to add. We'll also want to add a FileUpload control like we discussed earlier in this chapter. When you are done, your page should look similar to this:

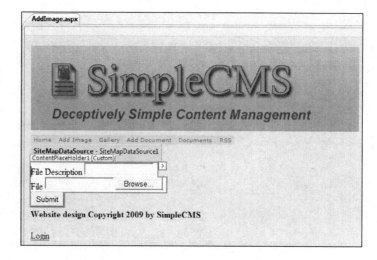

And your HTML view should look similar to this:

```
<%@ Page Language="VB" MasterPageFile="~/SimpleCMS.master"
AutoEventWireup="false"
CodeFile="AddImage.aspx.vb" Inherits="AddImage" title="Untitled Page"
%>
<asp:Content ID="Content1" ContentPlaceHolderID="head" Runat="Server">
</asp:Content>
<asp:Content ID="Content2" ContentPlaceHolderID="ContentPlaceHolder1"
Runat="Server">
    File Description <asp:TextBox ID="txtFileDescription"
runat="server"></asp:TextBox><br />
    File <asp:FileUpload ID="fuSiteFile" runat="server" /><br />
    <asp:Button ID="btnSubmit" runat="server" Text="Submit" />
</asp:Content>
```

You can always come back at a later point and arrange the controls into a style that fits your own design decisions, but for now, we'll just keep it simple. Notice that we also added a button for the user to click to submit their data. Now that we have the controls on the page, we need to make them do some actual work. Go into the code view for the page we just created. When you first enter it, you should see something similar to this:

```
Partial Class AddImage
        Inherits System.Web.UI.Page
End Class
```

Let's go ahead and choose the **btnSubmit** from the class selection drop-down and then choose the **Click** event from the method drop-down. When you do that you should see the Click event for the button generated, looking similar to this:

```
 Partial Class AddImage
     Inherits System.Web.UI.Page
Protected Sub btnSubmit_Click(ByVal sender As Object, _
        ByVal e As System.EventArgs) Handles btnSubmit.Click
End Sub
End Class
```

Now, we will want to create an instance of our BLL that we created earlier, and pass in all the values for the file to let the method do its thing and save our file to the database. The code for that could look similar to this:

```
Protected Sub btnSubmit_Click(ByVal sender As Object, _
        ByVal e As System.EventArgs) Handles btnSubmit.Click
        Dim bll As New SiteFilesBLL
        If bll.AddSiteFile(fuSiteFile.FileBytes, _
                fuSiteFile.FileName, _
                txtFileDescription.Text, _
                1, _
                Now, _
                Page.User.Identity.Name) Then
            ' All worked as expected
            Response.Redirect("~/Gallery.aspx")
        Else
            ' The upload failed.
        End If
    End Sub
```

You can see that I've added an IF/THEN check around the AddSiteFile() call to allow us to trap errors. I've also filled in all the values for the method. You may notice a couple of items in that list that may cause you to ask "why", so I'll discuss the purpose of each of the values briefly. The first value is the actual digital representation of the file, or the "bytes". The FileUpload control makes these available directly to us. The second parameter is the FileName, again coming directly from a property of the FileUpload control. The third parameter is the FileDescription, as entered in the text box by the user. The fifth value is a static integer of 1. In this case, we will use the 1 to represent images in our database. Remember that the database table will contain both images and documents. The sixth parameter is the "Created" date/time stamp. For this, you can use the Now() method that's prebuilt with .NET. The last parameter is the "Created By", or username, for the user who uploaded the file. That should complete our construction of this page, but wait. How would you get to the page? In order to access the page, we have to go back to the menu we created in Chapter 6 and add it. Open up the web.sitemap, and alter the items to include not only the AddImage.aspx, but we will also add the Gallery.aspx as well. When you are done, it should look similar to this:

```
<?xml version="1.0" encoding="utf-8" ?>
<siteMap xmlns="http://schemas.microsoft.com/AspNet/SiteMap-File-1.0"
>
  <siteMapNode url="" title="">
    <siteMapNode url="~/Default.aspx" title="Home"  description="Home"
/>
```

```
<siteMapNode url="~/AddImage.aspx" title="Add Image"  description="Add
Image" />
    <siteMapNode url="~/Gallery.aspx" title="Gallery"
description="Gallery" />
</siteMapNode>
</siteMap>
```

Let's go ahead and run our site now. Be sure to log in first (we'll come back to that shortly). From the menu, choose the **Gallery** page. As we haven't entered anything to this point, you should see a blank page like this:

From the menu, choose the **Add Image** item. You should see a page like this:

Go ahead and use the control to browse out and select an image from your computer. I'd suggest you select a JPEG file, just for ease of use. Fill in a description and click **Submit**. If all goes as expected, the file will be uploaded to the database. Of course, as we didn't tell the page to do anything after a successful save, it's difficult to know. Let's go back into the code for the Submit button Click, and change the result of the `IF/THEN` statement to have the page redirect to the Gallery page after an upload. It should look like this:

```
Partial Class AddImage
    Inherits System.Web.UI.Page
Protected Sub btnSubmit_Click(ByVal sender As Object, _
        ByVal e As System.EventArgs) Handles btnSubmit.Click
        Dim bll As New SiteFilesBLL
        If bll.AddSiteFile(fuSiteFile.FileBytes, _
                fuSiteFile.FileName, _
                txtFileDescription.Text, _
                1, _
                Now, _
                Page.User.Identity.Name) Then
            ' All worked as expected
            Response.Redirect("~/Gallery.aspx")
        Else
            ' The upload failed.
        End If
    End Sub
End Class
```

From the page menu, select the **Gallery** link and you should see a page similar to this:

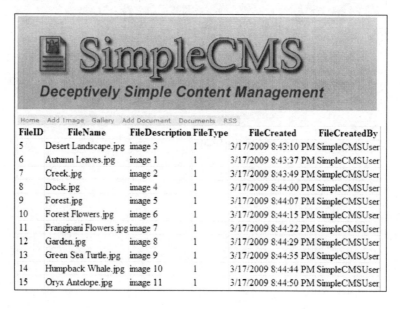

FileID	FileName	FileDescription	FileType	FileCreated	FileCreatedBy
5	Desert Landscape.jpg	image 3	1	3/17/2009 8:43:10 PM	SimpleCMSUser
6	Autumn Leaves.jpg	image 1	1	3/17/2009 8:43:37 PM	SimpleCMSUser
7	Creek.jpg	image 2	1	3/17/2009 8:43:49 PM	SimpleCMSUser
8	Dock.jpg	image 4	1	3/17/2009 8:44:00 PM	SimpleCMSUser
9	Forest.jpg	image 5	1	3/17/2009 8:44:07 PM	SimpleCMSUser
10	Forest Flowers.jpg	image 6	1	3/17/2009 8:44:15 PM	SimpleCMSUser
11	Frangipani Flowers.jpg	image 7	1	3/17/2009 8:44:22 PM	SimpleCMSUser
12	Garden.jpg	image 8	1	3/17/2009 8:44:29 PM	SimpleCMSUser
13	Green Sea Turtle.jpg	image 9	1	3/17/2009 8:44:35 PM	SimpleCMSUser
14	Humpback Whale.jpg	image 10	1	3/17/2009 8:44:44 PM	SimpleCMSUser
15	Oryx Antelope.jpg	image 11	1	3/17/2009 8:44:50 PM	SimpleCMSUser

As you can see, all the details on the file we uploaded are visible here, but the actual image itself isn't. That's because the image is stored in its raw form in the database, and hence the system will not automatically generate a column for this. We will need to manually do this. This is where things can get a little tricky. We will need to write a way to extract the raw data from the database and "recombine" it into a usable image. To accomplish this, we can create what's called a Stream to take the data out and allow us to work with it. Let's start by adding another Web Form to our page, same as we've done a number of times. However, this time let's make sure **not** to check the box that says **Select Master Page**. Call this new page `StreamFile.aspx`. You should get a new blank page that looks similar to this:

```
<%@ Page Language="VB" AutoEventWireup="false"
    CodeFile="StreamFile.aspx.vb" Inherits="StreamFile" %>
<!DOCTYPE html
    PUBLIC "-//W3C//DTD XHTML 1.0 Transitional//EN"
    "http://www.w3.org/TR/xhtml1/DTD/xhtml1-transitional.dtd">
<html xmlns="http://www.w3.org/1999/xhtml">
<head runat="server">
<title>Untitled Page</title>
</head>
<body>
    <form id="form1" runat="server">
    <div>
    </div>
    </form>
</body>
</html>
```

Change the HTML view of the page to look like this:

```
<%@ Page Language="VB" AutoEventWireup="false"
    CodeFile="StreamFile.aspx.vb" Inherits="StreamFile" %>
<%@ OutputCache Duration="60" VaryByParam="id" %>
<!DOCTYPE html
    PUBLIC "-//W3C//DTD XHTML 1.0 Transitional//EN"
    "http://www.w3.org/TR/xhtml1/DTD/xhtml1-transitional.dtd">
<html xmlns="http://www.w3.org/1999/xhtml">
<head id="Head1" runat="server">
<title></title>
</head>
<body></body>
</html>
```

We are simply eliminating all the unnecessary pieces of the page. We now need to go into the code view of the page. When we start, it will look like this:

```
Partial Class StreamFile
        Inherits System.Web.UI.Page
End Class
```

We'll need to add a Page_Load event to the code, and then we'll need to do some coding to retrieve the raw data from the database and stream it back out to the client. Here is a sample of one simple way of retrieving this stream, but there are other ways too:

```
Imports SiteFilesBLL

Partial Class StreamFile
    Inherits System.Web.UI.Page
Protected Sub Page_Load(ByVal sender As Object, _
        ByVal e As System.EventArgs) Handles Me.Load
        If Not Request.QueryString("id") Is Nothing AndAlso _
            Not Request.QueryString("type") Is Nothing Then
            Dim ID As Integer = CInt(Request.QueryString("id"))
            Dim FileType As Integer = CInt(Request.
QueryString("type"))
            If FileType = 1 Then      ' These are our Images
                Dim _SiteFile As New SiteFilesDS.SiteFilesDataTable
                Dim _SiteFilesBLL As New SiteFilesBLL
                _SiteFile = _SiteFilesBLL.GetDataByFileID(ID)
                Dim b() As Byte = _SiteFile(0).FileData
                Response.BinaryWrite(b)
            End If
        End If
    End Sub
End Class XE "image gallery:Page_Load event, adding to code"
```

Now that we have the page to return our image from the database, let's go back to the grid we put on our **Gallery** page. The code for it should look similar to this:

```
<%@ Page Language="VB" MasterPageFile="~/SimpleCMS.master"
AutoEventWireup="false"
CodeFile="Gallery.aspx.vb" Inherits="Gallery" title="Untitled Page" %>

<asp:Content ID="Content1" ContentPlaceHolderID="head" Runat="Server">
</asp:Content>
<asp:Content ID="Content2" ContentPlaceHolderID="ContentPlaceHolder1"
Runat="Server">
    <asp:GridView ID="GridView1" runat="server" AllowPaging="True"
    AutoGenerateColumns="False" DataKeyNames="FileID"
    DataSourceID="ObjectDataSource1">
    <Columns>
        <asp:BoundField DataField="FileID" HeaderText="FileID"
InsertVisible="False"
            ReadOnly="True" SortExpression="FileID" />
        <asp:BoundField DataField="FileName" HeaderText="FileName"
            SortExpression="FileName" />
        <asp:BoundField DataField="FileDescription"
HeaderText="FileDescription"
            SortExpression="FileDescription" />
        <asp:BoundField DataField="FileType" HeaderText="FileType"
            SortExpression="FileType" />
        <asp:BoundField DataField="FileCreated"
HeaderText="FileCreated"
            SortExpression="FileCreated" />
        <asp:BoundField DataField="FileCreatedBy"
HeaderText="FileCreatedBy"
            SortExpression="FileCreatedBy" />
    </Columns>
</asp:GridView>
```

Let's go ahead and add another column to the beginning of the grid to display our image. We'll add an `Image` column. Let's now set its properties using the following code:

```
<asp:GridView ID="GridView1" runat="server" AllowPaging="True"
    AutoGenerateColumns="False" DataKeyNames="FileID"
    DataSourceID="ObjectDataSource1">
    <Columns>
        <asp:ImageField DataImageUrlField="FileID"
            DataImageUrlFormatString="~/StreamFile.aspx?type=1&id={0}"
            ReadOnly="true" InsertVisible="false" ControlStyle-
Width="50" />
        <asp:BoundField DataField="FileID" HeaderText="FileID"
InsertVisible="False"
            ReadOnly="True" SortExpression="FileID" />
        <asp:BoundField DataField="FileName" HeaderText="FileName"
            SortExpression="FileName" />
        <asp:BoundField DataField="FileDescription"
HeaderText="FileDescription"
            SortExpression="FileDescription" />
        <asp:BoundField DataField="FileType" HeaderText="FileType"
            SortExpression="FileType" />
        <asp:BoundField DataField="FileCreated"
HeaderText="FileCreated"
            SortExpression="FileCreated" />
        <asp:BoundField DataField="FileCreatedBy"
HeaderText="FileCreatedBy"
            SortExpression="FileCreatedBy" />
    </Columns>
</asp:GridView>
```

Go ahead, run the site again, and go to the **Gallery** page. You should see the grid again, but this time with a small "thumbnail" of the image you selected. As many of the images we could be entering into our system may be large, and we wouldn't want the grid to become too cumbersome, we have set our grid to always keep the images to 50px in width. Now, we will want to allow the users the ability to see the full size image, so let's go back to the grid and add one more column. This time we'll add a `Hyperlink` column to the grid. Go ahead and add one so that it looks similar to this:

```
asp:GridView ID="GridView1" runat="server" AllowPaging="True"
    AutoGenerateColumns="False" DataKeyNames="FileID"
    DataSourceID="ObjectDataSource1">
    <Columns>
        <asp:HyperLinkField DataNavigateUrlFields="FileID"
```

```
                    DataNavigateUrlFormatString="~/StreamFile.
        aspx?type=1&id={0}"
                    InsertVisible="false" Text="View" Target="_blank" />
            <asp:ImageField DataImageUrlField="FileID"
                    DataImageUrlFormatString="~/StreamFile.aspx?type=1&id={0}"
                    ReadOnly="true" InsertVisible="false" ControlStyle-
        Width="50" />
            <asp:BoundField DataField="FileID" HeaderText="FileID"
        InsertVisible="False"
                    ReadOnly="True" SortExpression="FileID" />
            <asp:BoundField DataField="FileName" HeaderText="FileName"
                    SortExpression="FileName" />
            <asp:BoundField DataField="FileDescription"
        HeaderText="FileDescription"
                    SortExpression="FileDescription" />
            <asp:BoundField DataField="FileType" HeaderText="FileType"
                    SortExpression="FileType" />
            <asp:BoundField DataField="FileCreated"
        HeaderText="FileCreated"
                    SortExpression="FileCreated" />
            <asp:BoundField DataField="FileCreatedBy"
        HeaderText="FileCreatedBy"
                    SortExpression="FileCreatedBy" />
        </Columns>
    </asp:GridView>
```

Run the site again, and navigate to the **Gallery** page. This time you will see the **View** column. Click on it, and you should get another window that opens with just your image displayed.

We've now got a gallery added to our CMS site, as well as a way to add new images to it. Go ahead, add a few more, and you should see that when you add more than ten images, you will automatically have page numbers on the bottom of your grid for easier use. The **Gallery** and the **Add Image** pages are not the best looking ones out there, but they are fully functional. We will leave most of the "prettying up" to you so that you can incorporate the look and feel of your choice with your site.

The one last thing I want to mention in regards to Image and Photo Galleries is that there are a great deal of plug-ins out there on the Internet, many of which are free. I suggest that before you spend too much time enhancing your gallery, you spend a little time with your favorite search engine. You may find some great ones already built for you that you could easily plug into this site and use.

Document repositories

Document repositories work basically the same way as the image galleries. With this in mind, we will be able to utilize the work we've already done and simply enhance it to fill another need. Just like with the gallery work we did earlier, let's start down at the DAL level. Let's create another method on the SiteFilesTableAdapter in the SiteFilesDS. Right-click on the **SiteFilesTableAdapter** and select **Add Query**. Select the **Use SQL statements** option and then **SELECT which returns rows**. We'll want to modify the query that is generated to limit it to only our documents. Remember that images and documents are stored in the same location, so we need to filter out all the unwanted items. Modify the query so that it looks like this:

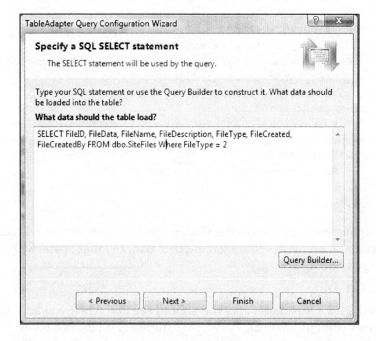

On the next page, let's name our methods **FillDocuments** and **GetDocuments**, as shown in the following screenshot:

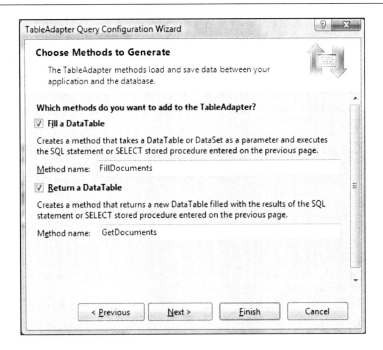

Click **Next** and then **Finish**, and we should have our new method to retrieve our documents for displaying later. Now we need to go to the BLL and give us a way to call the new method we wrote. We'll want to add a new method to the `SiteFilesBLL` class we created earlier to retrieve the documents from the DAL. Yours should look similar to this:

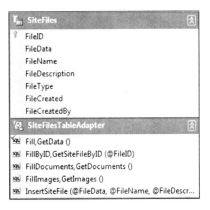

Now we're ready to create a page to add a document to the list, and then we'll want to add a page to view a list of all the documents. For adding a document, our page will be nearly identical to the **Add Image** page we created already. Add a new Web Form to the site, calling it `AddDocument.aspx`, and making sure to select the `SimpleCMS.master` as your Master Page. Open the new page you created in the HTML view and add the same series of controls you added for the **Add Image** page. It should look like this:

```
<%@ Page Language="VB" MasterPageFile="~/SimpleCMS.master"
AutoEventWireup="false"
CodeFile="AddDocument.aspx.vb" Inherits="AddDocument" title="Untitled
Page" %>

<asp:Content ID="Content1" ContentPlaceHolderID="head" Runat="Server">
</asp:Content>
<asp:Content ID="Content2" ContentPlaceHolderID="ContentPlaceHolder1"
Runat="Server">
    File Description <asp:TextBox ID="txtFileDescription"
runat="server"></asp:TextBox><br />
    File <asp:FileUpload ID="fuSiteFile" runat="server" /><br />
    <asp:Button ID="btnSubmit" runat="server" Text="Submit" />
</asp:Content>
```

Switch to the Code view for the page and add a `Page_Load` event. From there, we will need to instantiate the BLL class and add a call to the `AddSiteFile()` method just like before. However, this time notice that we change the `FileType` parameter from `1` to `2`, in order to indicate that it's a document and not an image. Yours should look similar to this:

```
Partial Class AddDocument
    Inherits System.Web.UI.Page
    Protected Sub btnSubmit_Click(ByVal sender As Object, _
        ByVal e As System.EventArgs) Handles btnSubmit.Click
        Dim bll As New SiteFilesBLL
        If bll.AddSiteFile(fuSiteFile.FileBytes, _
                fuSiteFile.FileName, _
                txtFileDescription.Text, _
                2, _
                Now, _
                Page.User.Identity.Name) Then
            ' All worked as expected
            Response.Redirect("~/Documents.aspx")
        Else
            ' The upload failed.
        End If
    End Sub
End Class
```

Notice that we also changed the successful code path to redirect to a different page, `Documents.aspx`. This will be the next page we create. Let's go ahead and add another Web Form just like before, calling it `Documents.aspx` and using the same `SimpleCMS.master` that we've been using. Rather than just use another grid to show how you could display the list of documents, we'll look at another control you could use. For this listing, we'll use the Repeater control. Go ahead and drag a Repeater control from the Toolbox onto your form inside the Content2 control. It should look like this:

Open the Tasks menu from the control and select **Datasource | New Datasource**. Choose the **Object** option and click the **OK** button. You'll then get a selection screen just like we got with the gallery. Choose the **SiteFilesBLL** and click **Next**. On the next screen, we need to define the Data Method we want to use. Select the **GetDocuments()** method from the drop-down list and click **Finish**. We've now told our Repeater to go to the database and get all the documents in it, but we haven't yet told it how to present the results to us. With the grid, it did a bunch of guesswork for us and laid out all the columns from the database in a nice grid fashion. However, the Repeater starts out empty, and we need to do the layout work ourselves. Open the HTML view for the `Documents.aspx` page and it should look similar to this:

```
<asp:Content ID="Content1" ContentPlaceHolderID="head" Runat="Server">
</asp:Content>
<asp:Content ID="Content2" ContentPlaceHolderID="ContentPlaceHolder1"
Runat="Server">
    <br />
    <asp:Repeater ID="Repeater1" runat="server" DataSourceID="ObjectD
ataSource1">
</asp:Repeater>
    <asp:ObjectDataSource ID="ObjectDataSource1" runat="server"
```

```
            DeleteMethod="DeleteSiteFile" InsertMethod="AddSiteFile"
            OldValuesParameterFormatString="original_{0}"
    SelectMethod="GetDocuments"
            TypeName="SiteFilesBLL" UpdateMethod="UpdateSiteFile">
        <DeleteParameters>
                <asp:Parameter Name="FileID" Type="Int32" />
            </DeleteParameters>
            <UpdateParameters>
                <asp:Parameter Name="FileID" Type="Int32" />
                <asp:Parameter Name="FileData" Type="Object" />
                <asp:Parameter Name="FileName" Type="String" />
                <asp:Parameter Name="FileDescription" Type="String" />
                <asp:Parameter Name="FileType" Type="Int32" />
                <asp:Parameter Name="FileCreated" Type="DateTime" />
                <asp:Parameter Name="FileCreatedBy" Type="Str ing" />
            </UpdateParameters>
            <InsertParameters>
                <asp:Parameter Name="FileData" Type="Object" />
                <asp:Parameter Name="FileName" Type="String" />
                <asp:Parameter Name="FileDescription" Type="String" />
                <asp:Parameter Name="FileType" Type="Int32" />
                <asp:Parameter Name="FileCreated" Type="DateTime" />
                <asp:Parameter Name="FileCreatedBy" Type="String" />
            </InsertParameters>
        </asp:ObjectDataSource>
    </asp:Content>
```

Let's go ahead and add some HTML formatting for us to display our documents in.
For this, we'll use a simple table tag. Let's add a header row to the table, with all the
columns we would want to display from the documents list. When you are done, it
should look similar to this:

```
<asp:Repeater ID="Repeater1" runat="server" DataSourceID="ObjectDataS
ource1">
    <HeaderTemplate>
        <table border="1" style="width:600px">
            <tr>
                <th>Document</th>
                <th>Created</th>
                <th>User</th>
            </tr>
    </HeaderTemplate>
    <FooterTemplate>
        </table>
    </FooterTemplate>
</asp:Repeater>
```

Notice that we put all this in the `HeaderTemplate` and `FooterTemplate` controls within the Repeater. The `HeaderTemplate` is only displayed once, which is what we want. Now we need to add an `ItemTemplate` to display the individual items from the list that we receive from the database. The `ItemTemplate` is repeated for every single item in the list that comes back. Go ahead and add your `ItemTemplate`, and fill in its contents so that it looks similar to this:

```
<asp:Repeater ID="Repeater1" runat="server" DataSourceID="ObjectDataS
ource1">
    <HeaderTemplate>
        <table border="1" style="width:600px">
            <tr>
                <th>Document</th>
                <th>Created</th>
                <th>User</th>
            </tr>
    </HeaderTemplate>
    <ItemTemplate>
        <tr>
            <td><%#Container.DataItem("FileName")%></td>
            <td><%#Container.DataItem("FileCreated")%></td>
            <td><%#Container.DataItem("FileCreatedBy")%></td>
        </tr>
    </ItemTemplate>
    <FooterTemplate>
        </table>
    </FooterTemplate>
</asp:Repeater>
```

We've now created the two pages we needed, but we still need to add them to our menu that we created earlier. Add them to your `web.sitemap`. Yours should look similar to this:

```
<?xml version="1.0" encoding="utf-8" ?>
<siteMap xmlns="http://schemas.microsoft.com/AspNet/SiteMap-File-1.0"
>
  <siteMapNode url="" title="">
    <siteMapNode url="~/Default.aspx" title="Home"  description="Home"
/>
    <siteMapNode url="~/AddImage.aspx" title="Add Image"
description="Add Image" />
    <siteMapNode url="~/Gallery.aspx" title="Gallery"
description="Gallery" />
    <siteMapNode url="~/AddDocument.aspx" title="Add Document"
description="Add Document" />
    <siteMapNode url="~/Documents.aspx" title="Documents"
description="Documents" />
  </siteMapNode>
</siteMap>
```

Go ahead and run the site now. Don't forget that until you actually go and add some documents to the site through the AddDocuments.aspx page, you won't get any results in your Documents.aspx list. Make sure to add a couple and then your resulting Documents.aspx should look similar to this:

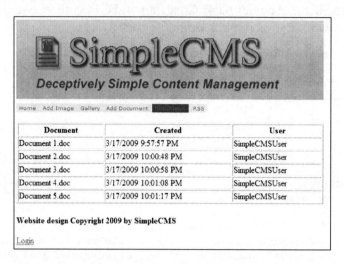

We can now see all the documents listed out, but we don't have the ability to actually open one of them. To accomplish this, let's go back to the HTML view for the repeater we put on our Documents.aspx page. Let's adjust the first column so that the name of the document is a link to actually open the document. For this we'll need to wrap it in an <A HREF> tag and call our StreamFiles.aspx page. Yes, that's right; we can reuse that same page for streaming out documents, as well as our images. Change the code for the first column so that it looks similar to this:

```
<asp:Repeater ID="Repeater1" runat="server" DataSourceID="ObjectDataS
ource1">
    <HeaderTemplate>
        <table border="1" style="width:600px">
            <tr>
                <th>Document</th>
                <th>Created</th>
                <th>User</th>
            </tr>
    </HeaderTemplate>
    <ItemTemplate>
        <tr>
            <td><a href="StreamFile.aspx?id=<%#Container.
DataItem("FileID") %>&type=2"
                target="_blank"><%#Container.DataItem("FileName")%></
a></td>
```

```
            <td><%#Container.DataItem("FileCreated")%></td>
            <td><%#Container.DataItem("FileCreatedBy")%></td>
        </tr>
    </ItemTemplate>
    <FooterTemplate>
        </table>
    </FooterTemplate>
</asp:Repeater>
```

We'll also need to go to the `StreamFile.aspx` code and add the functionality to retrieve the document from the database and present it to the user. For that we'll want to add another `IF` check to the existing method. Add the following code so that yours looks similar to this:

```
Protected Sub Page_Load(ByVal sender As Object, _
        ByVal e As System.EventArgs) Handles Me.Load
        If Not Request.QueryString("id") Is Nothing AndAlso _
            Not Request.QueryString("type") Is Nothing Then
            Dim ID As Integer = CInt(Request.QueryString("id"))
            Dim FileType As Integer = CInt(Request.
QueryString("type"))
            If FileType = 1 Then    ' These are our Images
                Dim _SiteFile As New SiteFilesDS.SiteFilesDataTable
                Dim _SiteFilesBLL As New SiteFilesBLL
                _SiteFile = _SiteFilesBLL.GetDataByFileID(ID)
                Dim b() As Byte = _SiteFile(0).FileData
                Response.BinaryWrite(b)
            ElseIf FileType = 2 Then     ' These are our Documents
                Dim _SiteFile As New SiteFilesDS.SiteFilesDataTable
                Dim _SiteFilesBLL As New SiteFilesBLL
                _SiteFile = _SiteFilesBLL.GetDataByFileID(ID)
                Dim b() As Byte = _SiteFile(0).FileData
                Response.Clear()
                Response.AddHeader("Content-Disposition", _
                    "attachment; filename=" & _SiteFile(0).FileName)
                Response.AddHeader("Content-Length", b.Length.
ToString())
                Response.ContentType = "application/octet-stream"
                Response.BinaryWrite(b)
                Response.Flush()
                Response.End()
            End If
        End If
    End Sub
```

You will notice the code handles this in a slightly different fashion from the original, but it just shows you one more alternative when storing your files within the database and streaming them out for use.

RSS feeds

These days, users want to be able to know what's going on with sites they visit, especially when it may routinely have new content such as articles, news, blog posts, and so on. For this continuous updating, many users have turned to the world of RSS. Before we go into too much depth on adding the functionality to our site, let's talk a little more about what RSS is and how it works. **RSS** typically stands for **Really Simple Syndication** and its purpose is just what its name indicates. It's a way for you to syndicate (distribute) your site in a standardized, simple format. An RSS feed is really nothing more than a properly formatted XML file, following a set of guidelines. We won't go into detail on the specifications for a proper RSS, but a quick search online with your favorite search engine should produce a plethora of information on the subject. For our purposes, we will stick with simply implementing the process and generating the XML output.

Now for the XML output for the Articles within our site, we have two basic options. We could create a physical XML file on the server and append a new entry to it each time a new article is added to the system. However, I've found that this method can be quite cumbersome and can create a great deal of headaches. Most of the problems around this can be related to the way the server has to open and close the file, the permissions on the file to do the work, possible caching issues with the file, and lastly the possibility of corruption of the file. For these reasons, I often opt for a second option, that is, generating the file "on the fly" in a very similar way to how we are retrieving images and documents within our CMS.

First thing we will need to do if we want to generate our file dynamically is to create a page to generate the output. Go ahead and add a new Web Form to your site and call it RSS.aspx. However, this time make sure to uncheck **Select master page**, just like we did for the other streaming page. Your newly-generated file should look like this:

```
<%@ Page Language="VB" AutoEventWireup="false"
    CodeFile="RSS.aspx.vb" Inherits="RSS" %>
<!DOCTYPE html PUBLIC "-//W3C//DTD XHTML 1.0 Transitional//EN"
    "http://www.w3.org/TR/xhtml1/DTD/xhtml1-transitional.dtd">
<html xmlns="http://www.w3.org/1999/xhtml">
<head runat="server">
<title>Untitled Page</title>
</head>
<body>
```

```
<form id="form1" runat="server">
<div>
</div>
</form>
</body>
</html>
```

We'll now want to trim out all the unnecessary HTML. Your page should now look like this:

```
<%@ Page Language="VB" AutoEventWireup="false"
    CodeFile="RSS.aspx.vb" Inherits="RSS" %>
<%@ OutputCache Duration="300" VaryByParam="none" %>
<!DOCTYPE html PUBLIC "-//W3C//DTD XHTML 1.0 Transitional//EN"
    "http://www.w3.org/TR/xhtml1/DTD/xhtml1-transitional.dtd">
<html xmlns="http://www.w3.org/1999/xhtml">
<head id="Head1" runat="server"><title></title></head>
<body></body>
</html>
```

Now, we'll need to open the code view of our newly-created page. Go ahead and add a `Page_Load()` event. Your code should now look similar to this:

```
Partial Class Rss
        Inherits System.Web.UI.Page

        Protected Sub Page_Load(ByVal sender As Object, _
            ByVal e as System.EventArgs) Handles Me.Load

        End Sub
End Class
```

From here the code can look intimidating, but all we are really doing is building our XML file one tag at a time. I'll try to break it down as we go. In order for us to be able to use XML and its built-in methods provided by the .NET Framework, we will have to first add an `Imports` statement to the top, as follows:

```
Imports System.Xml

Partial Class RSS
    Inherits System.Web.UI.Page
```

Next, we'll start off our code within the `Page_Load` method with some house cleaning. We'll want to add the `Response.Clear` line to clear any pre-existing output that the system may have already generated. Next, we'll add a new Response declaration to tell the user's browser what the file type is. Your code should look similar to this:

```
Protected Sub Page_Load(ByVal sender As Object, ByVal e As System.
EventArgs) Handles Me.Load

        Response.Clear()
        Response.ContentType = "text/xml"
```

Now, we'll need to instantiate the new XML output that we want to generate. To do this, we'll create our `XmlTextWriter` object, and will also create the starting tags, like this:

```
Dim objX As New XmlTextWriter(Response.OutputStream, Encoding.UTF8)
        objX.WriteStartDocument()
```

The next three lines of code we need are simply XML tags (better known as Elements) and some corresponding attributes necessary for RSS readers to properly parse the data. Your next three lines should look like this:

```
objX.WriteStartElement("rss")
objX.WriteAttributeString("version", "2.0")
objX.WriteStartElement("channel")
```

The next five lines in the XML output are "top level" items. This means they are in the file once and help to define what your RSS feed is all about. This is information like your site name, site/feed URL, site description, and copyright information. The code for this will look like this:

```
objX.WriteElementString("title", "Simple CMS")
        objX.WriteElementString("link", "http://www.YourSiteName.com/
rss.aspx")
        objX.WriteElementString("description", "Articles from
SimpleCMS.")
        objX.WriteElementString("copyright", "(c) 2009, yoursite.com.
All rights reserved.")
        objX.WriteElementString("ttl", "5")
```

That takes care of all the setup for the parent elements of the XML file. Now what we need to do is actually get all the latest Articles from our system into the feed. For this we will first need to instantiate the BLL layer for our Articles and call the method to retrieve the latest Articles. That would be a call like the following:

```
Dim _articlesBLL As New ArticlesBLL
For Each _article As ArticlesDataSet.ArticlesRow In _articlesBLL.
GetAllCurrentPublishedArticles
Next
```

Now that we have the collection of Articles we want to output in our feed, we just need to create the appropriate elements for each Article. The next eight lines of code create the element for the Article and fill in the child Elements with the values from the Article that was retrieved from the database. These items are the title, description (contents), link to the Article, date published/created, author, and the categorization. The code to populate this will look like this:

```
Dim _articlesBLL As New ArticlesBLL
        For Each _article As ArticlesDataSet.ArticlesRow In _
articlesBLL.GetAllCurrentPublishedArticles
            objX.WriteStartElement("item")
            objX.WriteElementString("title", _article.ArticleTitle)
            objX.WriteElementString("description", _article.
ArticleBody)
            objX.WriteElementString("link", "http://www.yoursite.com/
articles.aspx?id=" & _article.ArticleID.ToString)
            objX.WriteElementString("pubDate", CDate(_article.
ArticleCreatedDate).ToString("R"))
            objX.WriteElementString("author", _article.
ArticleCreatedBy)
            objX.WriteElementString("category", "Articles")
            objX.WriteEndElement()
        Next
```

All we have left to do now is close out all the XML Elements we've created. Go ahead and add these five lines to close the elements and close out the output for the user's browser. The code for that will look like this:

```
objX.WriteEndElement()
        objX.WriteEndElement()
        objX.WriteEndDocument()
        objX.Flush()
        objX.Close()
        Response.End()
```

That's it! Our CMS site's Articles are now available to the world through their favorite RSS reader. The only thing now is to provide a link on our menu so that the users can find our RSS Feed. Open the `web.sitemap` we created for our site and add the RSS link to it like this:

```
<?xml version="1.0" encoding="utf-8" ?>
<siteMap xmlns="http://schemas.microsoft.com/AspNet/SiteMap-File-1.0"
>
  <siteMapNode url="" title="">
    <siteMapNode url="~/Default.aspx" title="Home"  description="Home"
/>
    <siteMapNode url="~/AddImage.aspx" title="Add Image"
description="Add Image" />
    <siteMapNode url="~/Gallery.aspx" title="Gallery"
description="Gallery" />
    <siteMapNode url="~/AddDocument.aspx" title="Add Document"
description="Add Document" />
    <siteMapNode url="~/Documents.aspx" title="Documents"
description="Documents" />
    <siteMapNode url="~/RSS.aspx" title="RSS" description="RSS" />
  </siteMapNode>
</siteMap>
```

Go ahead and run the site now and click the RSS menu item. Depending on your browser, you may get an output that looks similar to this (IE7 version).

Summary

In this chapter, we covered a great deal about dynamically providing content to your users. We've explored streaming files and images from the database, as well as generating RSS feeds "on the fly". However, this is just a small sample of the different ways this can all be done. I highly recommend you spend some time with other research materials, and execute some different options within the code, in order to see what other things you can do. Once you master the concepts of creating the content dynamically, nearly anything is possible.

8

Administrator Control Panel

If the content is the "heart" of a good CMS, then the Administrator Control Panel is surely the "brain". It's the piece that lets all the other pieces do their jobs. Maintaining users, adjusting permissions, approving Articles, and viewing site settings and stats are all key aspects of the Control Panel. These are the pieces we will set up in this chapter, along with giving you a basis to extend these for your own site.

This chapter will cover the following:

- Creating the basic site settings table
- Creating the BLL and DAL classes
- User account management
- Article administration
- Basic site reporting
- Search Engine Optimization

Basic site settings

Most CMS sites have a number of settings that you can configure from within the Control Panel. These are typically the Site Name (as it appears on the header), the Site Image (again from the header), and the Footer text. In addition to these three, you will often also see settings to maintain the Theme, as well as a section for "additional header information", which you can use for any extra scripts you want to place in each page and also for things such as analytics scripts. For these items, we will need a way to maintain them and store these settings. Just as with our site content, we have a number of options for storing them, but for our CMS, we'll stick with using the database that we've already created. You should already be familiar with creating a new database table, so I won't go into great detail here. However, for our purpose, you will want to create the table, calling it `SiteSettings`, with the following columns/data types defined:

	Column Name	Data Type	Allow Nulls
🔑	SiteID	int	☐
	SiteName	varchar(250)	☐
	SiteImage	varchar(250)	☑
	SiteFooter	varchar(250)	☐
	SiteAdditionalHeaderInfo	text	☐
	SiteTheme	varchar(250)	☑

We now have the table created, but we need to go ahead and pre-load this table so that it's easier for us to work with later. For this you will do just like you did earlier in the book when you pre-loaded the Articles, by running the following simple Insert script:

```
Insert Into SiteSettings
(SiteID,SiteName,SiteImage,SiteFooter,SiteAdditionalHeaderInfo,SiteTh
eme)
values
(1,'SimpleCMS',Null,'Website design Copyright 2009 by
SimpleCMS','',Null)
```

Now that we have the new table and sample data created, we need a way to read and write the data to it. We've already created a number of DAL datasets, but for our usage here, we'll explore another way of doing the DAL, as a class, so that you can see another option available to you. Right-click on the **DAL** folder in your **Solutions Explorer** and choose **Add New Item**. From the options given, choose **Class** and give it a name of **SiteSettingsDAL.vb**. This will generate a new class that should look like this:

```
Imports Microsoft.VisualBasic
Public Class SiteSettingsDAL
End Class
```

While this class will eventually work very similar to the datasets you created earlier, we would expect it to carry out only a couple of basic functions—reading and updating. So, for these two functions, let's go ahead and create them. The first is the `ReadSiteSettings()` function, which will look similar to the following:

```
Public Shared Function ReadSiteSettings() As Data.DataSet
    Dim conn As New Data.SqlClient.SqlConnection( _
    ConfigurationManager.ConnectionStrings( _
    "SimpleCMSConnectionString").ConnectionString)
    Dim cmd As New Data.SqlClient.SqlCommand("Select * from
SiteSettings", conn)
    Dim da As New Data.SqlClient.SqlDataAdapter(cmd)
    Dim ds As New Data.DataSet()
    da.Fill(ds)
    Return ds
End Function
```

The other function we need is the `SetSiteSettings()` which, as the name implies, is our way of updating these settings for our system. That new function will look similar to this:

```
Public Shared Function SetSiteSettings( _
        ByVal SiteName As String, _
        ByVal SiteImage As String, _
        ByVal SiteFooter As String, _
        ByVal SiteAdditionalHeaderInfo As String, _
        ByVal SiteTheme As String) As Boolean
        Dim conn As New Data.SqlClient.SqlConnection( _
            ConfigurationManager.ConnectionStrings( _
            "SimpleCMSConnectionString").ConnectionString)
        conn.Open()
        Dim cmd As New Data.SqlClient.SqlCommand( _
            "Update SiteSettings set " & _
            "SiteName = @SiteName, " & _
            "SiteImage = @SiteImage, " & _
            "SiteFooter = @SiteFooter, " & _
            "SiteAdditionalHeaderInfo = @SiteAdditionalHeaderInfo, "
                                    & _
            "SiteTheme = @SiteTheme " & _
            "Where SiteID = 1 " _
            , conn)
```

```
        cmd.Parameters.Add("@SiteName", Data.SqlDbType.VarChar).Value
= SiteName
        If SiteImage = Nothing Then
            cmd.Parameters.Add("@SiteImage", Data.SqlDbType.VarChar).
Value = DBNull.Value
        Else
            cmd.Parameters.Add("@SiteImage", Data.SqlDbType.VarChar).
Value = SiteImage
        End If
        cmd.Parameters.Add("@SiteFooter", Data.SqlDbType.VarChar).
Value = SiteFooter
        cmd.Parameters.Add("@SiteAdditionalHeaderInfo", _
                Data.SqlDbType.Text).Value = SiteAdditionalHeaderInfo
        If SiteImage Is Nothing OrElse SiteImage.Length <= 0 Then
            cmd.Parameters.Add("@SiteTheme", Data.SqlDbType.VarChar).
Value = DBNull.Value
        Else
            cmd.Parameters.Add("@SiteTheme", Data.SqlDbType.VarChar).
Value = SiteTheme
        End If
        Return cmd.ExecuteNonQuery() = 1
    End Function
End Class
```

While this function may look a bit complicated, it really isn't. The basic premise of it is to simply take the incoming information—the site settings—and put them into an SQL statement for updating the database. We've added some additional pieces such as the parameters, for a couple of purposes. Firstly, they are there to protect you and prevent what's called an SQL injection, which you can find easily with a search from your favorite search engine. The second is to show you how you can easily take the code and elaborate on it, making it more robust, more secure, and more stable.

The next step in our process is to create a BLL class for us to access within our site when we want to actually do the work. Right-click on your **BLL** folder and select the **Add New Item** option, choosing the Class object and giving it the name **SiteSettingsBLL**. It should look similar to this:

```
Imports Microsoft.VisualBasic
Public Class SiteSettingsBLL
End Class
```

Just like with the DAL class we just created, we will need to create our read and write functions. Now, we could just create these functions to call directly into the DAL and pass the returning dataset back, but we will take a more object-oriented approach. First, we will need to create our `SiteSettings` object. Within the same `SiteSettingsBLL.vb` file, we will add the following code, but we will place it AFTER the closing "End Class" part of the existing code.

```
Public Class SiteSettings
    Private _SiteName As String
    Private _SiteImage As String
    Private _SiteFooter As String
    Private _SiteAdditionalHeaderInfo As String
    Private _SiteTheme As String
    Public Property SiteName() As String
        Get
            Return _SiteName
        End Get
        Set(ByVal value As String)
            _SiteName = value
        End Set
    End Property
    Public Property SiteImage() As String
        Get
            Return _SiteImage
        End Get
        Set(ByVal value As String)
            _SiteImage = value
        End Set
    End Property
    Public Property SiteFooter() As String
        Get
            Return _SiteFooter
        End Get
        Set(ByVal value As String)
            _SiteFooter = value
        End Set
    End Property
    Public Property SiteAdditionalHeaderInfo() As String
        Get
            Return _SiteAdditionalHeaderInfo
        End Get
        Set(ByVal value As String)
            _SiteAdditionalHeaderInfo = value
        End Set
```

```
            End Property
        Public Property SiteTheme() As String
            Get
                    Return _SiteTheme
            End Get
            Set(ByVal value As String)
                _SiteTheme = value
            End Set
        End Property
    End Class
```

This defines our `SiteSettings` object that we will use whenever we want to pass our settings around. Now that we have this object, we can look at the `SiteSettingsBLL` class we have. We already know we will need two functions — one for reading and the other for writing the settings. The function to read the settings will look similar to this:

```
Public Shared Function ReadSiteSettings() As SiteSettings
    Dim _SiteSettings As New SiteSettings
    Dim _dr As Data.DataRow = _
        SiteSettingsDAL.ReadSiteSettings.Tables(0).Rows(0)
    _SiteSettings.SiteAdditionalHeaderInfo = _
        _dr("SiteAdditionalHeaderInfo")
    _SiteSettings.SiteFooter = _dr("SiteFooter")
    If _dr("SiteImage") Is DBNull.Value Then
        _SiteSettings.SiteImage = "~/Images/SimpleCMSLogo.jpg"
    Else
        _SiteSettings.SiteImage = _dr("SiteImage")
    End If
    _SiteSettings.SiteName = _dr("SiteName")
    If _dr("SiteTheme") Is DBNull.Value Then
        _SiteSettings.SiteTheme = "SimpleCMSTheme"
    Else
        _SiteSettings.SiteTheme = _dr("SiteTheme")
    End If
    Return _SiteSettings
End Function
```

Note that we added some additional checks in place. Our settings allow us to have no image, as well as no theme selected, for which we use some predefined default values. The other function we need to create is the `SetSiteSettings()` function. For this the code would look similar to this:

```
Public Shared Function SetSiteSettings( _
    ByVal _SiteSettings As SiteSettings) As Boolean
    Return SiteSettingsDAL.SetSiteSettings( _
        _SiteSettings.SiteName, _
        _SiteSettings.SiteImage, _
        _SiteSettings.SiteFooter, _
```

```
        _SiteSettings.SiteAdditionalHeaderInfo, _
        _SiteSettings.SiteTheme)
    End Function
```

It's basically a reverse of the `ReadSiteSettings()` method — taking the `SiteSettings` object and breaking it apart to call the DAL class.

Now that we have our BLL, our DAL, and our database all set up, what do we do with this all? First off we need to consume the data. You will see that nearly all of these pieces we defined are part of our Master Page. Let's open up our `SimpleCMS.master` and look at the HTML in it. At the top of it we have:

```
<img src="Images/SimpleCMSLogo.jpg" />
```

Let's change this so that it's no longer a simple HTML image tag, but instead is an ASP.NET Image control. That will look like this:

```
<asp:Image ID="imgSiteImage" runat="server" />
```

While we're at it, let's go ahead and replace the hard-coded footer text so that it's using an ASP.NET Label control, like this:

```
<asp:Label ID="lblSiteFooter" runat="server" />
```

We also need to add a new control near the existing `head` ContentPlaceHolder. That will look like this:

```
<asp:ContentPlaceHolder id="head" runat="server">
</asp:ContentPlaceHolder>
<asp:Label ID="lblAdditionalInfo" runat="server" />
```

Now we need to open the Code view of the page. Look at the `Page_Load()` method and let's add the following code to it:

```
If Not IsPostBack() Then
    Dim _SiteSettings As New SiteSettings
    _SiteSettings = SiteSettingsBLL.ReadSiteSettings
    Page.Title = _SiteSettings.SiteName
    imgSiteImage.ImageUrl = _SiteSettings.SiteImage
    lblSiteFooter.Text = _SiteSettings.SiteFooter
    lblAdditionalInfo.Text = _
        _SiteSettings.SiteAdditionalHeaderInfo
End If
```

We've now made our SimpleCMS pull in our SiteSettings and use them for its page. In addition, we've set up our site so that we can change the Theme, which we built earlier in the application. To make the site use these new settings, we need to add the following to the code for each of our pages:

```
Protected Sub Page_PreInit(ByVal sender As Object, _
ByVal e As System.EventArgs) Handles Me.PreInit
    Page.Theme = SiteSettingsBLL.ReadSiteSettings.SiteTheme
End Sub
```

Okay, we have now set our site to use all these great new settings we've established, but we still have no way to alter the values of these settings, short of directly modifying them in our database. We have the `SetSiteSettings()` method created but we need a way of filling this. This comes back to the Administrator Control Panel, which is nothing more than a special page within our site. Go ahead and add a new page to your site, calling it `ControlPanel.aspx`, but make sure that you do not select a Master Page to use. You should have a standard ASP.NET Web Form. The first thing we need to do is to make sure that we limit the access to this new page to only those people we've set in the Administrator role. To do this, we will create the `Page_Load()` event and add the following code:

```
Protected Sub Page_Load(ByVal sender As Object, _
ByVal e As System.EventArgs) Handles Me.Load
  If Not Page.User.Identity.IsAuthenticated Then
    Response.Redirect("Login.aspx")
  Else
    If Not Page.User.IsInRole("Administrator") Then
      Response.Redirect("Default.aspx")
    End If
  End If
End Sub
```

We'll also need to add some input controls on the page to allow us to input our settings. We will need one for each of the SiteSettings we want to maintain. The HTML for the page will look similar to this:

```
<table>
  <tr><th>Site Settings</th></tr>
  <tr>
    <td>
      <table>
      <tr>
        <td valign="top">Name:</td>
        <td>
          <asp:TextBox ID="txtSiteName" runat="server" />
```

```
          </td>
        </tr>
        <tr>
          <td valign="top">Image:</td>
          <td>
            <asp:TextBox ID="txtSiteImage" runat="server" />
          </td>
        </tr>
        <tr>
          <td valign="top">Theme:</td>
          <td>
            <asp:TextBox ID="txtSiteTheme" runat="server" />
          </td>
        </tr>
        <tr>
          <td valign="top">Footer:</td>
          <td>
            <asp:TextBox ID="txtSiteFooter"
              TextMode="MultiLine" runat="server" />
          </td>
        </tr>
        <tr>
          <td valign="top">Add'l Header Info:</td>
          <td>
            <asp:TextBox ID="txtAdditionalInfo"
              TextMode="MultiLine" runat="server" />
          </td>
        </tr>
        <tr>
          <td colspan="2">
            <asp:Button ID="btnSave" runat="server"
              Text="Save" />
          </td>
        </tr>
        </table>
      </td>
    </tr>
  </table>
```

Now that we have the inputs defined, we need to actually do something with them. For this you will want to open up the Code view of the page and add an event for the `btnSave.Click()`. That should look like this:

```
Protected Sub btnSave_Click(ByVal sender As Object, _
    ByVal e As System.EventArgs) Handles btnSave.Click
End Sub
```

Within this new event that we've created, we need to read in the values. You will need to add the following code to your event:

```
Protected Sub btnSave_Click(ByVal sender As Object, _
    ByVal e As System.EventArgs) Handles btnSave.Click
    Dim _siteSettings As New SiteSettings
    _siteSettings.SiteName = txtSiteName.Text
    _siteSettings.SiteImage = txtSiteImage.Text
    _siteSettings.SiteTheme = txtSiteTheme.Text
    _siteSettings.SiteFooter = txtSiteFooter.Text
    _siteSettings.SiteAdditionalHeaderInfo = _
        txtAdditionalInfo.Text
    If SiteSettingsBLL.SetSiteSettings(_siteSettings) = _
        True Then
        ' All Saved OK.
    Else
        ' There was an error saving.
    End If
End Sub
```

The page would now accept your inputs and save them to the database, but we really don't want to have to re-enter all the values each time. So, let's add the following code to the `Page_Load()` event so that the existing values are put into the controls to get us started:

```
If Not IsPostBack Then
  Dim _siteSettings As New SiteSettings
  _siteSettings = SiteSettingsBLL.ReadSiteSettings
  txtSiteName.Text = _siteSettings.SiteName
  txtSiteImage.Text = _siteSettings.SiteImage
  txtSiteTheme.Text = _siteSettings.SiteTheme
  txtSiteFooter.Text = _siteSettings.SiteFooter
  txtAdditionalInfo.Text = _
      _siteSettings.SiteAdditionalHeaderInfo
End If
```

You should now be able to alter these settings at will. You do need to keep in mind a couple of items though, and these are areas that you may wish to extend in your site. The first is that the image you type in must exist in the path you gave it. This means that you need to get it uploaded to your site. You could use the techniques you learned in the earlier chapters on uploading images and apply them here. Another thing to remember is that the Theme you type in must exist within the `App_Themes` folder. You need to have a fully developed theme in place. There are additional code samples on the Internet that show how to read the contents of a folder. With this you could easily iterate through the `App_Themes` folder to get a list of Themes in your site, and then display this list in a DropDownList control, instead of using the TextBox control, to display the Theme list in the control panel.

User accounts

While we have already created a method for users to come to the site and sign up, there are still a few functions that an Administrator may want to accomplish—being able to disable users, approve users, and to set user groups/roles, just to name a few. To be able to do these, we will need to be able to list out the users, view the details on each user and, when necessary, be able to modify them. ASP.NET has a number of functions built in for us to make these things easier, so we'll take what they've done for us and build on top of it.

The first thing we'll need to do is adjust the Control Panel page to include a place for us to list out the users in the system. For our site, we'll keep it simple, as a series of hyperlinks in a Repeater. However, for your usage, you may want to look at other ways of presenting the list. Back to our site though, go ahead and add the following HTML to your Control Panel page, just before the closing `</table>` tag.

```
<tr style="background-color:Silver;">
  <th>User Administration:</th>
</tr>
<tr>
  <td>
    <asp:Repeater ID="rptrUsers" runat="server">
      <HeaderTemplate>
        <table cellpadding="4"><tr>
      </HeaderTemplate>
      <ItemTemplate>
        <td>
          <asp:HyperLink ID="hyUserName" runat="server" />
        </td>
        <asp:Label ID="lblNewLine" runat="server" />
```

```
        </ItemTemplate>
        <FooterTemplate>
          </tr></table>
        </FooterTemplate>
      </asp:Repeater>
    </td>
  </tr>
```

Now that we have a place to display the user list, we need to go into the Code view for the page and actually retrieve the list. Open the `ControlPanel.aspx.vb` and add the following two lines, right after the code we use to fill the SiteSettings in the `Page_Load()`:

```
rptrUsers.DataSource = Membership.GetAllUsers()
rptrUsers.DataBind()
```

We've now retrieved the list of users and bound it to our repeater, but we haven't told the repeater what to do with this list yet. For this we will need to add the following code to the `ControlPanel.aspx.vb` file.

```
Protected Sub rptrUsers_ItemDataBound( _
ByVal sender As Object, _
ByVal e As System.Web.UI.WebControls.RepeaterItemEventArgs) _
Handles rptrUsers.ItemDataBound
  If e.Item.ItemType = ListItemType.Item _
  OrElse e.Item.ItemType = ListItemType.AlternatingItem Then
    Dim _item As MembershipUser = _
      CType(e.Item.DataItem, MembershipUser)
    Dim hyUserName As HyperLink = _
      CType(e.Item.FindControl("hyUserName"), HyperLink)
    hyUserName.Text = _item.UserName
    hyUserName.NavigateUrl = _
      "Profile.aspx?user=" & _item.UserName

    If (e.Item.ItemIndex + 1) Mod 3 = 0 Then
      Dim lblNewLine As Label = _
        CType(e.Item.FindControl("lblNewLine"), Label)
      lblNewLine.Text = "</tr><tr>"
    End If
  End If
End Sub
```

The code above will take each user from the list that ASP.NET has generated for us, and display their username as a hyperlink. It will also, thanks to a little fancy math, add a `</tr><tr>` after every third item in the list so that you get a nice, well-formed grid. You may have also realized that the hyperlinks point to a page called `Profile.aspx`, which doesn't yet exist. This will be our next step in the process. Go ahead and add a new Web Form to the site, calling it `Profile.aspx` and using the `SimpleCMS.master` as its Master Page. We'll want to add some controls to the page to allow us to display the details of the user we've selected. Therefore, add the following HTML and WebControls to the page, and within the ContentPlaceHolder1, your code should look similar to this:

```
<table>
  <tr style="background-color:Silver;">
    <th colspan="2">User Profile:</th>
  </tr>
  <tr>
    <th align="right">Name:</th>
    <td><asp:Label ID="lblName" runat="server" /></td>
  </tr>
  <tr>
    <th align="right">LastLoginDate:</th>
    <td>
      <asp:Label ID="lblLastLoginDate" runat="server" />
    </td>
  </tr>
  <tr>
    <th align="right">IsApproved:</th>
    <td>
      <asp:CheckBox ID="chkIsApproved" runat="server" />
    </td>
  </tr>
  <tr>
    <th align="right">Email:</th>
    <td><asp:Label ID="lblEmail" runat="server" /></td>
  </tr>
  <tr>
    <th align="right">CreationDate:</th>
    <td><asp:Label ID="lblCreationDate" runat="server" /></td>
  </tr>
  <tr>
    <th align="right" valign="top">Roles:</th>
    <td>
      <asp:CheckBoxList ID="chkRoles" runat="server" />
    </td>
```

```
      </tr>
      <tr>
        <td colspan="2" align="right">
          <asp:Button ID="btnSave" runat="server" Text="Save" />
        </td>
      </tr>
    </table>
```

What we have is really not much more than a series of labels used to display the details for the user, but if you look close, there is also a Checkbox and a CheckboxList. The first is used to indicate if the user is "Approved" or not. This is how you can enable/disable users within your site. Also, the CheckboxList, as you'll see shortly, will contain a list of all the roles we've established within our site. And with a couple of lines of code, it will show you what roles the user is assuming. Again these Checkboxes will allow us to change the roles that a user is set up in.

Now that we've added the HTML and WebControls to the page, we need to go into the code file, Profile.aspx.vb, for the page. The first thing we need to do is add a Page_Load() event and put the following code into it:

```vb
Protected Sub Page_Load(ByVal sender As Object, _
ByVal e As System.EventArgs) Handles Me.Load
  If Not Request.QueryString("user") Is Nothing Then
    If Not IsPostBack Then
      Dim _user As MembershipUser = _
        Membership.GetUser(Request.QueryString("user"))
      lblName.Text = _user.UserName
      lblLastLoginDate.Text = _user.LastLoginDate
      chkIsApproved.Checked = _user.IsApproved
      lblEmail.Text = _user.Email
      lblCreationDate.Text = _
        _user.CreationDate.ToShortDateString()

      chkRoles.DataSource = Roles.GetAllRoles
      chkRoles.DataBind()

      For Each chk As ListItem In chkRoles.Items
        If Roles.IsUserInRole(_user.UserName, chk.Value) Then
          chk.Selected = True
        Else
          chk.Selected = False
        End If
      Next

      If Page.User.IsInRole("Administrator") Then
        chkRoles.Enabled = True
        chkIsApproved.Enabled = True
```

```
            btnSave.Visible = True
        Else
            chkRoles.Enabled = False
            chkIsApproved.Enabled = False
            btnSave.Visible = False
        End If
    End If
  End If
End Sub
```

This code will do a number of things. The first thing it does is check that a username was passed through the `QueryString()` to the page. The next thing it does is fill in all the details for the user into the WebControls we added to our page. You will see that it also calls another built-in property in ASP.NET to get a list of all the roles in our site. We take that list and bind it to the CheckboxList we added. Then we iterate through this list of Checkboxes and check if the user is in that role. If this is the case, we make sure that the Checkbox is selected. The last piece of this code is for us to check the user who is viewing the data and, if he/she is an Administrator, to enable the Checkbox, CheckboxList, and Button. If the user isn't an Administrator, we disable/hide these items.

Our next step is to put the code in place so that when an Administrator comes in and changes a user's `IsApproved` status or their roles, we can save the changes. For this we added a Button to our page, with the ID of `btnSave`. Add the following code to your page:

```
Protected Sub btnSave_Click(ByVal sender As Object, _
ByVal e As System.EventArgs) Handles btnSave.Click
  Dim _user As MembershipUser = _
    Membership.GetUser(Request.QueryString("user"))
  _user.IsApproved = chkIsApproved.Checked
  Membership.UpdateUser(_user)

  For Each chk As ListItem In chkRoles.Items
   If chk.Selected Then
    If Not Roles.IsUserInRole(_user.UserName, chk.Value) Then
     Roles.AddUserToRole(_user.UserName, chk.Value)
    End If
   Else
    If Roles.IsUserInRole(_user.UserName, chk.Value) Then
     Roles.RemoveUserFromRole(_user.UserName, chk.Value)
    End If
   End If
  Next
End Sub
```

That's user Administrator in its simplest form. You will probably want to extend the functionality to fit your needs, but this should be sufficient to get you started. You'll find that if you start to look through all the properties of the Membership, MembershipUser, and Roles functionality, there is a lot you can do, all pre-built for you by Microsoft to make your work easier. Look into the Profiles system within the ASP.NET framework, and with this, you could add additional pieces of information beyond the standard membership items. You could add pieces such as First/Last Name, Address, Phone, and even look at things such as User Avatars. These are all pieces that can give your site additional flare and make it feel more comfortable to your users, thereby ensuring their return visits, which is often the goal of a web site.

The last bit of User/Role Administrator I want to touch on in this section is the ability to add new roles to the system, without having to go through the ASP.NET Site Configuration tools you used before. While we don't have any functionality in place to use any new roles, you may find that your site will. For this purpose, let's go back to the `ControlPanel.aspx` page in its HTML view and add the following right before the `</table>` tag:

```
<tr style="background-color:Silver;">
  <th>Role Administration:</th>
</tr>
<tr>
  <td>
    <asp:TextBox ID="txtNewRole" runat="server" />
    <asp:Button id="btnSaveRole" runat="server" Text="Add" />
    <br />
    <asp:Label ID="lblRoles" runat="server"></asp:Label>
  </td>
</tr>
```

This is a simple piece, so we don't need to create an all new page for it. We'll just tuck it into our existing Control Panel. It's a simple TextBox for us to enter the name of a new role we want to create, a Button for us to call the system and tell it about the new role, and a Label that we'll use to show all of the roles we currently have in the system. First, let's populate the Label with the existing roles we've defined. In our `Page_Load()`, right before the first line of code that says `If Not IsPostback()`, we need to add the following:

```
lblRoles.Text = "<ul>"
For Each _role As String In Roles.GetAllRoles
  lblRoles.Text += "<li>" & _role & "</li>"
Next
lblRoles.Text += "</ul>"
```

This will take our Label and fill it with all the roles as mentioned with a nice bullet list, using the `<ul>` and `<li>` tags. Now, we'll need to open the `ControlPanel.aspx.vb` file and add the following event to it:

```
Protected Sub btnSaveRole_Click( _
ByVal sender As Object, _
ByVal e As System.EventArgs) Handles btnSaveRole.Click
   If txtNewRole.Text.Trim.Length > 0 Then
     If Not Roles.RoleExists(txtNewRole.Text) Then
       Roles.CreateRole(txtNewRole.Text)
     End If
   End If
End Sub
```

This piece of code will first check to see that they entered a new role's name, then if that role already exists, and lastly it will call the system and tell it to save this new Role. We now have a fully functional user and role administration system in place, and even an added benefit of the Profile page. The Profile can really make your users feel like they are part of the site, but more important is that these Profiles, when associated in roles, are the key to the functionality of the site. With proper assignments into roles and the implementation of the way to check the current user's assignment, you can enable and disable portions of the site. This can be exceptionally handy as your site grows, and you may need to allow responsibility to others to help with the maintenance. By granting special permissions through roles, you could split apart these maintenance features. Perhaps you want one group to be able to upload documents, another to upload images, and perhaps you would like two more groups to be approvers of these content sections. This is all easily done by using the pieces covered here.

Articles

Earlier in the book, we gave you the ability to create new Articles for the site. As part of the Articles, we set up the ability to allow them to be approved, through the use of the Published property. Now we need to give certain users the ability to go in and approve these Articles. As we've worked with UserControls for much of the Articles section of this book, we'll continue with that idea here. Let's go ahead and add a new UserControl to the `Controls` folder, calling it `ApproveArticles.ascx`. Now we need to add some HTML and WebControls to the new UserControl we created so that we can display the data. Add the following to the HTML of the `ApproveArticles.ascx`:

```
<asp:GridView Id="grdUnapprovedArticles"
    runat="server" DataKeyNames="ArticleID"
    AutoGenerateColumns="false">
```

```
    <Columns>
      <asp:BoundField DataField="ArticleTitle"
         HeaderText="Title" />
      <asp:BoundField DataField="ArticleSummary"
         HeaderText="Summary" HtmlEncode="false" />
      <asp:ButtonField ButtonType="Button"
         Text="Delete" CommandName="Delete" />
      <asp:ButtonField ButtonType="Button"
         Text="Approve" CommandName="Approve" />
    </Columns>
  </asp:GridView>
```

Now that we have the HTML and WebControl using the ASP.NET GridView, let's go the the `ApproveArticles.aspx.vb` code view and add the following so that you can see how this will work:

```
Protected Sub Page_Load(ByVal sender As Object, _
ByVal e As System.EventArgs) Handles Me.Load
  Dim _ArticlesBLL As New ArticlesBLL()
  grdUnapprovedArticles.DataSource = _
  _ArticlesBLL.GetAllUnpublishedArticles
  grdUnapprovedArticles.DataBind()
End Sub
```

In this code, we call out to the `ArticlesBLL`. However, the function we called, `GetAllUnpublishedArticles()`, doesn't exist yet. This is what we'll need to do now, but we need to start down at the DAL, in the ArticlesDataSet. Open the ArticlesDataSet and let's add a new query to the ArticlesTableAdapter. We'll use the SELECT statement option and then SELECT **which returns rows**. For the SQL statement that's generated, you will want to alter it so that it looks like this:

```
SELECT ArticleID, ArticleTitle, ArticleBody, ArticleSummary,
ArticleCreatedBy, ArticleCreatedDate, ArticlePublished,
ArticleExpirationDate
FROM Articles where ArticlePublished = 0
```

What this will do is limit the results to only those Articles from the database that have a 0 (or False) for the `ArticlePublished` value. We still need to give names to the new methods we created. For this we'll use `FillAllUnpublishedArticles` and `GetAllUnpublishedArticles`. Now, let's got to our `ArticlesBLL` and add the following function to the existing code:

```
' Get All Unpublished Articles Function
<System.ComponentModel.DataObjectMethodAttribute( _
System.ComponentModel.DataObjectMethodType.Select, True)> _
```

```
Public Function GetAllUnpublishedArticles() As _ ArticlesDataSet.
ArticlesDataTable
    Return Adapter.GetAllUnpublishedArticles()
End Function
```

With this we should now have a UserControl that will display all of the unpublished Articles in the system. While this control will now display our unpublished Articles, we don't have a way to interact with them yet. We'll need to add a couple of events to the code for this—one for deleting the articles and the other for approving them. For the delete operation, we can use the following piece of code:

```
Protected Sub grdUnapprovedArticles_RowDeleting( _
ByVal sender As Object, ByVal e As _
System.Web.UI.WebControls.GridViewDeleteEventArgs) _
Handles grdUnapprovedArticles.RowDeleting
  Dim _id As Integer = _
    CInt(grdUnapprovedArticles.DataKeys(e.RowIndex).Value)
  Dim _ArticlesBLL As New ArticlesBLL()
  _ArticlesBLL.DeleteArticle(_id)
  grdUnapprovedArticles.DataSource = _
  _ArticlesBLL.GetAllUnpublishedArticles
  grdUnapprovedArticles.DataBind()
End Sub
```

And for our approve operation, we can use the following code snippet:

```
Protected Sub grdUnapprovedArticles_RowCommand( _
ByVal sender As Object, ByVal e As _
System.Web.UI.WebControls.GridViewCommandEventArgs) _
Handles grdUnapprovedArticles.RowCommand
  If e.CommandName = "Approve" Then
    Dim _id As Integer = _
      CInt(grdUnapprovedArticles.DataKeys( _
      e.CommandArgument).Value)
    Dim _ArticlesBLL As New ArticlesBLL()
    Dim _article As ArticlesDataSet.ArticlesRow = _
      _ArticlesBLL.GetDataByArticleID(_id).Rows(0)
    _article.ArticlePublished = 1
    _ArticlesBLL.UpdateArticle( _
      _article.ArticleID, _
      _article.ArticleTitle, _
      _article.ArticleBody, _
      _article.ArticleSummary, _
      _article.ArticleCreatedBy, _
      _article.ArticleCreatedDate, _
```

```
      _article.ArticlePublished, _
       _article.ArticleExpirationDate)
    grdUnapprovedArticles.DataSource = _
    _ArticlesBLL.GetAllUnpublishedArticles
    grdUnapprovedArticles.DataBind()
  End If
    End Sub
```

Now that the control is fully functional, we need to add it to our `ControlPanel.aspx`. Open up your page, and at the top of the page, below the `<@...>` directive, add the following:

```
<%@ Register src="Controls/ApproveArticles.ascx"
tagname="ApproveArticles" tagprefix="uc1" %>
Then, down at the bottom of the page, right before the </table> tag,
add  the following:
<tr style="background-color:Silver;">
  <th>Unpublished Articles</th>
</tr>
<tr>
  <td>
  <uc1:ApproveArticles ID="ApproveArticles1" runat="server" />
  </td>
</tr>
```

We now have a fully functional Articles system, complete with adding, approving, and even deleting operations. While this code is fairly simplistic, it's all designed around the idea that you can take this and expand upon it, customizing it for your needs and experiences. There are any number of ways that all of these same pieces could be accomplished. We've shown you only a few different options. Find the one (or ones) that works for you and extend it to cover the other pieces. By taking the code and experimenting, you will find that your knowledge and understanding of how these pieces work will be greatly increased, and soon you should find yourself tweaking things you never would have imagined at the beginning.

While we have tried to cover many different options while presenting you with the samples for the Articles module, there are sure to be many others out there, but we hope the principles you've learned here will aid you in understanding them, and perhaps give you the advantages to take these different methods and methodologies, and incorporate them into your own code, both easily and effectively.

Reporting

Reporting for a web site can be as simple as you would like, or as complex as building the Empire State Building, and the ways to go about it are about as varied as anything out there. For the sake of time, and to keep you from being buried, we'll stick to a fairly simple approach, but we'll also touch upon some other suggestions and ideas.

To start off, we need to decide what exactly it is that we want to report on. A few simple, key items should be enough to get you started. In our site, let's track the page that's visited, when it's visited, and some basic browser information from the user. For this we will need to store this data someplace and our database is perfect. Let's create ourselves a new table, calling it SiteStats, with the following setup:

Column Name	Data Type	Allow Nulls
PageURL	varchar(500)	☐
VisitedDate	datetime	☐
BrowserInfo	varchar(1000)	☐

Like most of the pieces we've done to this point, we will need to create both a DAL and BLL for handling our data. As we're taking a very simplistic approach to our reporting, we'll go with a small, object-based system like we did for the SiteSettings. Go ahead and create a new class in your DAL folder, calling it SiteStatsDAL.vb. We'll need a method to add a new row to our table and a way to read the results. For the Add method, let's create a new function called AddStat(). We'll want it to look like this:

```
Public Shared Function AddStat( _
ByVal PageURL As String, _
ByVal VisitedDate As DateTime, _
ByVal BrowserInfo As String) As Boolean
  Dim conn As New Data.SqlClient.SqlConnection( _
    ConfigurationManager.ConnectionStrings( _
    "SimpleCMSConnectionString").ConnectionString)
  conn.Open()
  Dim cmd As New Data.SqlClient.SqlCommand( _
    "Insert Into SiteStats " & _
    "(PageURL,VisitedDate,BrowserInfo) " & _
    "values " & _
    "(@PageURL,@VisitedDate,@BrowserInfo) " _
    , conn)
  cmd.Parameters.Add("@PageURL", _
    Data.SqlDbType.VarChar).Value = PageURL
```

```
     cmd.Parameters.Add("@VisitedDate", _
       Data.SqlDbType.DateTime).Value = VisitedDate
     cmd.Parameters.Add("@BrowserInfo", _
       Data.SqlDbType.VarChar).Value = BrowserInfo
     Return cmd.ExecuteNonQuery() = 1
   End Function
```

The other method we need is the Get method. Let's go ahead and create a new function, calling it GetStats(), with code that looks like this:

```
Public Shared Function GetStats() As Data.DataSet
   Dim conn As New Data.SqlClient.SqlConnection( _
     ConfigurationManager.ConnectionStrings( _
     "SimpleCMSConnectionString").ConnectionString)
   Dim cmd As New Data.SqlClient.SqlCommand( _
     "Select * from SiteStats", conn)
   Dim da As New Data.SqlClient.SqlDataAdapter(cmd)
   Dim ds As New Data.DataSet()
   da.Fill(ds)
   Return ds
End Function
```

You may want to add other methods, getting only recent records or records for specific dates or pages, but we'll leave that for you to decide. We now need to create our BLL class and our object. In your BLL folder, add a new class, calling it SiteStatsBLL.vb. First, we'll need to create a new class in the file for the object. Place the following code right after the "End Class" in your file:

```
Public Class SiteStat
    Private _PageURL As String
    Private _VisitedDate As DateTime
    Private _BrowserInfo As String
    Public Property PageURL() As String
        Get
            Return _PageURL
        End Get
        Set(ByVal value As String)
           _PageURL = value
        End Set
    End Property
    Public Property VisitedDate() As DateTime
        Get
            Return _VisitedDate
        End Get
        Set(ByVal value As DateTime)
```

```
            _VisitedDate = value
        End Set
    End Property
    Public Property BrowserInfo() As String
        Get
            Return _BrowserInfo
        End Get
        Set(ByVal value As String)
            _BrowserInfo = value
        End Set
    End Property
End Class
```

Now, within the `SiteStatsBLL` class, we will need two methods just like we did for the DAL—an `Add` and a `Get` method. For the `Add` method, we'll use a function called `AddStat()`, with the following code:

```
Public Shared Function AddStat( _
ByVal PageURL As String, _
ByVal VisitedDate As DateTime, _
ByVal BrowserInfo As String) As Boolean
    Return SiteStatsDAL.AddStat( _
      PageURL, _
      VisitedDate, _
      BrowserInfo)
End Function
```

And for the `Get` method, we'll call the function `GetStats()`, and use the following:

```
Public Shared Function GetStats() As _
Generic.List(Of SiteStat)
    Dim _return As New Generic.List(Of SiteStat)
    Dim _ds As Data.DataSet = SiteStatsDAL.GetStats
      For Each _dr As Data.DataRow In _ds.Tables(0).Rows
        Dim _siteStat As New SiteStat
        _siteStat.BrowserInfo = _dr("BrowserInfo")
        _siteStat.PageURL = _dr("PageURL")
        _siteStat.VisitedDate = CDate(_dr("VisitedDate"))
        _return.Add(_siteStat)
    Next
    Return _return
End Function
```

Now that we've got all our classes and methods created, we need to actually put some code into our site to save the information. In the Code view of each page, we should already have a `Page_Load()` event. Paste the following into this event as the first line:

```
SiteStatsBLL.AddStat(Page.Request.Url.PathAndQuery, _

Now, Page.Request.UserAgent)
```

We are now logging every page hit in the site to our database. All we are missing now is a way to view the logs. While we could simply stick a small viewer into our Control Panel page, it's really something that is independent of this. For our use, let's simply create a new page for our site, calling it `StatReport.aspx` and use the `SimpleCMS.master` for our Master Page. Let's go ahead and add a GridView control, and use an ObjectDataSource to bind it. Our resulting HTML should look like this:

```
<asp:GridView ID="grdStatDetails" runat="server" AllowPaging="True"
AutoGenerateColumns="False" DataSourceID="ObjectDataSource1">
  <Columns>
    <asp:BoundField DataField="PageURL" HeaderText="PageURL"
      SortExpression="PageURL" />
    <asp:BoundField DataField="VisitedDate"
      HeaderText="VisitedDate"
      SortExpression="VisitedDate" />
    <asp:BoundField DataField="BrowserInfo"
      HeaderText="BrowserInfo"
      SortExpression="BrowserInfo" />
  </Columns>
</asp:GridView>
<asp:ObjectDataSource ID="ObjectDataSource1"
  runat="server" SelectMethod="GetStats"
  TypeName="SiteStatsBLL">
</asp:ObjectDataSource>
```

Go ahead and browse around the site a little, and then go to our new `StatReport.aspx` page (did you add it to your menu). You should get results similar to this:

There you have it, Site Reporting, albeit in its simplest form, for you to use.

As you may have noticed that the tracking we are showing you here is quite limited while completely functional. You will want to take this and extend it long before you ever put your site up. While most functions of a site can be added as you go along, there is a distinct flaw in that ideology when it comes to reporting. There is no way to go back and get additional data after the visit. By that I mean if you start to track another piece of data one day, let's say Default Language settings on the browser, you won't have any of this data from before the time you started to track it.

The key to reporting is data, and lots of it, all the time. The more you gather, the more you can know, as well as the better you can adjust your site to fit your users' needs. Take the time at the beginning of your site design to make sure you have covered all the things you will want to track. Get these pieces implemented early on, preferably before you even launch your site. I've found that it's better to gather more information than you may think you'll ever need, simply because you never know what you may want tomorrow.

A few pieces that I highly recommend you investigate adding from the start may be view-counts on the individual module content pieces you've built. Wouldn't it be nice to know how many times a particular Article has been viewed? Perhaps adding a counter to the documents and image pieces to track how many times they've been retrieved? These are pieces that, as mentioned, you can't go back and fill in later, so it's key to add these now. Perhaps you want to log all the errors that may have happened with your site and display these in a report. All of these pieces work under the same principle as the reporting section you've just written. You could look at using the same table in your database or even look at adding others — the choices are all up to you. This is why it's difficult for anyone else to tell you what you need to do here, but hopefully we've shown you enough to let you take the pieces and arrange them into something larger that will serve you well.

The last thing I want to briefly cover when it comes to the area of site stats and reporting is that there are a great number of third-party tools for this. There are some such as Awstats and web trends that sit on your server and intercept all the calls to your site and generate some beautiful reports. There are also things such as Google Analytics, which would plug right in to the Additional Header Information piece in our SiteSettings, which gives you some other wonderful tracking systems.

With these third-party applications, it takes all the work off you for maintenance, and since these applications are constantly being updated to include new browsers and anything else that might change, you can eliminate the need for any extra work on yourself. These tools are extremely well tested and will come with all the features you could think of. I highly recommend looking into these other types of reporting tools — maybe not as full replacements, but perhaps as additional sources. Let these other tools gather things such as browser versions, languages, and even what page they visited. However, continue to use your own tools to track specific pieces such as the view-counts, and you will find that you will get a much more robust view of the usage of your site.

Search Engine Optimization

While the idea of **Search Engine Optimization (SEO)** isn't really a function of the Administration of the site, it is another one of those key pieces that happen "under the covers" of a site. With that in mind, I thought it would be a good time to bring it up so that you can implement it when you are working on your site. Many developers will fail to take advantage of the little pieces that you can add, or simply do "right", to make their site better when it comes to SEO. If your site isn't going to be exposed on the Internet, being used on an internal network/intranet, perhaps you can skip over this, but otherwise I think it pays to take just a few moments to talk about it.

I'd probably start by saying that there is some much more detailed work available on the topic, and that you should spend some time researching it to learn more. Sites such as Google will provide you page after page all devoted to this topic, and sites such as Wikipedia.org are constantly being updated to give you the most up-to-date information available. Beyond that I'll give you the quick rundown. SEO is, simply put, making your site easier for the search engines to classify, categorize, parse, and generally "learn" about. Sites with poorly implemented SEO techniques will find themselves almost unreachable when someone opens their favorite search engine. This would mean less visitors, and less visitors means less usage. If people can't find, or find out about your site, then they can't come to it and read all the information you've made available to them.

While I'm not going to cover all the details of SEO, I will try to cover a few of the big hitters and help you start off on the right track.

- **Create a unique title for your page:**

  Every page in your site will have the ability to have its own unique title (the `<title>` tag that's part of the header and/or page declaration). By giving each of your page its own title, the search engines will know that these pages are different, and therefore will be classified/tracked independently. This gives a much more detailed breakdown of your site for the searching users. This title is also one of the key fields that the search engines base their results on, typically the first priority key. Be detailed in your page title, but make sure it's to the point.

- **Add a <meta> description tag**:

  Within the `<head>` tag of your pages, in addition to the `<title>` tag, you can also add what's referred to as a `<meta>` tag. This is a piece of additional information that really doesn't show to the site user, but is crucial for many search engines. A sample of the `<meta>` tag may look something like this:

  ```
  <head>
  <title>...</title>
  <meta name="description" content="Simple CMS" />
  </head>
  ```

  In this sample, the `<meta>` tag is for the description of the site. This is what many search engines will use when parsing the contents of your page. A good `description` tag, when it's filled with detailed, useful information, will be all that your user needs to know they've found what they need when searching. In our sample, I used `Simple CMS` as the content of the description, but this would actually be a bad example. You will want to build your content section so that it's as detailed as possible.

Now there are a number of other pieces you could dig into for proper SEO, but if you take on these first two properly, you may find that you've already covered most of the basics. The other items I just want to mention to look into would be proper URL paths and the use of a SiteMap. These are additional pieces that many search engines will crawl through when evaluating your site.

Summary

In this chapter, we covered a number of items quite quickly, and by now you should be getting more familiar with the tools and the methodology of the site, but just because we covered them quickly does not mean they are not important items. The Administrator Control Panel is really an intricate part of your site. It allows you, as an Administrator, to control a number of aspects of your site and gives you the ability to customize nearly all of it. Take what you've learned here and expand it, and I think you will find that there is a wonderful opportunity for you to create a site that is truly unique, but at the same time one that can be based on some shared principles of reusability. A simple control panel adjustment here and there, and you've suddenly got an entirely new site, all without a single line of code or even a deployment of your site. We hope that you can take these pieces and grow them into something larger.

9
Further Possibilities

Now that you have a working CMS, where do you go from here? As you probably noticed throughout this book, we touched upon a number of different areas and mentioned a few other options along the way, but there are still a number of other possibilities yet to be discovered. In this chapter, we'll try to touch upon a few other options so that you can see just how you may want to extend your site.

At the end of this chapter, we will have covered:

- Possibilities for upsizing your SQL Server
- Suggestions for additional modules for your site
- Using base pages and inheritance
- Handling (trapping) errors

Upsizing to the SQL Server

The site we developed and designed in our book is based around the Microsoft SQL Express database engine. While this engine is quite robust, we mostly did this because of the cost involved, or lack thereof. Due to the nature of the database being a file-based engine, there are a number of hosting providers, and if you are going to use a third-party host, that may not allow you to use SQLExpress. You may also determine that your site will be a heavily used site with thousands of users. If this is the case, you may want to look at using the "full" version of Microsoft SQL Server. With this, you would have all of the additional capabilities, depending on the specific version you were to use, as well as the more robust engine. I highly recommend you go to the Microsoft web site and look at the different options available when choosing your database engine, and then use that in correlation with your needs and what your hosting provider may offer.

One of the best things about switching to the full version of SQL Server is that you don't have to change any of your code. SQL and SQLExpress have a shared "core" that does all of the database work, so all of the queries we've written within our application will work exactly the same way. The only piece of code within the application that you would need to update is the connection string within the `web.config` file.

To use the full version of SQL, you just need to first install it on a server. The full installation instructions for this will come with your SQL software. If you're using a hosting provider for your web site, then this has already been done for you. After that you have a couple of options. If you are starting off with a new web site, you can follow the same methods that were covered in Chapter 2, but if you are upsizing, it's even simpler. Open up your **SQL Server Management Studio**, connecting to your SQL Server. Expand the **Object Explorer** and you should see a number of folders in your tree, like this:

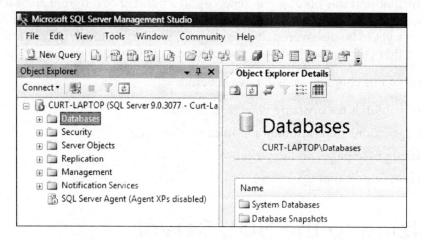

Right-click on the **Databases** folder and select the **Attach menu** option. Use the **Add...** button to browse to the **SimpleCMS.mdf** database file that you have for your existing site.

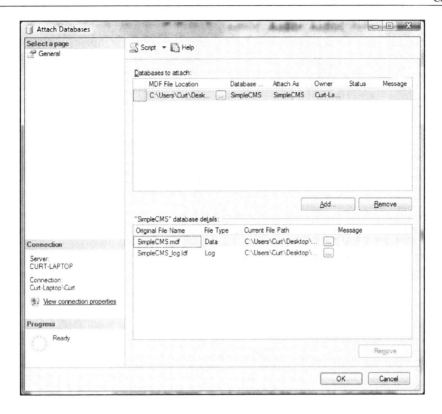

That's it. Your SQL Server Management Studio should now show your SimpleCMS database on your server.

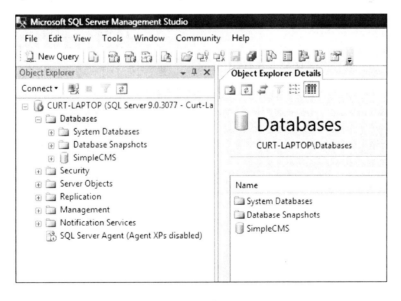

From here, you can open your site and go into your web.config. Open the <connectionStrings /> section and find your connection string.

```
<add name="SimpleCMS_DatabaseConnectionString" connectionString="Data
Source=.\SQLEXPRESS;AttachDbFilename=C:\Inetpub\wwwroot\
App_Data\SimpleCMS.mdf;Initial Catalog=SimpleCMS.mdf;User
ID=sa;Password=SimpleCMS" />
```

You will want to replace it with the following, making sure to use your SQL Server name:

```
<add name="SimpleCMSConnectionString" connectionString="server=YOUR_
SERVER;Integrated Security=True;Trusted_Connection=yes;database=Simple
CMS" providerName="System.Data.SqlClient"/>
```

If you need help with configuring your connection string, I highly recommend going on to the Internet for assistance. The web site www.ConnectionStrings.com is a great resource for all of this information. After you get your string configured, go ahead and run your application, and test it out. You may find that you get an increase in the performance because the full versions of SQL Server are much more optimized. Beyond simply connecting to the server, depending on the version of SQL Server you have, you may find a number of other options available to you. Automated backups, load balancing, and scheduled jobs are just a few things you may want to explore within SQL Server.

Additional modules

Beyond the Articles and Files (Documents and Gallery) Modules we've created within the site, you may want to look at adding some others. Many CMS sites will offer options such as Forums, Messaging, and Videos. These are all ideas you may want to incorporate within your site. For these, or any others you may think of, it's just a matter of following the same patterns we've been using throughout this site.

Start with planning out your Module. It's crucial to know how you want it to work before you start off, or you may find yourself rewriting large pieces of code (and I'm sure that no one really wants to do that). Once you have your concepts all laid out, start by creating the individual pieces. If you need some new tables in your database, get those created first.

Next, you'll want to take the time and get your DAL all "wired up" using the Typed Dataset option, as we did with the Articles module, or you may want to use the Object-based system like we did with the SiteSettings module—it's up to you. I highly recommend that whichever method you go with, you use it for all your modules. We purposely used differing methods in this book, simply to show you different possibilities. However, maintaining a site using a mixture of methodology is quite difficult at times.

The next step, just as we've done before, would be to create your BLL. Make sure to keep your specific business rules within the context of your BLL and not in the UI, just to make things easier for yourself as you expand and grow your site. In addition, you will want to make sure to write detailed validation rules to ensure your site is always getting the best possible data. Another item that I strongly recommend you incorporate into your BLL is the use of comments. Whenever possible, add a simple comment or note to your code explaining what, and why, that piece of code is there. This is because as your site grows and expands, you will always know what that piece is for. This will also allow other developers to come into a piece of code and know immediately why it was designed and what it's purpose is—a "must have" in any multi-developer situation.

Once the layers are in place, go ahead and create your UI. Take into account the Master Page(s) you may have created, the CSS/Skin/Theme files you've incorporated, and all the other shared bits. The UI is all the user ever sees, and while it's typically very straightforward, it's really your only chance to gain your users'/customers' attention. The best written code with a poor UI will suffer dramatically.

The key to using the module-based approach, as we've done here, is that these pieces are really designed to be implemented with as little direct impact on the rest of the site. By doing this, you ensure the stability of your site, which is critical. Along with this, you also ensure that when you've got the new pieces completed, you don't have to spend hours testing all the other pieces of your site again.

Base pages

The concept of inheritance is one that is at the root of all object-oriented programming. All the pages in our site are currently "inheriting" from the `System.Web.UI.Page` class that is part of the ASP.NET framework — but they don't have to. One concept that you will find in many applications is the use of a "base" class. The idea behind this is that if you have all of your classes (or pages in our case) inheriting from a single class of your own, then you have given yourself a shared place for many things to reside. Just like in the idea behind the Master Page, we can do this ourselves. Create a new class in your `app_code` folder, calling it `SimpleCMSBasePage.vb`. It will start off simple and empty like this:

```
Imports Microsoft.VisualBasic
Public Class SimpleCMSBasePage
End Class
```

What you can do now is set it up so that it inherits from `System.Web.UI.Page`. (You'll come to know the reason in a while.) To do this, change the Class definitions to look like this:

```
Imports Microsoft.VisualBasic
Public Class SimpleCMSBasePage
    Inherits System.Web.UI.Page
End Class
```

Now, let's take a look at all our existing pages. You'll see that every one of them has the following piece of code in them:

```
Protected Sub Page_PreInit(ByVal sender As Object, _
ByVal e As System.EventArgs) Handles Me.PreInit
    Page.Theme = SiteSettingsBLL.ReadSiteSettings.SiteTheme
End Sub
```

Copy that piece from one of the pages and put it into our new class so that it looks like this:

```
Imports Microsoft.VisualBasic
Public Class SimpleCMSBasePage
    Inherits System.Web.UI.Page

    Protected Sub Page_PreInit(ByVal sender As Object, _
    ByVal e As System.EventArgs) Handles Me.PreInit
        Page.Theme =  SiteSettingsBLL.ReadSiteSettings.SiteTheme
    End Sub

End Class
```

Open the code (`****.aspx.vb` file) for each of our pages in our site. Remove the code that we just copied from all of them. And here comes the really cool part. Take the line that says:

```
Inherits System.Web.UI.Page
```

and change it so that it now reads:

```
Inherits SimpleCMSBasePage
```

What we've just done is make all our pages inherit from the `SimpleCMSBasePage` class that we've created, which in turn inherits from the `System.Web.UI.Page` class. We get all the functionality of the ASP.NET Page class in addition to any extra code we want to put into our own base class. Beyond using it just for the simple event we did above, you could easily add any number of things to this class. Functions, properties, and even other events are all available to you to put in this new class and remember, anything you put here will automatically be available to you from any of your pages. Perhaps you want to do additional logging of the visits to your pages, and this would be a great place to put that logger.

Another thing that you may want is a place to store static constants for use in your site. This would be another time when the base page would be useful. Now, isn't that pretty cool, but wait...there's more. Not only can we do this with our Page classes, but we can also do this with all our DAL and BLL classes. By having all your BLL classes inherit from a single one, you could write some of your functionality here, thereby not having to repeat it in each BLL class. The same thing goes for your DAL classes. You can create any number of extra inheritance layers that you need as well. These additional layers can add a nice way of separating code and keeping things from getting overly cumbersome in a single file, but be careful not to overdo it, as you can easily cross the line and turn the code into something tough to weed through. When you add too many layers, it's not always easy to track down where a problem may originate, and none of us want to spend more time than necessary on that kind of a thing.

Error trapping

One key concept that we really only briefly touched upon in our site is how you want to handle errors that may occur. There are a number of different methodologies that you may come across if you do some searching on the Internet, but the one thing you will nearly always see is that you need a common way of handling them for your application. Whether you log them into the Event Viewer in the Operating System of the server, write them to a table in your database, or even both. However, you will want to make sure you do this consistently. In addition, you will also want to make sure that your users always know how to find any information on an error that may impact them.

There are two basic concepts when it comes to errors in an application. The first is "handled" errors. These are things that you can expect to happen. Validation failures, missing data, incomplete data, and so on, are all common occurrences of a "handled" error. We have numerous points within our application where an IF/THEN check may produce a failure for us. For these you will want to:

1. Log the error appropriately.
2. Let the user know.

For logging the error, I'd suggest you put a simple LogError() method in the new SimpleCMSBase* classes that we created earlier. This one method can be called from any of the other classes that have inherited from this one, giving you a single, unified point for logging these messages. Beyond simply logging these errors, you will want to make sure the user knows what to do. For this, the best way is simply to put a message on the screen telling them what happened and what they can do, if anything. By using a consistent place on the screen to display these messages, and by displaying them in a consistent way (same color, font, and so on), your users will hopefully be able to handle most situations themselves.

The second type of error is what's called an "unhandled" error. These are errors that you haven't specifically coded for, but that doesn't mean they aren't expected. No matter how much time you spend making your site just perfect, and regardless of the countless hours you spent testing your site (you did test it—all right?), there is always the possibility of an error. For this you will want to look at a few key pieces—the Page, the web.config, and the global.asax file. I won't go into great depth on these, as you will surely find more information than you would ever want with a quick Internet search, but briefly:

- The Page has a few built in methods for handling errors. `OnError()` and `Page_Error()` are both exposed to us for use within the `Page` class.

- The `global.asax` file, if you add one to your site, will have some methods of its own that are called any time an error occurs, specifically the `Application_Error` event.

- Lastly, but certainly not least, is the `web.config`. Within this file is a `<customErrors />` section. This is where you can tell your application to do specific things such as redirect to special pages in your site, whenever certain types of errors occur.

Handling errors and properly logging them is really only half of the puzzle. Now you, as the person in charge of the code, need to know that an error occurred. Many sites will incorporate some messaging, through email, to let a specific user know whenever an error occurred. This lets you to be quickly responsive to your site and correct errors before many users may even report them.

In addition, I recommend that you have some way of reviewing your error logs, either manually or in a special error page in your site. We've briefly touched on this in the last chapter, but it's worth repeating a little here. A good report to view the errors, and perhaps a way to flag/mark a status on them, is incredibly useful. You will want to check this report frequently so that you can ensure your users are getting the best experience they can. I suggest that you even publish some of these to an Article on your site, so if a user is getting an error, he/she can know that it is being looked into, and you will especially want to let the users know when these fixes have been put into the site. This gives your users some feeling that they are part of a solution and not just a problem. These users will be your best interactions. This is because when they feel more comfortable, they will share their experiences more, and will be happy to share with you, any errors they may receive. By being vigilant, you can continuously work on making your site better, and that's what everyone wants in the end.

Summary

Now that you've got your site completed, modules written, UI looking sharp, interfaces running smoothly, and are feeling all-around good about the work you've done, what should you do now? The simple answer is "keep going". Take time to review what you've done. Re-evaluate the code you wrote. Nearly every developer out there finds that when he/she completes a project that they are a better developer than they were at the start. With that in mind, the code you did at the beginning is probably not as "good" as what you wrote at the end. See if you can make it better. Take the time to optimize the code, combine any duplicate code into shared functions, or make them into custom controls if they are pieces for your pages. Take time to look around the Internet at other sites with similar usages as yours, and look for ideas. Talk with your users and ask them what they like or don't like in the site, and see if you can improve upon it. Find out what new functionality may benefit the people who use your site and see what it would take to incorporate these concepts into your code.

The basic idea is that a web site, or really any application, is never really "done". Every good site out there is making improvements, or should be, on a continuing basis. There are always new techniques, new functionality, and new options available to developers to help them make better applications. Take time to see what's out there, collect that information, and see what it can do for you and your site.

Index

X

XML output, RSS feeds 216

Z

Zones
  body Zone 175, 177
  footer Zone 175, 176
  header Zone 175, 176
  setting up 177
  side Zone 176
  three column layout 175
  two column layout 175

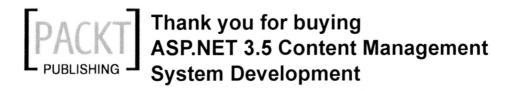

About Packt Publishing

Packt, pronounced 'packed', published its first book *"Mastering phpMyAdmin for Effective MySQL Management"* in April 2004 and subsequently continued to specialize in publishing highly focused books on specific technologies and solutions.

Our books and publications share the experiences of your fellow IT professionals in adapting and customizing today's systems, applications, and frameworks. Our solution based books give you the knowledge and power to customize the software and technologies you're using to get the job done. Packt books are more specific and less general than the IT books you have seen in the past. Our unique business model allows us to bring you more focused information, giving you more of what you need to know, and less of what you don't.

Packt is a modern, yet unique publishing company, which focuses on producing quality, cutting-edge books for communities of developers, administrators, and newbies alike. For more information, please visit our website: www.packtpub.com.

Writing for Packt

We welcome all inquiries from people who are interested in authoring. Book proposals should be sent to author@packtpub.com. If your book idea is still at an early stage and you would like to discuss it first before writing a formal book proposal, contact us; one of our commissioning editors will get in touch with you.

We're not just looking for published authors; if you have strong technical skills but no writing experience, our experienced editors can help you develop a writing career, or simply get some additional reward for your expertise.

ASP.NET 3.5 Social Networking

ISBN: 978-1-847194-78-7   Paperback: 580 pages

An expert guide to building enterprise-ready social networking and community applications with ASP.NET 3.5

1. Create a full-featured, enterprise-grade social network using ASP.NET 3.5

2. Learn key new ASP.NET topics in a practical, hands-on way: LINQ, AJAX, C# 3.0, n-tier architectures, and MVC

3. Build friends lists, messaging systems, user profiles, blogs, message boards, groups, and more

4. Rich with example code, clear explanations, interesting examples, and practical advice – a truly hands-on book for ASP.NET developers

ASP.NET MVC 1.0 Quickly

ISBN: 978-1-847197-54-2   Paperback: 256 pages

Design, develop, and test powerful and robust web applications with MVC framework the agile way

1. Rapid guide to building powerful web applications with ASP.NET MVC framework

2. Covers all facets of web application development including requirement analysis, design, building, testing, and deployment

3. Explore the ASP.NET MVC framework with several newly released features including WebForms, Script Combining, jQuery integration, and ASP.Net MVC AJAX helpers

Please check **www.PacktPub.com** for information on our titles

ASP.NET 3.5 Application Architecture and Design

ISBN: 978-1-847195-50-0 Paperback: 260 pages

Build robust, scalable ASP.NET applications quickly and easily.

1. Master the architectural options in ASP.NET to enhance your applications

2. Develop and implement n-tier architecture to allow you to modify a component without disturbing the next one

3. Design scalable and maintainable web applications rapidly

4. Implement ASP.NET MVC framework to manage various components independently

Enhancing Microsoft Content Management Server with ASP.NET 2.0

ISBN: 978-1-904811-52-7 Paperback: 224 pages

Use the powerful new features of ASP.NET 2.0 with your MCMS Websites

1. Get Microsoft Content Management Server Service Pack 2 up and running

2. Use the most exciting features of ASP.NET 2.0 in your MCMS development

Please check **www.PacktPub.com** for information on our titles

Lightning Source UK Ltd.
Milton Keynes UK
UKOW010334101012

200315UK00003B/18/P